The
Battleship
Book

Also by Robert M. Farley

Grounded: The Case for Abolishing the United States Air Force

The Battleship Book

Robert M. Farley

The Wildside Press

Rockville, Maryland

The Battleship Book

This book is dedicated to my uncle, Paul Farley,
who helped nurture my interest in these great ships.

Edited by Leigh Grossman
www.swordsmith.com

Cover design by Steve Coupe
Special thanks to John Betancourt

ISBN 978-1-4794-0556-5
Ebook ISBN 978-1-4794-0557-2

Published by:
Wildside Press
9710 Traville Gateway Drive #234
Rockville, MD 20850
www.wildsidepress.com

First Wildside Press edition: September 2015

10 9 8 7 6 5 4 3 2 1

Table of Contents

I. The Pre-Dreadnoughts

II. The World War I Era

III. The World War II Era

List of Sidebars

The
Battleship
Book

Introduction

This book is about battleships, or more specifically, what battleships meant to the world.

The steel "battle" ship began to emerge as a type in the second half of the nineteenth century, as steam and iron replaced sail and wood, and advances in gunnery technology made possible the construction of heavy, breechloaded turret guns. By the early 1890s, the pre-dreadnought battleship had taken shape. These ships typically displaced over 13,000 tons, and carried a mixed armament built around two heavy twin gun turrets, one fore and one aft. Variations on this type spread across the globe quickly, with most of the major naval powers adopting the template (allowing for some regional variation). The pre-dreadnought competed, for a time, with the armored cruiser, which carried lighter guns on a similar displacement but could make greater speed.

Two events in 1905 threw the battleship world into disarray. In May, Admiral Togo Heihachiro, leading a fleet of four battleships and several armored cruisers, utterly destroyed a larger Russian battlefleet at Tsushima. The battle, involving ships of recent vintage, demonstrated the effectiveness of the combination of speed and heavy gunnery. Togo had

showed that a battle squadron, correctly employed, could destroy a vast store of national wealth and power in just a few hours. New battleships would incorporate the lessons of Tsushima, carrying heavier armaments optimized for long-range engagements. Designers and strategists took note.

In October, the Royal Navy laid down HMS *Dreadnought*, the first battleship equipped with a single caliber main armament in multiple turrets. Dreadnought carried ten 12" guns in five turrets, and could make 21 knots. At the insistence of First Sea Lord John "Jacky" Fisher, the builders finished *Dreadnought* in a year. Although the Japanese and Americans had already begun work along similar lines, the example electrified naval architects and strategic thinkers around the world.

The great battleship race had begun. It would continue, in one form or another, until the commissioning of HMS *Vanguard* in 1946. The race would consume enormous resources worldwide, as great and small powers competed with one another in number, size, and sophistication of battleships. Paused for World War One, the race would eventually lead to a landmark arms control negotiation, as well as a redefinition of the nature of naval power. Along the way, scores of graceful, powerful warships would move from slip to sea, and eventually to scrapyard (the lucky ones, anyway).

Purpose of this book

This book focuses on the strategic and political relevance of the "castles of steel" that so many nations built in the first half of the twentieth century. Battleships represented a tremendous investment of state resources, sometimes to the extent of bankrupting national coffers for an extended period. Unsurprisingly, the names that governments give them reflect national priorities, and sometimes intra-national conflicts. Consequently, each entry includes a discussion of how the ship acquired its name, and what that name meant to the nation (and navy) at the time.

The entries also attempt to convey the strategic problems the ship in question was intended to solve. Governments don't commit massive investments to weapons for no reason, even if the primary reasons may sometimes elude us. Governments often bought battleships in the expectation that they would fight other battleships. In other cases, they were expected to fight cruisers, or escort aircraft carriers, or show the flag, or demonstrate that the nation in question was a major international player.

The book does not focus on the technical aspects of the world's battleships. Many other volumes already do this. Instead, the narratives discuss how the ships related to contemporaries, as well as to past and future battleships. Each entry also includes a brief stat bloc that gives the basic facts, including displacement, weaponry, and dates of construction, reconstruction, and loss. These stats reflect the original condition of the ships, before any modifications and reconstructions. While this book acknowledges and explores the distinctions between pre-dreadnoughts, dreadnoughts,

USS Oregon, October 12, 1898.

battlecruisers, super-dreadnoughts, and fast battleships, it generally uses the catch-all term "battleship" in reference to all of them.

How to Read This Book

This book includes more than sixty entries, each devoted to a particular battleship. While the book concentrates on the dreadnought era, it includes several pre-dreadnoughts, one "post" dreadnought, and two battleships converted to aircraft carriers.

The selection of ships is simultaneously systematic and idiosyncratic. Every country to own a battleship received at least one entry (in a couple cases, the entry completely exhausts that nation's battleship fleet). The rest of the choices include ships that had remarkable stories, or that had a major effect on naval architecture, or that took unusual names, or that had particularly profound national meaning. The length of entries is less reflective of the historical importance of a battleship than it is of how the interesting story of that ship's career was.

In addition to the ship entries, the book includes three interlude chapters focused on events that affected a great number of battleships: the Battle of Jutland, the Pearl Harbor attack, and the impact of the interwar naval limitation treaties. Each of these events had an outsized effect on battleship construction, design, and employment.

The reader, and especially the reader new to the history of the battleship form, should feel free to abandon the chronological ordering and wander across entries of interest. Each entry tells its own story, but the stories of different ships are inextricably interwoven with one another. Readers will find some repetition with respect to historical, legal, and technical developments, as these events rarely had uniform effect across ships and nations. Often, the reader will find two sides of the same battle.

Origins of this book

This volume does not use scholarly standards of evidence or citation, although I hope that it will spark interest for future scholars of these great vessels. The book draws upon some scholarly work on battleships (and includes an extensive reading list), but does not include exhaustive citation of the scholarly or technical literature on battleship employment and construction. My own scholarly work touches upon how the interest in battleship construction and ownership spread across the globe in the early twentieth century, but that investigation is only tangential to the entries in this volume.

The foundations for the book were laid in 2006, when I began the series "Sunday Battleship Blogging" at the group blog Lawyers, Guns, and Money (lawyersgunsmoneyblog.com). The series began with HIJMS *Mutsu*, a Nagato class battleship that exploded and sank while at anchor in 1943 (*Mutsu* and a very few others didn't make the cut in this volume). It continued for over a year, developing entries at greater length before finally concluding with USS *Wisconsin*. Most of the entries in this book represent substantial revisions of those early efforts. Elements of the book draw on other posts at Lawyers, Guns, and Money, as well as writing originally published at the Diplomat: APAC, War is Boring, and the National Interest.

My affection for these huge ships stems from my grandfather, who served in the Pacific in World War II and told me stories of the great warships. He hailed from Missouri, and so he shared a favorite battleship with Harry Truman. My grandmother and grandfather were fans of Johnny Horton, and I listened to Horton's "Sink the Bismarck" hundreds of times while growing up. Over the years, I've had the good fortune to visit USS *Massachusetts*, USS *New Jersey*, and USS *Wisconsin*, and the museums dedicated to their preservation.

Thanks are due to the other contributors

to Lawyers, Guns, and Money, including Scott Lemieux, David Watkins, Erik Loomis, David Noon, David Brockington, Charli Carpenter, Steve Attewell, and Scott Eric Kaufman. The commenters to LGM, who corrected errors and contributed a great deal of enthusiasm, also deserve much thanks. Finally, the host of anonymous editors at Wikipedia deserve a great deal of credit for the work they've accomplished. While the resource can often be uneven, the community that has chosen to work on battleships has done a remarkable job of filling gaps in the public record, and an equally remarkable job of finding and posting photographs of the world's most beautiful ships.

I

The Pre-Dreadnoughts

HMS Victoria

Laid Down: 1885
Launched: 1887
Completed: March, 1890
Displacement: 11,000 tons
Main Armament: two 16.25" guns (one twin turret)
Secondary Armament: one 10" gun, twelve 6" guns (individual mounts)
Speed: 16 knots
Major Actions: None
Treaty: Pre-Washington Naval Treaty
Fate: Rammed and sunk, June 22, 1893

HMS Victoria in 1887. From the book, Life of Vice Admiral Sir George Tryon KCB *by Rear Admiral C. C. Penrose Fitzgerald*

In 1861, HMS *Warrior* set the state of the art in Line of Battle Ship. Combining steam engines, advanced guns, and an iron hull, she was substantially superior to her ironclad counterparts in France and the United States. The Royal Navy developed the ironclad type for the next twenty years, with the *Colossus* class of 1882 being the first to resemble what became known as the classic "pre-dreadnought." Experimentation on the battleship form continued until the *Royal Sovereign* class of 1891, which set a new template for battleship construction. Between 1891 and 1905, nearly all the battleships in all navies in the world followed the pattern set by *Royal Sovereign*; four heavy guns in two turrets, one fore and one aft, with a heavy secondary armament, reciprocating engines, and a speed of around 16 knots.

HMS *Victoria* preceded *Royal Sovereign* by four years, and was originally intended to carry the name HMS *Renown*. In a decision that would become heavy with irony, the Royal Navy determined to honor Queen Victoria on the occasion of the Queen's Golden Jubilee by renaming the ship after her. *Victoria* was the first battleship to use vertical triple expansion engines, which significantly reduced her coal consumption. The enormous 16.25" guns were not directly comparable to later naval artillery; the expected range of engagement was no longer than a couple of miles. Loading took five minutes for each shot. Successor ships carried smaller, more easily manageable weapons.

Upon commissioning HMS *Victoria* became flagship of the Royal Navy Mediterranean squadron, which represented an overwhelming concentration of naval power. The Mediterranean squadron was intended to offset the growth of the Italian Navy, which had recovered from the embarrassment of Lissa to field a squadron powerful enough to threaten British communications (via Suez) with India. In 1891 the Mediterranean Fleet fell to Admiral George Tryon, an innovator whose main enthusiasm was signaling. The Royal Navy system of signaling, the Admiral felt, had ossified since the days of Nelson, leaving the captains of individual ships little room for initiative and threatening an entire system collapse in response to unforeseen events during battle. Accordingly, Admiral Tryon pursued a much simpler system of signal that gave credit to the professionalism of captains and allowed them some command latitude.

On June 22, 1893 the Mediterranean squadron was engaged in maneuvers off Tripoli (part of modern Lebanon). Deployed in two columns, the fleet was returning to anchor when some confusion arose. The exact details remain unclear; Robert Massie suggests that Admiral Tryon was attempting a complex

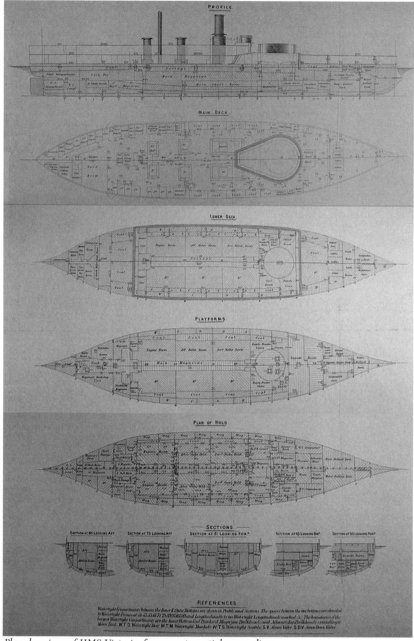

Plan drawings of HMS Victoria, from court-martial proceedings.

maneuver might be quite dangerous, but Admiral Tryon was inattentive, and Admiral Markham (commander of the second column) did not wish to cross Tryon. By the time that Tryon realized what was happening, a collision was unavoidable.

HMS *Camperdown*, equipped with a ram bow, struck HMS *Victoria* on the starboard side, then reversed engines to disengage. This doomed *Victoria*, as *Camperdown* left an enormous hole below the waterline. Thirteen minutes after the collision, *Victoria* rolled over and sank, carrying 358 sailors with her. Admiral Tryon did not survive, and his innovative system of signaling was discarded following the accident, even though it had not contributed to the collision. HMS *Victoria* now sits in five hundred feet of water just off the coast of Lebanon, with her bow buried in the sand and her stern pointing toward the surface.

Commander John Jellicoe escaped the sinking *Victoria* seconds before her loss. Just short of twenty-three years later, Jellicoe would command the Grand Fleet at the Battle of Jutland, where poor signaling would contribute to the loss of three British battlecruisers and to the escape of the High Seas Fleet.

maneuver that involved the two columns weaving into one another, while Andrew Gordon makes the altogether more plausible argument that Tryon simply miscalculated the distance between the columns. In any case, the maneuver set HMS *Victoria* on a collision course with HMS *Camperdown*, the lead ship of the second column. Several officers on both *Camperdown* and *Victoria* suggested that the

TERRIBLE NAVAL DISASTER. - SINKING OF H.M.S. VICTORIA, July 1, 1893. The Illustrated Australian News. Courtesy of State Library of Victoria

Author's Note

As far as I know, HMS *Victoria* is the only ship ever named after a sitting monarch to sink during the reign of that monarch. For obvious reasons, warships are only rarely named after reigning monarchs; another example is the *Alfonso XIII*, renamed *España* after the deposition of King Alfonso XIII.

I wonder how Queen Victoria reacted to the news of the loss of her namesake. The queen was seventy-four years of age in 1893, but had demonstrated the typical attentiveness of a British monarch to naval affairs. One would hope that whomever argued for changing the name of the ship from *Renown* to *Victoria* suffered some degree of professional mishap.

HMS *Victoria* is an interesting ship with respect to the evolution of the battleship type. The character of the line of battle ship was in flux until the early 1890s. After that point, it became remarkably programmatic, both within navies and around the world. The battleships of 1907 were superior to those of 1892, but resembled them very closely in basic form. That would change radically in the years after 1905.

Related Entries

Inspired... USS *Oregon*
Nearly killed the future commander at... Jutland
Shared a naming convention with... *España*

USS Oregon

Laid Down: 1891
Launched: 1893
Completed: July, 1896
Displacement: 10,300 tons
Main Armament: four 13" guns (two twin turrets)
Secondary Armament: eight 8" guns (four twin turrets)
Speed: 15 knots
Treaty: Pre-Washington Naval Treaty
Major Engagements: Straits of Magellan, Battle of Santiago de Cuba
Fate: Scrapped, 1956

Third ship of the *Indiana* class, *Oregon* was the second warship of the name to serve in the United States Navy (the first was a brig used primarily for exploration), although CSS *Oregon* had run blockades for the Confederacy. In the 1890s and 1900s, the USN used state names for both battleships and armored cruisers. At the time the two ship types were roughly the same size, with battleships carrying a heavier armament at the expense of speed. The types diverged over time, and in 1912 the USN renamed the remaining armored cruisers after cities, in order to free up state names and unofficially recognize the pre-eminence of the battleship.

Oregon was laid down in 1891, immediately in the wake of the publication of the first volume of Alfred Thayer Mahan's *Influence of Sea Power Upon History*. *Oregon* and her sisters were designed primarily for coastal defense work, but carried a main armament comparable with the most advanced foreign battleships. Nevertheless, although a reasonable effort for a navy unused to constructing line of battle ships, *Oregon* and her sisters did not compare favorably with foreign counterparts, the cream of which were represented by the British *Royal Sovereign* class. The *Royal Sovereigns* were 3,000 tons larger, carried 13.5" guns, and could make a knot and half faster than *Oregon*. Nevertheless, *Oregon* represented a start, and the USN would, with the

USS Oregon, 1898. From The History and Conquest of the Philippines and our Other Island Possessions; Embracing Our War with the Filipinos in 1899 *by Alden March.*

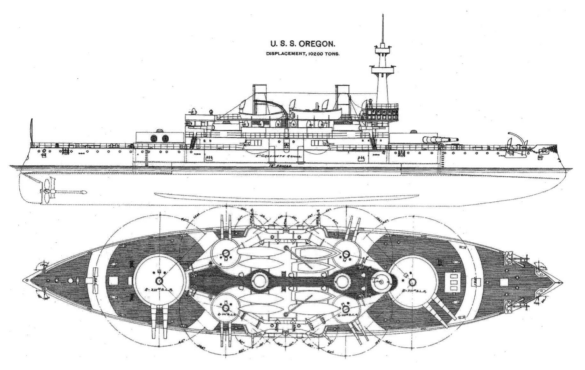

USS Oregon, 1893 line drawing.

help of Mahan and several committed presidential administrations, follow through with the creation of one of the world's most powerful navies.

Built in San Francisco, *Oregon* was commissioned in 1896 and immediately deployed to the Pacific. The Pacific Squadron was expected to support the Asiatic Squadron, which secured US interests in China and the rest of the Far East. On February 15, 1898, in the context of increasing tensions between Spain and the United States over Spanish control of Cuba, the armored cruiser *Maine* blew up in Havana. Thanks in part to the advocacy of William Randolph Hearst's network of newspapers, the United States went to war with Spain in April. Expecting the conflict to escalate, USS *Oregon* set sail for Cuba from San Francisco on March 19.

Oregon was not designed to withstand the rigors of a high speed trip around South America. Captain Charles Edgar Clark, who had only taken command of *Oregon* a few weeks before, opted to take the treacherous Straits of Magellan to save time. This placed the battleship in serious jeopardy when a major gale struck, forcing *Oregon* to anchor in uncertain conditions. Nevertheless, *Oregon* survived and arrived in the Cuba theater of operations on May 24. Now nicknamed "McKinley's Bulldog," *Oregon* participated in several actions against Spanish positions in Cuba before the war ended, including the Battle of Santiago de Cuba, which destroyed the bulk of the Armada España.

The story of *Oregon*'s experience circling South America was critical in building support for the construction of the Panama Canal, as access to a canal would have cut three weeks off the travel time. Consequently, the United States fomented a rebellion in Colombia that led to the independence of Panama, and purchased French equipment and property in what came to be known as the Canal Zone.

Oregon was redeployed to the Pacific after the war, and spent considerable time in East Asia, including duty on station during the Boxer Rebellion. An uncharted rock nearly sent her to the bottom in 1900. In 1906, the same year that HMS *Dreadnought* entered service, *Oregon* was decommissioned. Badly obsolete, she was refit and recommissioned in 1911, decommissioned again in 1914, and commissioned/decommissioned several more time before 1920. In 1923, *Oregon* was demilitarized and loaned to the state of Oregon as a floating museum. She was moored in the Willamette River for what was expected to be a permanent stay in Portland. However, World War II intervened, and the USN decided that *Oregon* was more useful as scrap metal than as a war monument. No less than Representative Lyndon Baines Johnson delivered the keynote upon her sale to a local scrapyard.

Strangely enough, the story doesn't end there. The Navy determined that it didn't actually need the scrap, and halted the process after *Oregon*'s guns and superstructure had been removed. The hulk was reclassified and used as a munitions ship in the Pacific campaign. Moored in Guam after the war, her hulk broke free during a storm in 1948, and floated about the Pacific for a month. In 1956 *Oregon* met her end as she was sold for scrap to a Japanese shipyard. *Oregon*'s foremast survives today in Tom McCall Waterfront Park in Portland, Oregon.

Author's Note

In 1992, I convinced a young woman that the entire battleship was actually buried beneath the Park, with only the mast above ground. I carry no guilt from this deception.

There's no question that USS *Oregon* would have better served the long-term interests of the United States Navy as a memorial in Portland than as scrap, especially given that most of the ship ended up in Japan. Had she

USS Oregon mainmast, Tom McCall Waterfront Park, August 27, 2005. CCA, Cacaphony.

survived, *Oregon* would have been the last representative not only of the early USN, but also of an era of battleship architecture.

We tend to think of our era as one of accelerating technological development, but it's interesting that *Oregon* went from construction and commissioning to decommissioning and obsolescence in a mere ten years. In twenty, she was an archaic relic. By comparison, we now expect *Nimitz* and *Ford* class aircraft carriers to serve as front line units for fifty or sixty years.

Related Entries

Contemporary of... HIJMS *Mikasa*
Inspired... *España*
Preceded... USS *Michigan*

HIJMS Mikasa

Laid Down: 1899

Launched: 1900

Completed: March, 1902

Displacement: 15,300 tons

Main Armament: four 12" guns (two twin turrets)

Secondary Armament: fourteen 6" guns (single mounts)

Speed: 18 knots

Treaty: Pre-Washington Naval Treaty

Major Engagements: Battle of Yellow Sea, Battle of Tsushima

Fate: Preserved as memorial

In 1894, the Imperial Japanese Navy (IJN) annihilated a Chinese fleet at the Battle of Yalu. The victory helped establish Japanese power on mainland Asia, and served as an announcement to the Western powers that Japan would play an important role in the brawl over the decaying corpse of Qing China.

The victory also highlighted some defi-ciencies in the IJN. Established in 1869, during the Meiji Restoration, the IJN had modeled itself around British and French tactics and doctrine, and had purchased ships from several European countries. The IJN initially preferred the French model, concentrating on small, fast cruisers and torpedo boats. At Yalu, however, two Chinese battleships proved almost unsinkable, pushing the Japanese back toward the British model. Accordingly, the IJN ordered half a dozen battleships from British yards, and accompanied this purchase with that of a large number of other, smaller warships. By 1903, Japan possessed an impressive battlefleet, competently trained and exhaustively drilled.

The last ship delivered to Japan before 1904 was *Mikasa*, a 15,000 ton battleship based on the British *Majestic* class. Named after a mountain, like many Japanese ships of the period, *Mikasa* closely resembled most battleships of the era, with a main armament disposed in two twin turrets and a powerful secondary battery. Before Tsushima, it was believed that battleships ought to have a mix of heavy and light guns, as the rate of fire of the

HIJMS Mikasa, 1905. Imperial Japanese Navy photo.

Mikasa, 1960

smaller guns, especially at short ranges, would make up for the reduced weight of their shells. *Mikasa*'s experience in the Russo-Japanese War would demonstrate the inadequacy of this model.

Russia, Germany, and France had worked together in 1895 to force Japan to cede much of its gains from the Sino-Japanese War back to China and to an independent Korea. Subsequently, Russia occupied most of the territory that Japan had given up. This caused friction between Japan and Russia, and led to the deployment of a powerful Russian naval squadron at Port Arthur. In February 1904 tensions boiled over, and Japan launched a surprise attack against the Russian fleet. The attack succeeded in damaging several Russian ships, but left much of the force intact. Japanese naval activity for the next several months concentrated on preventing the escape of the Russian ships. Minefields took their toll on both sides, the Russians losing one and the Japanese two battleships.

On August 10 the Russians made a break for it. *Mikasa*, under command of Admiral Heihachiro Togo, led the Japanese squadron that confronted the Russians. The Japanese crossed the Russian "T," meaning that they could use all of their guns while the Russians could only fire their forward batteries. In spite of superior Russian numbers, the Japanese prevailed and forced the Russian fleet back into Port Arthur with severe losses. The admiral of the Russian fleet was killed by a shell from *Mikasa*, which itself suffered significant damage.

In 1904, countries like Japan simply did not win wars against countries like Russia. Accordingly, the Tsar dispatched his Baltic Fleet to the Far East with orders to combine with surviving Russian ships at Vladivostok and destroy the IJN. The Russian fleet left on October 15, 1904. Along the way the fleet mistook a group of British fishing boats off Denmark for Japanese torpedo boats, and almost started a war with the United Kingdom. Although the new Russian fleet was not as technically advanced as the IJN, it included eight battleships, double the size of the Japanese fleet.

Admiral Togo decided to intercept the Russian fleet in the Tsushima Straits, between Korea and Japan. The Russians intended to push through the Straits as quickly as possible in an effort to reach Vladivostok and refit. The long transit had slowed the Russian ships and exhausted their crews, while the Japanese ships were repaired and fresh. The Japanese intercepted the Russians on May 27, 1905, and used its superior speed to outmaneuver the Russian task force. As the two fleets came into long distance gunnery range, the Japanese ships turned hard to port, allowing them to cross the Russian "T." This later became known as the "Togo Turn." Within hours, most of the Russian fleet was ablaze and sinking. Leading the Japanese line, *Mikasa* took heavy damage but managed to make it back to port without difficulty. The engagement was conducted almost entirely with the long range main batteries of both sides, lending credence to the "all-big gun" theories of Jackie Fisher. Isoruku Yamamoto, then a young officer on the cruiser *Nisshin*, lost two fingers in the battle.

Four of the five largest Russian battleships sank on the first day. The last, along with the most of the rest of the Russian fleet, was rounded up over the next day. The Japanese sank 21 Russian ships and captured seven, including four battleships. Tsushima was one of the last naval engagement in which a significant portion of the defeated fleet surrendered. From 1905 on, most defeated ships would scuttle themselves rather than strike colors and be boarded. The captured Russian ships were incorporated into the IJN in various capacities, with several serving until the 1920s.

Memorial dedication ceremony of Mikasa, May 27, 1961

Tsushima was the twentieth-century equivalent of Trafalgar, a battle of annihilation in which one fleet was almost completely destroyed with little or no damage to the other.

The Tsar was successfully dissuaded from dispatching the Black Sea Fleet to the Far East, and a peace was concluded with President Roosevelt serving as broker. Japan had to give up many of its territorial gains, but assumed control of Port Arthur and began to annex Korea.

In September 1905 *Mikasa* exploded and sank in port. Salvaged and returned to service, her responsibilities were steadily reduced until she was decommissioned in 1923. Nearly sunk in the Great Kanto Earthquake, *Mikasa* was scheduled for scrapping under the terms of the Washington Naval Treaty. At Japanese request, however, Britain and the United States approved the retention of *Mikasa* as a museum ship, and in 1925 she was converted into a memorial.

Mikasa suffered damage from US bombing in World War II, and following the Japanese surrender was disarmed by US occupation forces. A movement for restoration began in the mid-1950s, and gained the support of Admiral Chester Nimitz and other prominent Americans. Americans may have seen *Mikasa* as an acceptable symbol of Japanese nationalism, all the more so because of her service against Russia. Using many of the fittings from the Chilean battleship *Almirante Latorre*, *Mikasa* was restored and reopened as a memorial in 1962. She is now one of three World Memorial Ships, along with HMS *Trafalgar* and USS *Constitution*.

Author's Note

Several of *Mikasa's* half-sisters also survived into World War II, albeit in greatly altered condition. Togo's victory at Tsushima stands not only as one of the greatest naval triumphs in history, but also as a harbinger of the battleship age. The German, American, British, and Japanese navies would try to recreate Tsushima in World War I and World War II, generally to no great effect.

That *Mikasa* has survived to the present day is a testament not only to the preservationist instincts of the Japanese, but also to the good sense of the American occupiers, who surely appreciated that sending her to the scrapyard would be like pouring a bottle of fine wine into the Pacific. Fortunately she remains, a last link to the era of the pre-dreadnought battleship.

Related Entries:

Contemporary of... USS *Oregon*
Preceded... HIJMS *Kongo*
Related to... *Almirante Latorre*

SMS Schleswig-Holstein

Laid Down: 1905

Launched: 1906

Completed: July, 1908

Displacement: 13,200 tons

Main Armament: four 11" guns (two twin turrets)

Secondary Armament: fourteen 6.7" guns (casemates)

Speed: 19 knots

Major Actions: Battle of Jutland, Battle of the Danzig Bay

Treaty: Pre-Washington Naval Treaty

Fate: Sunk by British aircraft, December 18, 1944; wreck scuttled, refloated, used as target until 1966

SMS *Schleswig-Holstein* was the fourth of the *Deutschland* class, the last pre-dreadnought battleships built by Germany. The *Deutschlands* were authorized by Admiral Alfred Von Tirpitz's Fleet Acts, designed to provide Germany with a large, powerful navy capable of challenging the British. The idea of a powerful navy appealed to a wide swath of German society, including not only ideologically minded nationalists, but also labor and big industry. The prospect for a larger overseas empire also excited Kaiser Wilhelm II, who saw colonies as the path to world power. Like many German battleships of the era, *Schleswig-Holstein* took her name from a province, much of which had belonged to Denmark prior to 1864.

The commissioning of *Dreadnought* in late 1906 rendered most battleships in the world obsolete. This helped to obscure the fact that *Schleswig-Holstein* and her sisters were completely outclassed, upon completion, by foreign competition. The British *King Edward VIIs* were much larger and carried a heavier main armament. The same could be said of the American *Connecticut* class, and even the

SMS Schleswig-Holstein. Photo taken from USS Arkansas at Kiel, Germany, July 1930.

SMS Schleswig-Holstein. Photo taken from USS Arkansas *at Kiel, Germany, July 1930.*

Japanese *Mikasa*, completed six years earlier, compared favorably with the German design. Moreover, the German ships were utterly inferior to the last generation of pre-dreadnought warships, mostly completed after *Dreadnought*, and including the British *Lord Nelsons*, the French *Dantons*, and the Austrian *Radetzkys*. These ships generally carried a more coherent armament, better armor, and could make a higher speed than previous pre-dreadnoughts.

No one knew quite what to do with pre-dreadnought battleships after the completion of *Dreadnought*. The USN continued to employ pre-dreadnoughts in front line roles until it operated enough dreadnoughts to push the older battleships into the second line. Some pre-dreadnoughts, like the *Radetzky* class, had the speed to keep up with their dreadnought cousins, and could stay in a fleet role. The British employed pre-dreadnoughts in any number of different roles, including

coastal defense, cruiser hunting, and in the Dardanelles operation. By 1914, Germany had an embarrassment of dreadnoughts for any mission other than fighting the Royal Navy. Most German pre-dreadnoughts were committed to training operations or coastal defense. The *Deutschland* class, however, were retained as a squadron in the High Seas Fleet, and regularly performed maneuvers with the German dreadnought fleet.

Thus, *Schleswig-Holstein* was part of the High Seas Fleet in late May of 1916, when the German Navy sortied in an effort to catch and destroy a portion of the Grand Fleet of the Royal Navy. The inclusion of the six pre-dreadnoughts (the five *Deutschlands* and the earlier *Hessian*) was controversial; these ships were slower than the German dreadnoughts, and many believed that they didn't add enough firepower to be of consequence. Scheer included them because of the overwhelming firepower deficit the High Seas Fleet suffered respective to the Grand Fleet. *Schleswig-Holstein* and her sisters were at the end of the German line, and did not suffer from severe gunfire damage. However, one of their number, *Pommern*, was hit by a torpedo and sank, taking 839 sailors with her.

After the High Seas Fleet returned to port, *Schleswig-Holstein* and her sisters were removed from the front line in favor of other duties. At the end of the war, the best of the High Seas Fleet was dispatched to Scapa Flow, where it eventually scuttled itself. The rest of the German dreadnoughts were turned over to other allied powers, which either sank the German ships as targets or sold them as scrap. By the terms of the Treaty of Versailles, Germany was allowed to keep only a few pre-dreadnought battleships, including *Schleswig-Holstein*. The replacements allowed for these ships were even smaller than the pre-dreadnoughts themselves. Thus, the Kriegsmarine retained *Schleswig-Holstein* as an active unit for the entire interwar period.

In late August 1939, *Schleswig-Holstein* was dispatched to Gdansk for a "courtesy visit." On the morning of September 1, 1939 the aging battleship opened fire on a Polish Army barracks, opening World War II. *Schleswig-Holstein* continued to bombard Polish positions for the next five days, taking some damage from Polish shore batteries in the process. The rest of *Schleswig-Holstein*'s career was relatively unevently, although she did participate in the occupation of Denmark in early 1940. The Kriegsmarine used the old battleship as a training ship for the rest of the war.

On December 19, 1944, *Schleswig-Holstein* was hit by three bombs, caught fire, and sank in shallow water. The crew later set off scuttling charges, causing some additional damage. This damage did not dissuade Russia from refloating *Schleswig-Holstein*, renaming her *Borodino*, and turning her into a target ship. She continued in that service until 1948, when the Soviet Navy scuttled her. The wreck remained visible above water for almost two decades, continuing to provide a target for Soviet marksmanship.

Author's Note

Schleswig-Holstein is notable mainly for an era-spanning career. A contemporary of *Dreadnought*, *Schleswig-Holstein* fought at Jutland, survived the Treaty of Versailles, delivered the first shots of World War II, managed to make it almost to the end of the conflict, and even played a useful role in the postwar era. Only a very few ships have experiences as varied.

It's interesting that the Germans didn't devote greater resources to modernization in the intewar period. There was obviously a hard limit on what could be done, but *Schleswig-Holstein* and her sister were the largest platforms available. The Kriegsmarine decided to conserve resources, but a more aggressive modernization strategy might have increased their speed and considerably modified their armament.

Related Entries:

Contemporary of... HMS *Dreadnought*
Related to... *Admiral Scheer*
Fought at... Jutland

Danton

Laid Down: 1906
Launched: 1909
Completed: July, 1911
Displacement: 18,750 tons
Main Armament: four 12" guns (two twin turrets)
Secondary Armament: twelve 9.5" guns (six twin turrets)
Speed: 19.5 knots
Major Actions: None
Treaty: Pre-Washington Naval Treaty
Fate: Sunk by German U-boat, March 19, 1917

Georges Jacques Danton.

The *Dantons* were the last pre-dreadnoughts constructed by the French Navy. They were also the only pre-dreadnoughts to employ turbines, and the only twentieth-century battleships to have five funnels. In addition to her main armament of 12" guns, *Danton* carried a very heavy secondary armament of 9.5" guns arrayed in twin turrets, rather than in casemates. The French believed that Tsushima demonstrated the decisiveness of a large secondary armament, but no other major battleship builder shared this view. The speed and armament made the ships a good match for the Austro-Hungarian *Radetzkys*, which were about a knot faster but carried reciprocating

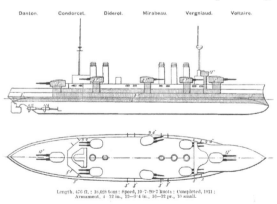

Danton. Brassey's Naval Annual 1915.

machinery. *Danton* was named for Georges Danton, first President of the Committee of Public Safety. At the time, French battleships were named after major figures from French history, and the *Dantons* came into service at a moment in which the Revolution was held in high esteem.

The *Dantons* were excellent specimens of the pre-dreadnoughts, but suffered all of the basic limitations of the type. The biggest problem with the six ships of the *Danton* class was that they occupied the main French building slips for about two years each, meaning that France lost critical time in the dreadnought race. It is commonly argued that they were obsolete prior to completion; in fact, despite their heavy armament and good speed, they were obsolete prior to being laid down. *Dreadnought* was larger, faster, and carried more guns and heavier armor. The *Courbets* (the first French dreadnoughts) were not competitive with the second generation American, British, or German designs when they entered service in 1913 and 1914.

Danton's World War I career was largely uneventful. The French Navy had come to a pre-war agreement with the Royal Navy to concentrate in the Mediterranean, while the British managed the North Sea. *Danton* and the other French battleships spent most of their time protecting convoys traveling to and from North Africa. Especially in the early part of the war, the French were concerned that the Austro-Hungarian Navy would sally forth and

Danton. Histoire de la Marine française illustrée, Marius Bar.

attack the convoys. No such operation ever materialized, however.

Danton also helped guard the Dardanelles in order to prevent a sortie by *Yavuz Sultan Selim*, the former German battlecruiser *Goeben*. She did not, however, participate in the naval campaign to force the straits, which used a large number of old French and British battleships. On the afternoon of March 19, 1917, *Danton* cruised into the patrol area (just south of Sardinia) of *U-64*, a German submarine operating from Austria-Hungary. Danton would become one of *U-64* s forty-six victims; 296 men would sink with her. *Danton* was one

Danton, torpedoed March 19, 1917 by U-64. Le Miroir.

of several pre-dreadnought battleships lost to submarines in World War I, all in French and British service. Curiously, no dreadnoughts were lost until World War II. *U-64* was herself destroyed on June 17, 1918.

During surveys for a trans-Mediterranean pipeline, the wreck of Danton was discovered in an excellent state of preservation. Although the ship apparently rolled over several times on her way down, she landed upright, and retains many of her guns and superstructure. Plans for the pipeline were moved by about 300 meters at the request of the French government, which views the wreck of Danton as a war grave.

Author's Note

In retrospect, the decision to go with an all-big-gun armament seems obvious. Mixed armaments required different types of ammunition, created problems with training and fire control, and reduced a battleship's overall "punch." At the time, however, the immaturity of armor and fire control schemes made a mixed armament plausible. The high rate of fire of the smaller weapons appealed to many officers, who believed that the destruction of the unarmored superstructure of enemy ships would leave them helpless. As battleship protection became optimized around heavy calibers, however, the utility of large secondary armaments declined.

Related Entries:

Contemporary of... HMS *Dreadnought*
Preceded... *Bretagne*
Shared a fate with... HMS *Barham*

Battlecruiser, Dreadnought, Super-dreadnought, Fast Battleship

The pre-dreadnought and the armored cruiser dominated the naval landscape in the years preceding the construction of *Dreadnought*. The ship types were relatively close in size Both fleets at Tsushima had examples of each, and most major navies kept both in the line. Tsushima helped demonstrate the pre-dreadnought's advantages over the armored cruiser, although naval architects in the United States and elsewhere had already begun to notice shortcomings of the type.

In any case, HMS *Dreadnought* and HMS *Invincible* made both pre-dreadnoughts and armored cruisers obsolete. This inaugurated two types of capital ship: the dreadnought and the battlecruiser. Dreadnoughts would compose the line of battle fleet, while battlecruisers would use their greater speed to act as fleet scouts and to perform other necessary duties.

The dreadnought was soon superseded by the super-dreadnought, which essentially cleaned up all the architectural problems with the earliest modern battleship. Reciprocating engines and wing turrets were out; super-dreadnoughts took advantage of superfiring weapons, and rationalized the armor scheme. They largely kept the same speed as dreadnoughts, meaning that the battleship/battlecruiser distinction remained useful. Even among battlecruisers, however, second-generation ships (super-dreadnought battlecruisers, essentially) were distinctly different, better balanced than their earlier sisters.

And then came the fast battleships. The first real fast battleship was probably HMS *Hood*, which was classified as a battlecruiser but much more heavily armored than earlier ships. The Japanese followed up *Hood* with HIJMS *Nagato*, which could make 26 knots. They also reconstructed the *Kongo* class ships in an effort to bring them up to battleship standards. The first post-treaty fast battleships were the *Dunkerques*, which combined high speed, heavy armament, and heavy armor. The battleships of the Second World War were distinctly superior to their predecessors, both because of more optimized armor and armament schemes, but also because they effectively combined the characteristics of dreadnought and battlecruiser.

II

The World War I Era

HMS Dreadnought

Laid Down: 1905

Launched: 1906

Completed: December, 1906

Displacement: 18,200 tons

Main Armament: ten 12" guns (five twin turrets)

Secondary Armament: twenty-seven 3" guns (single mounts)

Speed: 21 knots

Treaty: Pre-Washington Naval Treaty

Major Engagements: Sinking of *U-29*

Fate: Scrapped, 1923

State of the art battleship armament in the late nineteenth century involved a mix of large and small caliber weapons. Naval architects

believed that most engagements would take place within the range of the smaller guns, and that a variety of guns would combine penetrating power with volume. Indeed, some argued that large armored ships with small weapons (armored cruisers, which were roughly the same size as battleships) could defeat battleships by saturating them with fire.

However, developments in optics and improvements in gun accuracy at the beginning of the twentieth century began to tilt the balance toward heavier guns. The increased accuracy meant that ships could engage and expect hits at previously unimagined ranges. Moreover, the high rate of fire of smaller guns was mitigated by the fact that it was difficult to acquire the range by gun splashes when there were so many splashes around the target. Indeed, the presence of smaller weapons made it more difficult to get hits with larger guns. In

HMS Dreadnought

1904, the Japanese and the Americans began thinking about "all big gun" ships, which would carry a larger main armament at the expense of the secondary weapons. *Satsuma*, laid down in 1905, was designed to carry twelve 12" guns, but ended up carrying four 12" and twelve 10" because of a shortage of 12" barrels. The Americans didn't lay down *South Carolina* (which would carry eight 12" guns in four twin turrets) until December 1906, about the time that HMS *Dreadnought* entered service.

In October 1905 John "Jackie" Fisher became First Sea Lord. Fisher was, in organizational terms, a committed revolutionary. He retired many older Royal Navy ships and set others to reduced commission. His vision of the Royal Navy centered on a new kind of ship, the battlecruiser, that would have the speed and armament to either destroy or run away from any potential foe. This would answer the threat posed by German merchant cruisers (or French armored cruisers), while also providing for a powerful offensive capability. The Admiralty agreed to pursue the battlecruiser project, but also called for significant attention to the line of battle. Fisher compromised on a new design for a battleship, to be called *Dreadnought*. The Royal Navy has used the name *Dreadnought* (meaning "fear nothing") throughout its history (a *Dreadnought* served with Nelson at Trafalgar), with the 1906 version being the sixth to carry the moniker. The name was later applied to the Royal Navy's first nuclear attack submarine.

Dreadnought, like *Satsuma* and *South Carolina*, would carry a single main armament of large guns, rather than the mixed armament of previous ships. But Fisher wanted more than big guns. What distinguished *Dreadnought* from *South Carolina* or *Satsuma* was the decision to use turbines instead of reciprocating engines, resulting in a higher speed, faster cruising, and less vibration. It was this contribution that helped make *Dreadnought* a revolutionary design. Neither the Americans nor the Japanese had envi-

Admiral Sir John Fisher, December 28, 1915. Bain News Service.

sioned their new ships as part of a fundamental break with the past. USS *South Carolina* was built onto the hull of a *Connecticut* class pre-dreadnought with what amounted to a re-arranged armament. She could have (and eventually did) operated at the head of a squadron of pre-dreadnoughts without difficulty or embarrassment.

Dreadnought, on the other hand, rendered the previous battleships of the world obsolete at a stroke. Carrying a large number of heavy, long range guns and having a higher speed than any contemporary meant that she could destroy extant battleships at range. Later battleships would have to be modeled upon *Dreadnought*; thus, she gave her name to a

Dreadnought and Victory at Portsmouth. Henry J. Morgan, 1907.

type of warship.

The British didn't believe that superfiring turrets would work (and, in their defense, superfiring experiments in American battleships had yielded poor results), so arranged the turrets one fore, two aft, and one on each wing. This gave *Dreadnought* an eight gun broadside and six gun head on fire in either direction. *Dreadnought* was armored on roughly the same scale as the *Lord Nelson* class pre-dreadnoughts.

Dreadnought became Fisher's political cause. Fisher began stockpiling material for *Dreadnought* before finalizing the design, and delayed all other construction to accelerate her completion (*Lord Nelson* and *Agamemnon* were so delayed by this concentration that they didn't commission until 1908). Laid down in October 1905 (five months after *Satsuma*), she was launched in February 1906. HMS *Dreadnought* was commissioned in December 1906 (accounts vary as to whether on the third, sixth, or eleventh of the month).

Dreadnought represented what theorists of design refer to as an "architectural innovation." Her planners took a set of pre-existing technologies and re-arranged them into something transformative, without necessarily exploring new innovation in any one of these categories. As such, it was not difficult for other countries to adopt the same architecture. Her construction forced the navies of the world to reappraise their own battleship

designs, with the result that *Dreadnought* remained the most powerful ship in the world for only a brief period of time. By 1910, even Brazil (through British contracts) owned more powerful battleships than *Dreadnought*. But however quickly other ships might have eclipsed *Dreadnought*, she so clearly outclassed everything that had come before that the preceding ships were considered obsolescent and virtually useless for front-line service.

Her actual war career was less consequential. *Dreadnought* served as flagship of the Home Fleet until 1912, eventually taking a secondary role as newer and larger battleships entered service. Still, she remained a squadron flagship while she stayed with the Grand Fleet.

On March 18, 1915, the German submarine *U-29* slipped into Pentland Firth (in the Orkneys) to attack the Grand Fleet at exercise. The U-boat inadvertently surfaced after firing her torpedoes, and the nearby *Dreadnought* rammed her at speed, sinking the German submarine. *Dreadnought* is the only battleship to ever sink a submarine. Ironically, the number of dreadnoughts sunk by submarine in World War I is smaller than the number of submarines sunk by *Dreadnought*.

Dreadnought missed Jutland while in refit, and served for a while as flagship of a squadron of pre-dreadnoughts stationed on the Thames, intended to deter German battlecruisers from bombarding English coastal towns. Although she returned to the Grand Fleet in March 1918, she was placed in reserve when the war ended, and scrapped in 1923. She survived First Baron John Fisher (who had taken "Fear god and dread nought" on his family's coat of arms) by three years.

Author's Note

It's interesting to consider what modern battleships would have been called if another ship had preceded *Dreadnought*. I doubt, for example, that the navies of the world would have come to call their ships "South Carolinas."

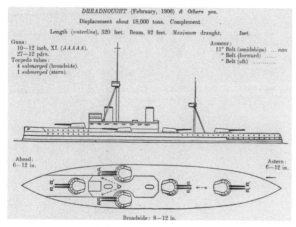

HMS Dreadnought. Jane's Fighting Ships, 1906-07.

Satsuma has a decent ring to it, but Japan is probably too remote for the name to catch on. *Dreadnought* was followed on the slips by HMS *Bellerophon* and HMS *Temeraire*, neither of which, I suspect, would have become popular.

The notion that a warship could go from being the world class to obsolete in a decade (perhaps less, given how quickly new ships outclassed *Dreadnought*) is almost entirely alien to modern sensibilities. Between 1905 and 1915, this essentially happened twice in a ten year period. HMS *Queen Elizabeth* was probably as far ahead of *Dreadnought* in terms of raw power as *Dreadnought* was ahead of the latest pre-dreadnoughts, although in the case of the former the innovation was more incremental (fast incremental) than disruptive. This degree of innovation was outmatched by everything except the fighter aircraft design industry during the twentieth century. Remarkably, however, many of the ships built just a decade after *Dreadnought* remained in service until the mid-1940s.

Related Entries:

Contemporary of... *Danton*
Inspired... SMS *Ostfriesland*
Served alongside... HMS *Iron Duke*

Turrets

In the pre-dreadnought era, naval architects faced few difficult choices with respect to arranging the main guns. Nearly every pre-dreadnought carried two twin turrets, one fore and one aft. *Dreadnought*, with five turrets, presented a much more complicated problem. Different potential turret arrangements each had their own benefits and drawbacks.

Wing turrets promised heavy end-on fire, but typically could only fire on one broadside. Some designs kept firing space open on either side, but this often caused blast damage and put strain on the hull. Wing turrets also created the need for more ammunition spaces, which increased weight and made the ship more vulnerable to explosion. Nevertheless, many early dreadnoughts and battlecruisers adopted wing turrets, especially in Germany, Japan, and the United Kingdom. *Dreadnought* herself sported a pair of wing turrets, giving her six gun end on fire, but only an eight gun broadside.

Other navies decided on superfiring turrets, which positioned one turret above and slightly behind another. The first dreadnoughts to carry superfiring turrets were the US *South Carolina* class, which carried eight 12" guns on four turrets, two forward and two aft. This gave them the same broadside as *Dreadnought*, on a smaller displacement. Several navies resisted the move to superfiring turrets because they were concerned that blast from the lower guns would throw off the aiming of the upper, but experience demonstrated that these concerns were groundless.

Still other navies adopted triple turrets, which were more complex than twin, but promised a savings in weight and space. The first ship to carry triple turrets was *Dante Alighieri*, which carried four non-superfiring triple turrets along the centerline. The first seven Russian dreadnoughts adopted the same arrangement. The Austrian *Tegetthoff* class combined superfiring with triple turrets, giving it a twelve gun broadside and six gun end on fire. Some navies preferred to stick with less complex, quicker firing twin turrets. Others, including the Royal Navy and the Marine Nationale, opted for quadruple turrets.

Over time, certain practices faded; wing turrets fell out of favor by the beginning of World War I. Center turrets (not on either end) were big during the super-dreadnought era, but eventually faded as well. Most fast battleships used a three turret arrangement, with two superfiring turrets fore and one aft, but even this practice varied.

HMS Invincible

Laid Down: 1906

Launched: 1907

Completed: March, 1909

Displacement: 17,250 tons

Main Armament: eight 12" guns, four twin turrets

Secondary Armament: sixteen 4" guns (single mounts)

Speed: 26 knots

Major Actions: Battle of the Falklands, Battle of Jutland

Treaty: Pre-Washington Naval Treaty

Fate: Sunk by German gunfire, May 31, 1916

Lord Fisher was not content with the invention of *Dreadnought*, the all big gun battleship which would render the fleets of the world obsolete. Indeed, even before the construction of *Dreadnought* Fisher had favored he development of a larger, faster warship. The mission of the Royal Navy was not limited to the destruction of the enemy battlefleet, and Fisher worried that smaller, less capable navies might attack British trade through the use of

Invincible anchored at Spithead, 1909.

commerce raiding armored cruisers. These cruisers (examples of which existed in the French, Russian, German, American, and Japanese navies) could outpace even *Dreadnought*, making the defense of Britain's trade lifeline difficult. Accordingly, before *Dreadnought* even left the slip, Fisher commissioned a design for a new kind of ship, the battlecruiser. HMS *Invincible* was the first of this kind.

Although roughly the same size as *Dreadnought*, *Invincible* sacrificed one turret and a lot of armor for six extra knots of speed. She carried one turret fore, one aft, and one on each wing. At her commissioning, *Invincible* could either outgun or outrun any ship in the world. She was almost literally invincible against armored cruisers, with huge advantages in speed and firepower. Facing battleships, she could use her speed to harass and withdraw. The Royal Navy would build eleven more battlecruisers, culminating in HMS *Hood*. The German Navy, feeling the need to match the British, built seven, while the Japanese eventually constructed four.

HMS *Invincible* began the war with the First Battlecruiser Squadron, based in Britain. Her first action was the Battle of Heligoland Bight, in which a group of British battlecruisers intercepted and destroyed a few patrolling German light cruisers. Developments in the Far East, however, drew HMS *Invincible* away. At the beginning of World War I, Germany controlled a naval base at Tsingtao. A crack squadron including *Scharnhorst* and *Gneisenau*, Germany's two best armored cruisers, had been stationed in Tsingtao before the war. The position in Asia was untenable, however, as British and Russian forces could easily occupy the German territory in China, and Japan clearly coveted Germany's Pacific empire. Admiral Graf Maximilian von Spee decided to take his squadron into the Pacific in an effort to do as much damage as possible to British convoys and communications. There was a small chance, if the Germans were lucky, that they might make it home. Spee's squadron wreaked havoc in the Southeast Pacific for a couple of months before the British were finally available to collect the ships necessary to track it down. The first Royal Navy effort ended in disaster, however: The British cruisers became separated from a pre-dreadnought battleship, and were destroyed at the Battle of Coronel. This defeat outraged British public opinion, and the Admiralty decided to deal with Spee by sending HMS *Invincible* and HMS *Inflexible* to the South Atlantic.

Admiral Graf von Spee's squadron attacked Stanley, in the Falkland Islands, on the morning of December 8, 1914. The admiral had no idea that *Inflexible* and *Invincible* were in port. Had the Germans launched an immediate and all-out attack, they might have had a chance of seriously damaging or even crippling the British ships. On the other hand, Admiral Graf von Spee can hardly be blamed for retreating before an overwhelmingly superior force. The British Admiral, Frederick Sturdee, was unfazed by the initial German attack, and ordered the crew to take in breakfast while the battlecruisers raised steam. When *Inflexible* and *Invincible* were ready, they proceeded to leave Stanley, track down the German cruisers (they

HMS Invincible, 1907.

had an advantage of 3-4 knots) and destroy them at range. The ensuing battle was deeply unsporting, but *Scharnhorst* and *Gneisenau* did manage to score a number of hits on their poor-shooting hunters before sinking.

HMS *Invincible* returned to Great Britain, but missed the Battle of Dogger Bank. In May 1916, *Invincible* was flagship of the Third Battlecruiser Squadron, temporarily operating with the Grand Fleet out of Scapa Flow rather than with the rest of the battlecruiser squadrons. Her commander was Read Admiral Horace Hood, part of a family with a long history in the Royal Navy. *Invincible* did not arrive at Jutland early enough to participate in the "Run to the South." Hood led the Third Battlecruiser Squadron into the fight ahead of the Grand Fleet, joining his ships to Beatty's

HMS Inflexible

HMS Invincible in poor condition, Battle of Jutland, May 31, 1916.

surviving battlecruisers. *Invincible* began to hammer SMS *Lutzow*, the flagship of Admiral Hipper's German battlecruiser squadron, with uncanny accuracy.

Unfortunately, the Germans noticed *Invincible*'s excellent gunnery, which distinguished her from the rest of Beatty's battlecruisers. *Lutzow* and *Derfflinger* poured fire onto *Invincible*, and a salvo from *Lutzow* hit the British ship on its middle turret. *Invincible* was not designed to take heavy fire from battleships, but the admirals of neither the Grand Fleet nor the High Seas Fleet could resist pressing their battlecruisers into front line combat. *Invincible* exploded and sank, taking all but six of her crew of 1,021 with her, including Admiral Hood. That was twice the number of survivors of the battlecruiser *Hood*, destroyed almost twenty-five years later. A much larger number of sailors probably survived the initial explosion, but it was not the policy of the Royal Navy to pick up survivors during battle. *Invincible* came to rest in two pieces, with her stern protruding just above the water. As the rest of the Grand Fleet passed by, the name *Invincible* was clearly visible on the stern of the wreck.

HMS Invincible.

Author's Note

In the years after Jutland, examination of the details of the losses of the three battlecruisers indicated that weapons storage and handling played a major role in the fatal explosions. Still, the eggshell thin armor on the early ships (such as *Invincible*) surely contributed to their loss. The passage of time would serve to vindicate Fisher's interest in the battlecruiser type, however, as faster ships consistently played a more active role in naval warfare (in both world wars), than their slower, more well-armored cousins.

The United Kingdom has insisted on retaining the name *Invincible* for its capital ships, despite the embarrassing loss of the battlecruiser at Jutland. The most recent *Invincible*, a light carrier, served honorably in the Falklands War, just as her namesake had served seventy years earlier.

Related Entries:

Contemporary of... HMS *Dreadnought*
Inspired... SMS *Goeben*,
Sunk by... SMS *Lutzow*

São Paulo

Laid Down: 1907

Launched: 1909

Completed: July, 1910

Displacement: 19,000 tons

Main Armament: twelve 12" guns (six twin turrets)

Secondary Armament: twenty-two 4.7" guns (casemates, individual mounts)

Speed: 21.5 knots

Major Actions: Revolt of the Lash

Treaty: Pre-Washington Naval Treaty

Fate: Sank while en route to scrapping, 1951

The commissioning of *Dreadnought* set the navies of the world to zero, or close enough. *Dreadnought* represented no great technical revolution. Rather, she combined a set of available technologies in a single platform, resulting in a ship that was simply larger, faster, and more heavily armed than any predecessor. The capacity to build a dreadnought type battleship was easily within the capabilities of any nation that could construct and maintain pre-dreadnoughts. Accordingly, the French, Russian, US, and German navies immediately began construction on their own dreadnoughts. Those countries without the capacity to build large armored ships simply bought them from others, most often from Great Britain. This group included Brazil, which ordered three battleships from British yards in the years before the First World War. *Minas Gerais* and *São Paulo* were delivered to Brazil in 1910, but the third ship, to be named *Rio De Janiero*, had another path.

Minas Gerais and *São Paulo* were very similar to *Dreadnought* in appearance and design, although they were slightly larger and carried two extra 12" guns, with superfiring turrets. When presented to Brazil, the two ships were probably the most powerful in the world. They were certainly superior in speed and armament to the latest class of US battleships (the *South Carolinas*), although the US Navy commissioned four dreadnoughts in 1910 and two each in 1911 and 1912. The purchase of these ships spurred a minor naval race between Brazil and its Southern Cone neighbors, as Argentina ordered two ships from the United States in 1910, and Chile one from the UK in 1912 (although the Chilean battleship, *Almirante Latorre*, served in the Royal Navy as HMS *Canada* for four years before delivery).

Other than HMS *Canada*, none of these ships ever saw combat. For the Southern Cone navies (as well as for some others) battleships served no meaningful military purpose. Any war between the three states would be decided

São Paulo uring sea trials, 1910. Brazilian Navy photo.

São Paulo. Brazilian Navy photo.

on land. The possession of a pair of dreadnoughts, even if the ships were state-of-the-art, would not long dissuade a major naval power from intervention; as noted above, the US possessed eight such ships by 1912, would commission another eight by 1918, another five by 1923. At the Battle of Jutland, the Grand Fleet deployed thirty-seven dreadnoughts and the High Seas Fleet twenty-one. São Paulo and her kin were symbols, meant to indicate to foreign and domestic audiences that Brazil was a modern, powerful player on the world stage. In 1910, with Mahan's *The Influence of Sea Power on History* being read by one and all, being modern meant possessing a dreadnought.

Mere possession did not convey the resources for maintaining a dreadnought, however. In 1910, Brazil fell into a devastating economic recession. This put immense pressure on the armed forces, which had to reduce personnel, pay, and procurement. This led to an increase in lashing, a punishment then regarded as standard in the Brazilian Navy. In the Navy, lashing fell most heavily on black sailors, many of them recent descendants of slaves. In November 1910, a particularly brutal incident of lashing led to a revolt, which began upon *São Paulo*'s sister ship, *Minas Gerais*. The revolt, concentrated among black enlisted personnel, quickly spread to *São Paulo* and several other ships. The sailors threatened to turn the guns of the two great battleships upon Rio de Janeiro, which was unprepared for bombardment. The government still controlled some torpedo boats, but attacking the rebels would have run the risk of destroying the most valuable property owned by the Brazilian state.

Four days into the revolt, the government acceded to most of the rebel demands, and issued a blanket amnesty. Shortly thereafter, however, the government went back on its

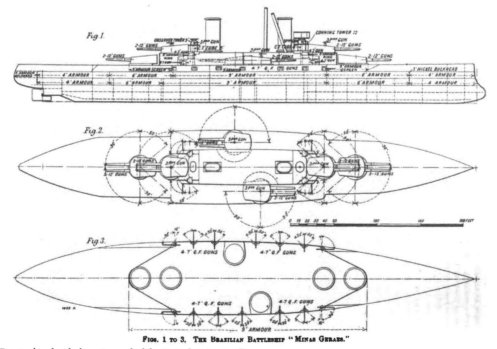

Minas Gerais class battleships. Journal of the United States Artillery, 1910.

word, expelling most of the rebel leaders from the navy and imprisoning them in brutal conditions. (In 2008, the Brazilian legislature would reaffirm the 1910 amnesty, in what labor activists saw as a victory for the history of worker's rights.)

In the wake of the revolt, the Brazilian government drastically reduced the readiness of the fleet, decreasing exercises and removing the firing pins from the main guns of *São Paulo* and *Minas Gerais*. Nevertheless, Brazil continued to pursue a relatively activist foreign policy, joining World War I on the Allied side. Upon Brazil's declaration of war in 1917, it was thought sensible to deploy *Minas Gerais* and *São Paulo* with the Grand Fleet. Sadly, the two ships were in such poor condition that they had to be refit in order to be made battleworthy. The refits lasted nearly two years, extending well after the end of the war. The rest of the Brazilian Navy made a genuine contribution to the war effort by patrolling for U-boats in the South Atlantic.

Jose Candido. Gazeta de Noticias, December 31, 1912.

The rest of *São Paulo*'s career was uneventful. In 1922 she helped suppress a soldiers' revolt in Rio de Janeiro, and in 1924 her crew mutinied again. This time, *Minas Gerais* did not go along, and *São Paulo* fired upon both her sister and some shore installations before surrendering.

In the 1930s the Brazilian Navy decided to modernize both of the ships. Between 1931 and 1935 *Minas Gerais* was extensively reconstructed. *São Paulo*, however, was in such bad shape that modernization was pointless. She served her last twenty years as a stationary defense ship, until being sold for scrap in 1951. In a storm off the Azores, *São Paulo* broke her tow line and disappeared. No evidence of the wreck, or of the eight man caretaker crew, was ever found.

world, rather than ships that would have proven more manageable on their budgets, stands in contrast to the practice of most of the other naval powers. That these ships saw most of their action in revolts (also true of the Chilean *Almirante Latorre*) was hardly accidental.

The prospect of *Minas Gerais* and *São Paulo* serving in the Grand Fleet is surely interesting, perhaps more for the different fleet and training procedures than for the material contribution they might have made. Of course, during the interwar period the Royal Navy would suffer from its own mutiny problem.

Author's Note

The desires of the Southern Cone navies to acquire the most powerful dreadnoughts in the

Related Entries:

Inspired by…HMS *Dreadnought*
Contemporary of… *Rivadavia*
Meant to fight… *Almirante Latorre*

USS Michigan

Laid Down: 1905
Launched: 1906
Completed: May, 1908
Displacement: 16,000 tons
Main Armament: eight 12" guns (four twin turrets)
Secondary Armament: twenty-two 3" guns (individual mounts)
Speed: 18.5 knots
Major Actions: None
Treaty: Pre-Washington Naval Treaty
Fate: Scrapped, 1924

Dreadnought was the first modern battleship completed, but not the first designed. That honor went to a pair of American battleships, *South Carolina* and *Michigan*. Congress limited the size of *Michigan* to more-or-less the same as that of the *Connecticut* class pre-dreadnought battleships, 2,500 tons smaller than *Dreadnought*. Onto that small frame the architects managed to pack eight 12" guns in four twin turrets. Larger only than the *España* class dreadnoughts, *Michigan* minimally, if efficiently, fulfilled the requirements of the dreadnought form.

The most advanced element of the design was turret distribution. While most other navies played with wing turrents (gun turrets set off the center line, and thus incapable of firing a broadside in either direction), *Michigan* was built with superfiring turrets, where the second turret on each side of the ship was elevated above the first. This allowed all of the guns to fire in a broadside in either direction. The Royal Navy and others believed that the blast from the lower gun would throw off the aim of the upper, but tests on the American ships were very successful. This arrangement was maintained in the rest of the US battleship fleet, and eventually spread to the rest of the world's navies.

Unfortunately, because of her small size *Michigan* lacked the machinery to make more than 18 knots. *Dreadnought*, on the other hand, could make 21 knots. The next class of American battleships (and all that followed them) could also make 21 knots, which had the effect of rendering *South Carolina* and *Michigan* obsolete shortly after their completion. Unable to keep up with the main US battle squadron, *Michigan* generally operated with squadrons of pre-dreadnoughts.

Michigan and *South Carolina* were also notable for being the first US battleships constructed with cage masts. Earlier US ships had been built with more conventional masts, although by 1910 most had been refitted with cage masts. Cage masts distinguished American ships from those of any other navy in the world. They were extremely fire resistant (shells simply passed through them), but tended to restrict angles of fire for anti-aircraft guns, although this was not an important consideration in 1908. Every battleship up until *West Virginia* (completed in 1922) carried cage masts. The experience of *Michigan* also, indirectly, helped lead to the end of the cage mast era. In 1918, gale force winds bent the forward mast of *Michigan* all the way down to the deck, killing six men and injuring twice as many. US battleships modernized during the interwar period lost their cage masts, although four of the ships at Pearl Harbor (*California*, *Tennessee*, *Maryland*, and *West Virginia*) still had theirs on the day of the attack. Two ships (*Maryland* and *Colorado*) would retain their cage masts all the way until their disposal dates in 1959.

In any case, *Michigan* never saw combat outside of the action off Vera Cruz in 1914, when Woodrow Wilson unleashed most of the firepower of the US Navy against a small Mexican city. In World War I, *Michigan* conducted convoy escort and training ops. *Michigan* was taken out of service shortly after World War I, and was scrapped under the requirements of the 1922 Washington Naval Treaty.

Collapsed cage mast, January 28, 1918. US Naval Historical Center.

USS Michigan underway, 1918. Enrique Muller, War Department photo.

Author's Note

Michigan was a nice, well-designed little battleship, more of a coda to the pre-dreadnought era than an introduction to the new form. US battleship architects habitually underrated speed relative to armor and armament. While other states had begun to develop fast pre-dreadnoughts, the United States built slow dreadnoughts. The US built no battlecruisers, and kept tight parameters for the speed of the "standard type" battleships.

But oh, the glory of cage masts. Unlike superfiring turrets, these were a design dead end. But nevertheless, the era of cage masts was wonderful from an aesthetic point of view. The masts set US dreadnoughts visually apart from all of their foreign contemporaries, lending a sense of uniqueness and authenticity to the American battlefleet. It's too bad they collapsed in strong winds, were bad for anti-aircraft fire, and had a variety of other fatal problems.

USS Michigan in 1912. National Archive and Records Administration.

Related Entries:

Contemporary of... HMS *Dreadnought*
Preceded... USS *Utah*
Inspired... SMS *Viribus Unitis*

SMS Ostfriesland

Laid Down: 1908

Launched: 1909

Completed: August, 1911

Displacement: 22,400 tons

Main Armament: twelve 12" guns, six twin turrets

Secondary Armament: fourteen 6" guns (single mounts)

Speed: 21 knots

Major Actions: Battle of Jutland

Treaty: Pre-Washington Naval Treaty

Fate: Sunk as target by US Army aircraft, July 21, 1921

SMS *Ostfriesland* was the second ship of the *Helgoland* class, the second group of German dreadnoughts. Germany had been taken aback by the appearance of HMS *Dreadnought* and HMS *Invincible*. The Kiel Canal, which provided for quick, safe transit between the Baltic and the North Sea, could not accommodate vessels of *Dreadnought's* girth. The Germans dawdled a bit before finally deciding to enlarge the canal, and in 1907 laid down their first modern battleships. The construction of HMS *Dreadnought* turned out to be a blessing in disguise, because while the Germans trailed badly in naval strength in 1906, *Dreadnought* reset the race; everybody went back to zero, and the Germans were well-positioned to make a game of it.

German warship naming practice of the time used states and regions for battleships. Accordingly, *Ostfriesland* was named after East Frisia, a region along Germany's North Sea coast. Like her predecessors in the *Nassau* class, *Ostfriesland's* main armament was arranged in hexagon fashion, with turrets fore and aft and four wing turrets. This meant that *Ostfriesland* only had a broadside of eight 12" guns, the same as the much smaller USS *Michigan*. The Brazilian *São Paulo* and the Argentinian *Rivadavia* each had ten-gun broadsides, and the Hungarian *Szent Istvan* and Italian *Dante Alighieri* each managed a twelve-gun broadside on a smaller displacement than the German ship. However, like all German ships, *Ostfriesland* was very well armored, and capable of sustaining a great deal of damage.

Ostfriesland's career mirrored that of the rest of the High Seas Fleet. It was thought at the time that encounters at sea were particularly susceptible to what became known as the Lanchester Equations, in which numerical advantage has exponential, rather than additive, effect. A naval battle, unlike a land battle, suffers from relatively few natural impediments. Thus, it was thought that any encounter would quickly become a match of competing battle lines. In such a match, the side with more heavy guns would cause damage above ratio to the other fleet. A small numerical advantage would mean a large victory; if sixteen ships met thir-

Ostfriesland in American service

teen, the ships would not simply cancel each other out, and the smaller side would be devastated at a relatively light cost to the larger. Because the High Seas Fleet could never match the Grand Fleet in numbers, its admirals were loath to sortie.

The only major clash between the dreadnoughts of the two fleets came at the end of May, 1916, at the Battle of Jutland. *Ostfriesland* played a relatively small part in the battle, taking no damage but probably scoring a hit on HMS *Warspite*. On the way back to port, *Ostfriesland* hit a mine, but did not suffer crippling damage. The High Seas Fleet made only a couple more minor sorties, and mutinied when ordered on a near-suicide mission in late 1918.

A relatively old ship, *Ostfriesland* escaped internment at Scapa Flow at the end of the war. The surviving German fleet was parceled out among the great powers, with *Ostfriesland* going to the United States. A forty-two-year-old US Army aviator, Brigadier General William "Billy" Mitchell, had been arguing since the end of the war that aircraft could destroy surface naval units. In July of 1921, US military authorities allowed him to put this to the test. Along with a number of other naval units, including the pre-dreadnoughts *Alabama* and *Iowa*, *Ostfriesland* was attacked by successive waves of US Army Air Force bombers.

How realistic were the tests? *Ostfriesland* was older than most of the American battleships

of the day, but not all, and not much older. If bombers could sink her, then they could likely sink all but the most modern of the American standard type battleships. Three other issues made the exercise problematic, however. First, *Ostfriesland* was stationary, considerably simplifying the problem of bombing. Although Mitchell insisted that bombing a moving ship would be easier than a stationary target, no one took this claim seriously.

Second, *Ostfriesland* was in poor shape, and lacked a crew. German battleships were well-known for their thorough compartmentalization and their watertight integrity, but looters and poor maintenance had made sealing *Ostfriesland* impossible. The battleship was already taking on water before the bombing began. More importantly, with no damage control teams on board, even relatively minor damage could prove lethal. Finally (and in the only point that supports Mitchell) *Ostfriesland* had no munitions aboard. This rendered the battleship effectively immune to loss through catastrophic explosion, although the bombs used by the Army Air Service probably couldn't have penetrated the magazines anyway.

The first attacks by the bombers caused relatively light damage, but later attacks by heavier aircraft caused extensive flooding, eventually causing *Ostfriesland* to roll over and sink. Reportedly, several USN admirals wept at the sight of her destruction.

Ostfriesland sinking

Ostfriesland in American service

USN was already obsolete as of the early 1920s.

The US Navy rejected this, arguing that the German ship was old, small relative to new US ships, carried no anti-aircraft armament, and could not maneuver. A fleet under steam, the admirals argued, could not be so destroyed. But both services took the tests seriously. In battleship refits after 1921, the US Navy substantially increased the anti-aircraft weaponry of its main units. Mitchell was surely correct that aircraft would eventually take a devastating toll on battleships; aircraft would sink at least fourteen battleships in World War II, the largest single cause of loss.

Mitchell violated the rules of the exercise, but not to the extent that it made much of a difference to the outcome. The Army Air Service sank *Ostfriesland* and a variety of other old American and German vessels, helping both services to learn a great deal about targeting and bomb damage. Mitchell's interest was in propaganda, however; he used the sinking of the old battleship to argue that surface vessels of any kind were effectively obsolete in the face of determined air attack. It bears note that Mitchell was not predicting that surface ships would become vulnerable at some point in the future. He made clear his belief that the

Author's Note

SMS *Ostfriesland* has become a footnote in the history of American naval aviation. Sailors, soldiers, and airmen bitterly debated the rules and process of her sinking, as well as precisely what could be learned from her loss. Mitchell's career ended in recrimination and disgrace, although he helped set the terms on which the Air Force would win its independence after World War II.

As a battleship, she was an effective but not particularly inspired unit. The Japanese also adopted the hexagon turret distribution patter for a time, despite its inefficiency. Even had the Washington Naval Treaty not intervened, it's not likely that *Ostfriesland* would have survived long beyond 1921.

Related Entries:

Preceded... SMS *Friederich der Grosse*
Contemporary of... USS *Utah*
Fought at... Jutland

Ostfriesland in American service

SMS Goeben
Yavuz Sultan Selim
Yavuz Selim

Laid Down: 1909

Launched: 1911

Completed: June, 1912

Displacement: 23,000 tons

Main Armament: ten 11" guns (five twin turrets)

Secondary Armament: twelve 5.9" guns (casemates)

Speed: 27 knots

Treaty: Pre-Washington Naval Treaty

Major Engagements: Mediterranean Pursuit, Bombardment of Sevastopol, Dardanelles, Battle of Imbros,

Fate: Scrapped, 1973

After the abortive hybrid armored cruiser *Blücher*, Germany responded to the British *Invincible* class battlecruisers with *Von der Tann*, a 20,000 ton warship carrying eight 11" guns, capable of 27 knots. As the Royal Navy continued to build battlecruisers, the Kaiserliche Marine determined to keep pace with its own battlecruiser squadron, alongside the larger dreadnought battlefleet.

Germany followed up *Von der Tann* with two ships of the *Moltke* class, *Moltke* and *Goeben*. Because Germany lacked a long naval tradition, the ships of Kaiserliche Marine took their names from famous German generals. *Goeben* was named after August Karl von Goeben, a Prussian infantry commander from the Franco-Prussian War. The *Moltkes* represented an incremental improvement over *Von der Tann*, but all of the German battlecruisers of the First World War demonstrated stability, longevity, and the ability to absorb damage.

The battlecruisers (along with their armored cruiser predecessors) were, by virtue of their speed, more flexible than the dreadnoughts, and capable of deployment on stations distant from the North Sea. In the years prior to the war, Germany deployed naval squadrons around the world to protect its burgeoning colonial empire. War came so quickly that some of these squadrons were trapped in unfriendly waters, chased by superior British forces.

Goeben and the light cruiser *Breslau* amounted to a respectable, if not formidable, German presence in the Mediterranean. Germany had two allies in the Med—Italy and Austria—but Berlin worried the two traditional enemies might fight each other in preference of France. After twenty-two months on station, *Goeben* badly needed a refit, not to mention the more immediate desire for coal, and Mediterranean allies weren't eager to accommodate.

The German squadron began the war at the Austro-Hungarian port Pola, but even though the war began on Austria-Hungary's terms, Vienna still hoped it could avoid war with Britain. *Goeben* headed for Brindisi, arriving on August 1, but the Italians were indifferent-to-hostile. In desperate need of fuel, *Goeben* (then joined by *Breslau*) traveled the next day to Messina, where Italian authorities again denied them fuel. The German crews literally tore apart several German merchant ships in search of coal, eventually finding sufficient stores to move on.

Admiral Wilhelm Souchon, who would later command a squad-ron in the High Seas Fleet, led the German detachment. He had few choices, none of them good. He could attack French convoys, head back to Austrian safe havens, or make a run for Turkey. His official orders encouraged interference with convoys of French troops coming from North Africa, but French and British naval superiority in the Med made any concerted offensive action nearly suicidal. Sitting out the war with the Kaiserliche und Königliche Kriegsmarine (Austria-Hungary's navy) held little strategic appeal, as Souchon understood that adding two German ships would not tilt the military balance in the Med.

And so Souchon set off for Turkey, a choice that—surprisingly—would add nearly fifty years to his flagship's lifespan. Thus began an epic pursuit across the Mediterranean, with effects that reverberated across World War I.

The Admiralty appreciated the threat posed by *Goeben* and *Breslau*, and had made preparations. Souchon's squadron faced a trio of Royal Navy battlecruisers, as well as a squadron of armored cruisers. The Royal Navy expected Souchon to break west, in search of the convoys and in hope of making his way into the Atlantic. The battlecruisers *Indomitable* and *Indefatigable* guarded the western exit of Messina, *Inflexible* patrolled off Tunisia, and the squadron of armored cruisers patrolled the eastern approaches.

The first and best chance to stop *Goeben* came when this squadron, consisting of four British armored cruisers and eight destroyers under Admiral Ernest Troubridge, sighted the ship and considered closing for combat. *Goeben*, a battlecruiser, could both outrun and outgun any individual Royal Navy cruiser. However, she could not beat an entire squadron.

In 1914, the size gap between armored cruiser and capital ship remained relatively small. Each of Troubridge's cruisers displaced nearly 13,000 tons, with a heavy armament of 9.2-inch guns. However, the cruisers lacked *Goeben*'s speed, as well as the armor to protect them from the German's 11-inch shells. At the very least, Troubridge might have forced the Germans to expend more fuel and ammunition than they could afford. But Troubridge, concerned that *Goeben* might just pound the British ships from long range, avoided contact and planned to launch a torpedo attack after nightfall.

Against all expectations, Souchon continued toward the Dardanelles. The Royal Navy cruisers and battlecruisers pursued, but managed to fire just a few shells. The German

Yavuz Sultan Selim in the Bosphorus

ships arrived in Turkish waters on August 10 and waited for Ottoman authorities to decide what to do.

And then the Germans scored a diplomatic coup. In order to avoid legal problems associated with transiting ships through the straits, the Turks formally transferred *Goeben* and *Breslau* to the Ottoman navy. This had the added advantage of humiliating Britain, which had seized a pair of battleships under construction for the Ottoman Empire in British yards. In late October, still under the command of Souchon, *Yavuz Sultan Selim* and *Midilli*—the former *Goeben* and *Breslau*, respectively—attacked a Russian naval installation on the Black Sea.

Their raid was Turkey's first military action of World War I. Some historians have overstated the diplomatic impact of the transfer. The Ottoman government under Enver Pasha would likely have joined the Central Powers in any case. But the dramatic German offer undoubtedly had a popular impact, making it easier for Pasha to push his government into war.

Yavuz Sultan Selim had an active war career. The Russian Navy has historically been crippled by exceptionally bad geography, and Turkish entry into the war exacerbated the problem. The Black Sea fleet could not move through the Dardanelles and play any larger role in the war while the Ottoman Empire continued to fight, nor could the other members of the Entente supply Russia with war material. In essence, the Black Sea became a large lake which the Turks and Russians fought over for four years. For the first year, *Yavuz* was the big fish in the small pond. The Black Sea Fleet included five pre-dreadnoughts, none of which could equal *Yavuz* but which were, in numbers, capable of hurting her. One of the Russian battleships was named *Panteleimon*; its name, before 1905, had been *Potemkin*. *Yavuz's* political importance made her service particularly delicate, as it was thought that her loss might demoralize the Turkish people. Thus, the Germans and Turks were careful. When *Yavuz* hit a mine in late 1914, shipyard workers elaborately concealed the damage.

In the long term the Russians had the upper hand, as they had three dreadnoughts under construction in Black Sea yards. The Ottoman Empire also faced a threat from the Mediterranean. Winston Churchill got it into his head that Royal Navy battleships, if able to penetrate the Dardanelles, could force Turkey from the war. If Constantinople could be bombarded, he reasoned, the Ottoman government would collapse. To this purpose he launched a series of attacks on the Dardanelles. The most spectacular naval attack, on March 18, 1915, was led by the new British super-dreadnought *Queen Elizabeth* and included the battlecruiser *Inflexible* and fourteen French and British pre-dreadnoughts. In case the Allied fleet broke through, Admiral Souchon was instructed to fight to the death in defense of Constantinople. But the Allied operation was not a success: Six of the battleships hit mines and three sank.

Churchill was not the sort of man to be dissuaded by failure. He reasoned that ground troops might seize critical points along the passage and allow for the movement of the battleships down the strait. British, French, Australian, and New Zealander troops invaded in April of 1915. The scattered Turkish defenders were commanded by a thirty-four-year-old colonel named Mustafa Kemal. The land battle

Yavuz Sultan Selim, Midilli and other ships from the German airship SL 10, June 15, 1916.

for the Dardanelles was brutal on both sides, and eventually cost the Allies 45,000 dead and the Ottomans 88,000 dead. The Allied troops, unable to make progress, withdrew in January of 1916.

Yavuz tangled with the Russian battle squadron three times in the first year of the war, but was never able to corner and destroy it piecemeal. The five Russian ships, conversely, lacked the speed to force an engagement with *Yavuz*. The balance of power in the Black Sea tipped decisively towards the Russians in the latter part of 1915, however, with the commissioning of *Imperatritsa Maria* and *Imperatritsa Ekaterina Velikaya*, two new dreadnoughts. Each was more powerful than *Yavuz*, and the Russian fleet the capacity to deploy three different squadrons capable of destroying the annoying Turkish/German battlecruiser. *Yavuz* exchanged fire with *Imperatritsa Maria* to little effect in early 1916. Fortunately for the Germans and Turks, the Russian fleet was none too careful with its gunpowder: *Imperatritsa Maria* exploded and sank at anchor in late 1916.

Then, in March 1917, Russia went and had a revolution. *Imperatritsa Ekaterina Velikaya* became *Svobodnaya Rossiya*, and a third new dreadnought, *Imperator Alexander II*, became

Volya. *Panteleimon* became *Potemkin* again, briefly, then *Boretz Za Svobuda*. Russian operations steadily grew more sporadic as the revolution took its toll, and *Yavuz* resumed its predominance in the Black Sea. The Bolshevik Revolution of late 1917 completely shut the Russian fleet down. Admiral Souchon departed in September 1917 to claim the command of a squadron in the High Seas Fleet.

In January 1918 the prospects of the Turkish/German navy looked bright. The Germans were on the verge of seizing the Russian dreadnoughts (they eventually captured and pressed into service *Volya*). However, things were going poorly for the Turks on the ground. The new German admiral hoped that a foray by *Yavuz* and *Midilli* (formerly *Breslau*) into the Mediterranean would draw the Royal Navy from the supporting positions it had taken around Palestine. The Dardanelles were defended by several old British and French ships, including the advanced pre-dreadnoughts *Agamemnon* and *Lord Nelson*. The British admiral, however, had divided his fleet and was left with only *Lord Nelson* to engage *Yavuz*. Fortunately for the Royal Navy, *Yavuz* and *Midilli* ran into a minefield. *Midilli* struck a mine first, and *Yavuz* hit a mine while attempting to tow *Midilli* to safety. *Yavuz* broke off the operation, allowing *Midilli*, her partner in operation after operation since 1913, to sink. *Yavuz* then hit another mine, but managed to make it back to the strait before running aground because of a navigational error.

Badly damaged by mines, *Yavuz Sultan Selim* required four months of repair work at Constantinople. Given Allied domination of the North Sea and the Mediterranean, *Yavuz* could serve no more meaningful purpose in the war. Transferred to German-controlled Sevastopol, *Yavuz* was again placed in drydock for permanent repairs. In June, only partially repaired, *Yavuz* oversaw the surrender of the last remnant of the Russian fleet at Novorosiisky, although most of the ships were scuttled by the time of *Yavuz*'s arrival. *Yavuz* returned to Istanbul for further repairs, but peace interfered. Knowing that the war was coming to an end, the German crew of *Yavuz* transferred the ship to a Turkish crew on November 2, 1918.

At the end of the war, Turkey was required by treaty to turn over *Yavuz Sultan Selim*. However, a nasty little war had begun for control of Asia Minor. The ship was not scuttled or turned over, but instead left in an inactive state. The Allied desire to carve up the Ottoman Empire did not end with the Empire's Arab possessions. Greece, France, Italy, Bolshevik Russia, and the United Kingdom all sought territorial concessions within Anatolia itself. The Allies had substantial control over the rump Ottoman state, but elements within the Army, led by Mustafa Kemal, resisted the allied incursions. Through a long series of extraordinarily adroit political and military maneuvers, Kemal managed to force all the Allies out of Anatolia, although the Turks sold out Armenia to the Bolsheviks in return for arms and leverage. The Treaty of Lausanne ensured the independence of the new Republic of Turkey (under the rule of Kemal, now known as Ataturk), and provided for the return of *Yavuz* to the Turkish Navy In 1923, Great Britain turned formal possession of *Yavuz Sultan Selim* over to the new Turkish government.

Battleship technology had developed con-

TCG Yavuz and USS Missouri, Istanbul, April 1946. USN photo.

TCG Yavuz, Istanbul, 1947. USN photo.

siderably since 1910. *Yavuz Sultan Selim* was no longer a state-of-the-art ship, even as the naval treaties froze battleship development. *Yavuz* sat in reserve for several years as the Turkish government struggled to gather funds for a major refit. The Turks could not pay for a radical reconstruction of the sort that many other navies were carrying out, but they did intend a modest modernization, rendering *Yavuz* capable of defeating anything that the Soviet Union or Greece, Turkey's most likely two enemies, could put to sea.

The project was a financial disaster, and brought down Turkey's naval ministry. Turkey was on the verge of giving up on *Yavuz* when, in September 1928, Greece gave the Turkish Navy a wonderful gift. In an effort to intimidate Turkey, the Greeks undertook a massive naval exercise near Turkish waters. The maneuvers included *Kilkis* and *Lemnos*, a pair of pre-dreadnought battleships that the Greeks had acquired from the United States in 1914. Ataturk was enraged, and ordered the immediate refit of *Yavuz*, as well as the acquisition of modern destroyers and patrol ships. In 1930 she returned to service, flagship of the Turkish Navy.

Much had changed since *Yavuz* last served, however. As the rest of the High Seas Fleet lay at the bottom in the British naval base of Scapa Flow, *Yavuz* was the last remaining German-built battleship. Technology had moved forward, as the newest battleships operated by Japan, the United States, and the United Kingdom displaced nearly twice the tonnage of *Yavuz* and carried 16" guns. The battlecruiser concept itself had come into question, after the Royal Navy's disaster at Jutland. Advances in propulsion and hull technology had allowed naval architects to largely solve the speed vs. armor dilemma. The modern battlecruisers of the Royal Navy and the Imperial Japanese Navy outclassed *Yavuz* on every metric, as did the new generation of fast battleships that the great powers would lay down in the 1930s.

Obsolete does not mean useless, however. The Greek *Kilkis* and *Lemnos* were no match for the Turkish battlecruiser either alone or in tandem. *Yavuz* could not claim similar superiority over the Russian Navy in the Black Sea, as the battleship *Parizhya Kommuna* had arrived in early 1930. Nevertheless, *Yavuz* gave the Turks rough equality with the Russians. In 1936 *Yavuz* led a Turkish naval squadron to Malta, an event that helped re-inagurate Anglo-Turkish friendship. This meant that the Turks had little to fear from the far larger Italian Navy.

At 9:05 AM on November 10, 1938,

Ataturk died of cirrhosis of the liver. General stress and a lifetime of heavy drinking had taken their toll. TCG *Yavuz* bore Ataturk's body to its final resting place. One of Ataturk's legacies was a preference for a modest foreign policy, and suspicion of the fascist movements in Italy and Germany. Consequently, Turkey remained neutral during World War II, at least until February 1945. Even then, the declaration of war against Germany and Japan had no effect other than to secure Turkey's position in the United Nations. Bulgaria and Rumania had already left the war, securing the Black Sea, and the rump fascist Italian state no longer possessed a navy in the Mediterranean. TCG Yavuz thus engaged in no combat missions during World War II.

With the war over, most of the navies of the world decommissioned their old battleships. The oldest Royal Navy ships were sent to the scrapyard by 1949. The United States either sank or scrapped its most elderly ships. *Yavuz* became part of an odd sorority of ancient battleships possessed by second rate navies. *Yavuz's* new "sisters" included the Soviet *Novorossiysk*, the Argentine *Rivadavia*, the Brazilian *São Paulo*, and the Chilean *Almirante Latorre*. Even among these Yavuz was an anachronism, as she was the only one to have coal propulsion rather than oil. Nevertheless, *Yavuz* would remain the flagship of the Turkish Navy until 1954, two years after Turkey joined the NATO alliance.

There was little compelling military logic for keeping *Yavuz* in service. Turkey's admission into the NATO alliance essentially gave it naval superiority against any opponent other than Greece. The Soviet Union had recently acquired the Italian *Giulio Cesare*, but she was used mostly for training purposes, and it's unlikely that a Turko-Soviet dispute in the Black Sea would have been decided by battleship combat in any case.

Yavuz lay in reserve for eight years before, in 1962, the Federal Republic of Germany offered to purchase her and turn the ship into a museum. Unfortunately, the Turkish government declined to sell *Yavuz* back to the Germans. By 1966 the Turks had changed their minds, but German politics had moved a bit to the left, and Imperial nostalgia had waned. *Goeben* was not tainted by association with Nazism, but she remained a symbol of German militarism in the twentieth century. As no other buyer willing to preserve Yavuz could be found she was sold in 1971, and scrapped between 1973 and 1976.

Author's Note

Goeben earns the longest entry in this book because of her longevity, because of how compelling her story is, and because of her importance to two different navies. Of all the ships that should have been preserved, and could have been preserved, *Goeben* stands out. It's unclear where *Goeben* would have been berthed, but I suspect either in Hamburg or near the Laboe Naval Memorial. It was a tragedy for naval history. One commentator argued that scrapping *Goeben* was roughly akin to finding, then eating, a complete, intact mastodon corpse.

Related Entries:

Inspired by… HMS *Invincible*
Contemporary of… HMS *Lion*
Replaced… HMS *Agincourt*

Dante Alighieri

Laid Down: 1909
Launched: 1910
Completed: January, 1913
Displacement: 19,500 tons
Main Armament: twelve 12" guns (four triple turrets)
Secondary Armament: sixteen 4.7" guns (twelve individual mounts, two twin turrets)
Speed: 22 knots
Major Actions: None
Treaty: Pre-Washington Naval Treaty
Fate: Scrapped, 1928

Naming a battleship is fraught with complication. A capital ship is more than just a weapon; it represents national power in its purest and most visible form. Names, therefore, carry with them deep political and symbolic implications. Warship names sometimes send a message to foes, but they just as often speak to domestic audiences.

The various navies of the world used different protocols to name their battleships. The United States Navy was probably the most programmatic; battleships were to be named after states, cruisers after cities, destroyers after people, submarines after fish, and aircraft carriers after famous battles. (This has changed in recent years.) The Germans named their battleships after former monarchs, great admirals, and German states. The Royal Navy took names from all manner of different sources, including great battles (Agincourt), military commanders (Nelson, Marlborough, Iron Duke), monarchs (Queen Elizabeth), and famous old ships (Dreadnought). The Soviets changed the names of all of Russian battleships to suitably revolutionary terms after 1920, then changed them back during World War II. Only the Italians seem to have named a battleship after a poet.

Dante Alighieri was the first Italian dreadnought, and one of the first battleships anywhere to carry its main armament in triple turrets. The disposition of the turrets (four down the centerline, but not superfiring) gave *Dante Alighieri* a particularly heavy broadside for her 19,500 ton displacement. However, her end-on fire amounted to only three guns on either side. Only the Americans trusted the idea of superfiring turrets enough to attempt it on their first dreadnoughts. Like many Italian warships, *Dante* could make a good speed (23 knots) but sacrificed protection.

Dante Alighieri had a relatively uneventful

RN Dante Alighieri. Dr. Dan Sangera

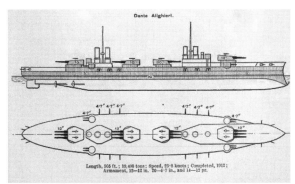

RN Dante Alighieri, line drawing. Brassey's Naval Annual 1923.

career. Designed to counter the dreadnoughts of the Austro-Hungarian Navy, *Dante* patrolled a great deal but never saw battle, as the Austrian ships rarely left port. The newer Italian battleship *Leonardo Da Vinci* wasn't so lucky, being blown up either by Austrian saboteurs or by an Italian ammunition accident in 1917. Italian frogmen replied by sinking the Austro-Hungarian battleship *Viribus Unitis* just after it had been transferred to the new Yugoslav Navy in 1918.

Dante Alighieri survived the war, but not

the peace. *Dante* and all of the other Italian dreadnoughts (including a refloated *Leonardo Da Vinci*) remained legal under the terms of the Washington Naval Treaty. Although the Regina Marina went to the trouble of putting her through a major reconstruction in 1923, it was clear that she would need another major modification in order to compete with the modernized super-dreadnoughts of the Royal Navy. Consequently, she was taken out of commission and sold for scrap in 1928.

Author's Note

Italian naval architecture is often dramatically underrated. The refusal to use superfiring turrets was a major problem with this design, but *Dante Alighieri* could make an impressive 22+ knots. The Austria *Tegetthoffs* (with superfiring triple turrets) had slightly more armor, but a lower speed and considerably less stability. In a line-of-battle engagement, *Dante* would have performed more than adequately.

The scrapping of *Dante* (and the failure to return *Leonardo Da Vinci* to service), meant that the Regia Marina would enter the 1930s understrength by two dreadnoughts. Given the dramatic transformations Italy worked upon its surviving dreadnoughts, there's little question that her naval architects would have been able to transform *Dante* into a useful unit. However, as Italy discovered in World War II, it simply lacked the material and economic resources to operate a major fleet for an extended period of time, meaning that even a modernized *Dante* likely would have sat at anchor for most of the war.

Related Entries:

Preceded... *Giulio Cesare*
Meant to fight... *Viribus Unitis*
Contemporary of... SMS *Ostfriesland*

RN Dante Alighieri

USS Utah

Laid Down: 1909
Launched: 1909
Completed: August, 1911
Reconstruction: 1925–26, 1931
Displacement: 23,000 tons
Main Armament: ten 12" guns (five twin turrets)
Secondary Armament: sixteen 5" guns (casemates)
Speed: 21 knots
Major Actions: Pearl Harbor
Treaty: Pre-Washington Naval Treaty
Fate: Sunk by Japanese carrier aircraft, December 7, 1941. Wreck preserved as museum

USS *Utah* (BB-31) was the sixth dreadnought battleship commissioned by the United States Navy. She entered service in August of 1911. *Utah* and her sister *Florida* were the first two US battleships to use steam turbines, although some later battleships (*New York*, *Texas*, and *Oklahoma*) would revert to reciprocating engines.

The battle squadron constructed by the United States between 1910 and 1921 avoided many of the problems of the Royal Navy, the High Seas Fleet, and the Imperial Japanese Navy. From *Delaware* on, the ships were all relatively heavily armed, armored, and consistent in speed. It was not difficult, therefore, for the fleet to operate as a unit. In contrast, the Royal Navy included battlecruisers, which, while useful for many operations, could not operate safely in the battle line. Also, the dreadnoughts of the Royal Navy varied widely in speed; this could be a handicap in battle, as faster ships could get separated from slower. The same problems existed in the High Seas Fleet and the IJN.

Utah, like many US ships of the period, engaged in her first combat action off Vera Cruz in April 1914. A contingent of sailors and marines were supported by offshore gunnery, and the men of *Utah* apparently distinguished themselves. *Utah* did not play much of a role in World War I, as she was not included in the squadron allocated to the Grand Fleet in 1917. *Utah* didn't arrive in Great Britain until September 1918, acting as a convoy escort. Like all other US battleships, she saw no combat.

The interwar period was relatively eventful for *Utah*. Twice, she served as the flagship of a squadron engaged in a goodwill cruise of South America. The second cruise included President-elect Herbert Hoover. *Utah* under-

USS Utah

USS Utah at Guantanamo Bay, 1920.

went modernization in 1925, losing her aft cage mast and receiving more anti-aircraft guns. Most of the rest of the period before 1930 was spent as a training ship.

Under the provisions of the 1930 London Naval Treaty, the United States needed to convert two battleships into auxiliaries. As one of the older ships in the fleet, *Utah* took on this role, losing most of her main armament through conversion to a gunnery training ship. *Utah* served in this capacity for eleven years. On December 7, 1941, *Utah* was moored some distance to the northwest of Battleship Row. The Japanese torpedo bomber pilots were rather less than interested in *Utah*'s demilitarized status, and at 8:01 AM she was hit forward

port by a single torpedo. Eleven minutes later, *Utah* rolled over and sank. Remarkably, only 64 of a crew of 471 died, with some sailors being rescued after their blowtorch-armed comrades cut through the bottom of the hull.

Utah was the oldest dreadnought to serve in World War II, but not the oldest to serve as a battleship, an honor which goes to USS *Arkansas*. *Utah*'s service in the war lasted about fifteen minutes. However, the service was not wholly irrelevant; the torpedo that hit *Utah* might have hit another US battleship, resulting in the deaths of more sailors. She remains at the bottom of Pearl Harbor today, although her memorial is visited far less frequently than *Arizona*'s.

USS Utah in original condition. Library of Congress.

USS Utah capsizing after torpedo hit, December 7, 1941

Author's Note

Utah's presence at Pearl Harbor is often forgotten because she had ceased to serve as a battleship at the time of the attack. However, her contribution to the preparedness of the Pacific Fleet was every bit as important as that of the other battleships of the line, and her sacrifice should be noted. Several relics of the ship adorn important government buildings in the state of *Utah*.

Related Entries:

Preceded... USS *Arkansas*
Contemporary of... *Bretagne*
Fought at... Pearl Harbor

Wreck of USS Utah. USN photo.

España

Laid Down: 1909
Launched: 1912
Completed: October, 1913
Displacement: 15,700 tons
Main Armament: eight 12" guns (four twin turrets)
Secondary Armament: twenty 4" guns (casemates)
Speed: 19.5 knots
Major Actions: None
Treaty: Pre-Washington Naval Treaty
Fate: Ran aground August 26, 1923

The battleship building fever that gripped the world in the wake of Mahan's *Influence of Sea Power Upon History* extended to small navies as well as large. Of course, smaller navies operated under much more severe constraints in terms of construction and maintenance costs. Spain, having lost much of its naval strength and virtually all of its overseas empire in the Spanish-American War, concluded that dreadnoughts were necessary for national defense. After several abortive efforts, it ordered three ships of the *España* class, which would become the smallest dreadnoughts ever constructed.

The British firm Vickers participated in the design process, but all three ships of the class were eventually built in Spanish yards. This was somewhat unusual for a navy as small as the Spanish, as most similarly situated powers simply placed orders at foreign yards. However, had Spain done this, the ships might have been seized by the Royal Navy at the beginning of World War I, as happened to Turkish and Chilean ships under construction in British yards. As it was, wartime material shortages delayed the completion of the final ship for eight years.

España was small, but her heavy armament made her more than equal to any pre-dreadnought battleship. Small and short of range, the *Españas* were not well-suited to any mission other than coastal defense, which occupied most of their service time. The three ships also engaged in shore bombardment of rebel positions in Morocco. Unfortunately, this mission proved hazardous. *España* hit a rock on August 26, 1923, and broke apart in an ensuing storm. Strangely, this accident happened exactly one year after the French battleship *France* had hit an uncharted rock and sank.

Seven years later, following the deposition of King Alfonso XIII, the sister ship *Alfonso XIII* was renamed *España*. The Armada Espanola floated various schemes for refit and modernization, including one ambitious plan for reconstructing *España* and her surviving sister along the lines of the German pocket battleships. However, these plans proved too

Jaime I, sister of España

Espana, ex-Alfonso XIII

expensive, and both ships were laid up until the beginning of the Spanish Civil War.

España lay in the territory claimed by Francisco Franco, and Nationalist forces quickly refurbished and returned her to service. While carrying out blockade operations, she hit a Nationalist mine and sank (all but five of her crew were saved). The third sister, *Jaime I*, had similar luck. Under Republican control, she suffered an internal explosion and sank in June, 1937.

After the end of World War I Spain considered, but rejected, a larger naval program. Expense was probably the largest reason, although the "naval holiday" declared by the Washington Naval Treaty undoubtedly played a part. The designs under study by the Spanish Navy would, if constructed, have been some of the largest battleships and battlecruisers in the world at the time. The existence of such ships would have made Spain's situation in World War II more complex, as they might have provided enough of a threat to British naval power to justify a preventative attack of the sort that the Royal Navy launched against the French fleet at Mers El Kebir.

Author's Note

The Spanish chose a very different route to naval sufficiency than the Southern Cone navies. Instead of buying advanced, large battleships, they concentrated on smaller, more manageable vessels. Unfortunately, they didn't fare much better than their Latin American brethren. The *Españas* are interesting chiefly for what they accomplished on an extremely small hull. They demonstrated that the dreadnought form could achieve a considerably more lethal unit than the pre-dreadnought, even on roughly the same displacement.

Related Entries:

Inspired by... HMS *Dreadnought*
Contemporary of... USS *Michigan*

HMS Lion

Laid Down: 1909
Launched: 1910
Completed: June, 1912
Displacement: 26,300 tons
Main Armament: eight 13.5" guns, four twin
    turrets
Secondary Armament: sixteen 4" guns (two
    individual mounts, fourteen casemates)
Speed: 28 knots
Major Actions: Battle of Heligoland Bight,
    Battle of Dogger Bank, Battle of Jutland
Treaty: Pre-Washington Naval Treaty
Fate: Scrapped, 1924

HMS *Lion* was the first of the Big Cats (also known as the "Splendid Cats"), and the sixth battlecruiser constructed for the Royal Navy. The Big Cats represented a leap ahead in battlecruiser construction, designed with centerline turrets in order to take advantage of a full broadside, and were nearly a third larger than the preceding *Indefatigable* class. *Lion*'s armor protection was poor, although better than that of the *Indefatigables*. The name "Splendid Cats" referred to the fact that three of the five ships authorized bore the names of large cats: *Lion*, *Tiger*, and *Leopard*. HMS *Lion* was one of the oldest, most renowned names in Royal

Navy history, reflecting the importance and expectations regarding this new class of ships. *Tiger*, however, was completed to an alternative design after the construction of the Japanese *Kongo*, and *Leopard* was never completed. The other two ships in the class were *Princess Royal* and *Queen Mary*, neither having particularly notable feline connotations.

HMS *Lion* became the flagship of David Beatty's battlecruiser squadron, intended to counter and destroy the German battlecruiser squadron. While the Grand Fleet battleships were based at Scapa Flow, Beatty's battlecruisers were stationed out of Rosyth, from whence they would be the first to intercept any movement by the High Seas Fleet.

Lion's first action came at the Battle of Heligoland Bight, where a group of British cruisers ambushed a group of German cruisers and destroyers conducting a routine scouting mission. *Lion* helped destroy the light cruisers SMS *Coln* and SMS *Ariadne* before retiring.

The early part of the war was characterized by various German schemes to lure out and trap part of the Royal Navy in an engagement against the whole of the High Seas Fleet. In December 1914, Admiral Franz Hipper dispatched his battlecruisers to bombard several English towns. The operation, which came off successfully, deeply irritated the British public, which wondered what, if not to protect England, the purpose of all the battlecruisers

HMS Lion, 1914. First appeared in Hugh Lyon, Encyclopedia of the World's Warships.

and battleships of the Royal Navy was. Hipper decided to launch a second raid in January 1915, but British intelligence caught wind of the operation, and the Royal Navy battlecruisers were ready. *Lion* led a group of five British battlecruisers against Hipper's force of three battlecruisers and one armored cruiser. In spite of their numerical superiority, the British managed to sink only the armored cruiser *Blücher*, and damage the remaining ships. *Lion*, at the head of the British line, was severely damaged, but managed to score a near-critical hit on the German battlecruiser *Seydlitz*. Only luck saved *Seydlitz* from a magazine explosion, although the Germans learned from the experience that battlecruiser magazines were vulnerable and had a tendency to explode.

Sixteen months later *Lion* would serve as Beatty's flagship at the Battle of Jutland. Although the Grand Fleet had been alerted to the German sortie, Beatty and his squadron were the first to intercept the Germans. Beatty's Rosyth squadron was supposed to consist of fifteen ships, including ten battlecruisers and the five *Queen Elizabeth* class fast battleships. However, HMAS *Australia* was under repair, *Queen Elizabeth* was in refit, and three older *Invincible* class battlecruisers had been dispatched to Scapa Flow for gunnery practice. Thus, Beatty only had six battlecruisers and four battleships available for the scrum. Beatty's questionable disposition of forces and poor British signaling meant that only the six battlecruisers would be involved in the opening skirmish with the Germans; the four fast battleships had received an incorrect signal and turned in the wrong direction.

Unaccountably, the British ships did not take advantage of their larger and longer ranged guns to engage the Germans at distance, and the two fleets began to fire simultaneously. More poor British signaling left the order of fire confused and one of the German ships unmolested. *Lion* suffered the first major wound of the battle, as a 12" shell hit her amid-

HMS Lion at the Battle of Dogger Bank. Willie Stoewer, 1915.

ships (or "Q") turret. The hit peeled back the roof of the turret, and very nearly started a magazine fire. Major Francis Harvey, who had lost both legs to the explosion, managed to order the magazine flooded before dying, a move that saved the ship (and condemned many of his men to drowning). Harvey received a posthumous Victoria Cross. Had *Lion* exploded, things might have gone poorly for the British. Two of Beatty's other battlecruisers would soon suffer magazine explosions, and the loss of the flagship would have left the British line in disarray. German fire would have been concentrated on fewer ships, and the British might well have lost at least one more battlecruiser (probably either *New Zealand* or *Princess Royal*) in addition to *Lion*.

Barham, Warspite, Malaya, and *Valiant* arrived to save Beatty and his ships from the Germans, and *Lion* was able to limp away. Another incidence of poor signaling prevented Beatty from reporting the size, position, and course of the German fleet to Admiral Jellicoe, a factor in the eventual escape of the High Seas Fleet. *Lion* continued to fire on German ships, although her role would never be as critical as in those first few minutes of the battle. After Jutland, David Beatty was promoted to command of the Grand Fleet. Much attention was paid to the failure of the British battlecruisers at Jutland, and future designs (including that of HMS *Hood*) were reworked to incorporate more armor. Regarding the battlecruiser concept, however, it is important to note that the German battlecruisers performed exceptionally well under fire, and that the battlecruisers that survived into World War II would all play useful roles when employed with care.

Lion had received severe damage, but returned to service by September, initially without a center turret. The Grand Fleet and High Seas Fleets would sortie several more times during the war, but never again met in force. Along with her surviving sister, *Lion* was scrapped in accordance with the Washington Naval Treaty of 1922.

Author's Note

The Splendid Cats, with their superfiring turrets and single tripod foremasts, were some of the most visually appealing battleships ever constructed. Long and sleek, they gave the feeling of speed, danger, and dignity. This sense would persist for the rest of the Royal Navy's battlecruisers; HMS *Tiger* was often called the most beautiful battleship ever built.

While *Repulse* and *Renown* were a tad too long and skinny, HMS *Hood* became the face of British naval power during the interwar period.

Lion and *Princess Royal* were at the very edge of suitability in the post-war world. World War I had given ample evidence that battlecruisers were fundamentally more useful than their dreadnought cousins; virtually every battlecruiser in German or British service received rough treatment during the war, often more than once. But the destruction of four battlecruisers at Jutland colored perceptions of the type, and the British decided to keep *Iron Duke* class super-dreadnoughts instead of *Lion*. Properly modernized, *Lion* could have supported cruiser squadrons and escorted aircraft carriers in World War II.

Related Entries:

Served alongside… HMS *New Zealand*
Inspired… HIJMS *Kongo*
Fought at… Jutland

Sevastopol
Parizhskaya Kommuna
Sevastopol

Laid Down: 1909

Launched: 1911

Completed: November, 1914

Displacement: 24,000 tons

Main Armament: twelve 12" guns (four triple turrets)

Secondary Armament: sixteen 4.7" guns (casemates)

Speed: 24 knots

Treaty: Pre Washington Naval Treaty

Major Engagements: Gulf of Finland

Fate: Scrapped, 1957

Until the invasion of Crimea, Russia expected to take into service in 2016 RFS *Sevastopol*, a 21,000-ton-displacement, French-built amphibious assault ship. The choice of name was odd, given that—until recently—the city of Sevastopol lay outside the borders of Russia. France has canceled the deal because of Moscow's aggression. But the ship formerly-to-have-been-known-as *Sevastopol* was not the first ship named for the great Russian naval base on the Crimean peninsula. Russian naval history is an intricate web of politics, geography, and foreign influence. Moscow has long struggled with the problems of maintaining four distinct, unsupportable fleets—and of an unreliable shipbuilding industry.

In May 1905, Admiral Heihachiro Togo destroyed the Russian Baltic fleet at Tsushima, putting a grim coda on a long, difficult journey around the Cape of Good Hope. Only Ottoman intransigence prevented Tsar Nicholas II from sending the five battleships of the Black Sea Fleet to the same fate.

However, the commissioning of HMS *Dreadnought* in early 1906 proved a blessing in disguise, rendering even the surviving Russian battleships obsolete. Prior to 1905, the Russian Imperial Navy had alternated between domestic and foreign battleship construction, purchasing vessels from both France and the United States.

Sevastopol in early condition. Courtesy of http://flot.sevastopol.info.

Now, needing entirely new Baltic and Pacific fleets, and needing to replace the obsolete Black Sea Fleet, Russia commissioned an international design contest, with the most competitive designs coming from the United Kingdom, Germany, and France. Russian domestic politics scotched an early proposal to go with a British design, and the final proposal came from a Russian builder, with engines and significant technical assistance provided by the British.

The resulting *Gangut* class most closely resembled the Italian battleship *Dante Alighieri*. Russia began construction of one class of four dreadnoughts in the Baltic, and another class of three slightly modified vessels in the Black Sea. Shipwrights laid down *Sevastopol*, named after the Crimean War siege of Sevastopol rather than after the city itself, in 1909. Inefficiency and corruption delayed *Sevastopol*'s completion until December 1914.

She carried a dozen 305-millimeter guns in four triple in-line turrets, meaning she had a twelve-gun broadside but only a three-gun end-on fire. Her 23.5-knot top speed was the only

real benefit of the design, but a curious attribute given the confined waters of the Baltic.

New foreign battleships left *Sevastopol* and her three sisters behind. The British *Iron Duke*, American *New York*, Chilean-British *Canada*, Austrian *Viribus Unitis*, Japanese *Kongo* and German *König* all entered service prior to Sevastopol and all exceeded her in size, armor, and armament.

Geography compounded Russian woes. After the war began in August 1914, the vastly superior German High Seas Fleet hemmed in the Russian Baltic fleet, leaving it with little to do. *Sevastopol* and her three sisters rusted in the Gulf of Finland for most of the war.

The revolutionary situation in Russia meant that maintenance, morale, and training suffered. By 1918, following a touch-and-go escape from ice-bound Helsinki, *Sevastopol* effectively left useful service. Following the Kronstadt Naval Rebellion, a change in management meant that Sevastopol became *Parizhskaya Kommuna* ("Paris Commune") in reference to the short-lived revolutionary committee that ran Paris at the end of the Franco-Prussian War.

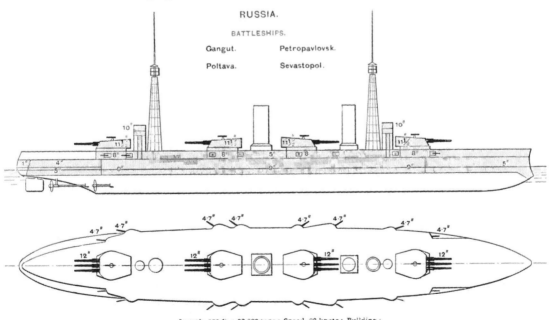

Length, 590 ft. ; 23,000 tons ; Speed, 23 knots ; Building ;
Armament, 12—12 in., 16–4·7 in. 4—3 pr.

Gangut class battleships. Brassey's Naval Annual 1912.

Sevastopol in early condition. Courtesy of http://flot.sevastopol.info.

The Soviet Union still recognized the need for sea power, however, and believed that both the Baltic and the Black Sea fleets required modern battleships. Serial plans for building a large, new battle fleet succumbed to fiscal reality—and to the USSR's diplomatic isolation. Accordingly, the Soviets slowly returned three of the four *Ganguts* to service.

In the Black Sea, the return to Turkish service of the recently refurbished TCG *Yavuz* —(the former German battlecruiser *Goeben*) —made the need for a heavy ship particularly acute. The USSR had lost all three of the improved *Ganguts* in either World War I or the Civil War, leaving only a rump fleet to offset the Turks, Romanians, and Bulgarians.

Consequently, after an overhaul and refit in 1929, *Parizhskaya Kommuna* returned to service and dispatched to the Black Sea. The journey did not go well. The Soviets had reconstructed *Parizhskaya Kommuna*'s bow, but the loss of expertise and experience resulted in design failure. *Parizhskaya Kommuna* nearly sank during a storm in the Bay of Biscay, and had to put into Brest for repairs.

Soviet authorities, embarrassed by the incident, mandated that only the crew could conduct the repairs. *Parizhskaya Kommuna* put back to sea three days later and almost sank again. After she returned to Brest, French workers performed adequate repairs. *Parizhskaya Kommuna* finally arrived in Sevastopol in January of 1930.

Upon her arrival in the Black Sea, *Parizhskaya Kommuna* became the largest and most powerful capital ship in the theater. Modernized several times, by 1938 *Parizhskaya Kommuna* had a mostly new superstructure, new oil-fired machinery, torpedo bulges, and a suite of anti-aircraft guns.

These modifications would serve the battleship well in World War II. *Parizhskaya Kommuna* played an active role in the defense of Crimea from the Wehrmacht in 1941 and

Sevastopol after reconstruction, 1947-48.

1942, supplying shore bombardment and transit for Red Army forces.

Eventually, however, the battleship became too tempting a target for German aircraft, and withdrew to the eastern reaches of the Black Sea. In late 1943, perhaps gripped by the reality that Paris Commune was a ridiculous name for a Russian warship defending the Black Sea, Soviet authorities renamed her *Sevastopol*.

After the war she became a training ship, and was scrapped in 1957.

Author's Note

The Kremlin's purchase of the assault ships RFS *Vladivostok* and RFS *Sevastopol*—and the construction of two additional ships under license in Russia—mirrors, in some ways, long-term Russian practice with respect to naval technology. Both Russian naval procurement and the Russian system of naming warships remain…complicated. The protestations of the shipbuilding industry notwithstanding, Russia still struggles to design and build large, modern warships that can compete with foreign contemporaries.

The Russian navy continues to contemplate filling its gaps by refurbishing aging hulks, rather than acquiring new platforms. And the name *Sevastopol* continues to resonate in difficult ways for Russia, and for Russia's neighbors.

Related Entries:

Preceded… *Volya*
Contemporary of… *Dante Alighieri*
Matched against… SMS *Goeben*

USS Arkansas

Laid Down: 1910

Launched: 1911

Completed: September, 1912

Displacement: 26,000 tons

Main Armament: twelve 12" guns (six twin turrets)

Secondary Armament: twenty-one 5" guns (five single mounts, sixteen casemates)

Speed: 20 knots

Treaty: Pre-Washington Naval Treaty

Major Engagements: Internment of the High Seas Fleet, Operation Torch, Operation Overlord, Okinawa

Fate: Sunk July 25, 1946 in atom bomb tests

USS Arkansas, February 1942

USS *Michigan* represented more of an evolutionary than a revolutionary design, with speed and size to match the preceding pre-dreadnought battleships. The next four classes of American battleships took the lessons of *Dreadnought* to heart, combining all big-gun armaments with speeds in excess of 20 knots. USS *Arkansas* and her sister USS *Wyoming* carried their main armament in six turrets, the most ever built onto an American battleship. The USN would not upgrade to 14" guns until the *New York* class, or to triple turrets until the *Nevada* class. Like all USN battleships,

Arkansas was relatively well armored and carried a well-distributed centerline armament, instead of resorting to wing turrets.

USS *Arkansas*'s first action was off Vera Cruz in 1914, where she bombarded Mexican positions and landed four companies of marines to participate in street fighting. Upon American entry into World War I, *Arkansas*'s first duty was defense of the East Coast. In July 1918 she was deployed to Scotland to serve with the Sixth Battle Squadron of the Grand Fleet, but saw no action apart from an unconfirmed U-boat sighting. At the end of the war, she helped escort the defeated German High Seas Fleet to Scapa Flow, where it would eventually scuttle itself. *Arkansas* was

USS Arkansas, 1918. National Archives and Records Administration.

USS Arkansas (left) with USS Texas, transiting the Panama Canal in 1919

USS Arkansas in final condition, 1945. USN photo.

USS Arkansas, November 1944

one of the eighteen battleships retained under the terms of the Washington Naval Treaty, and received a light modernization in 1926 that removed her cage mainmast and increased her anti-aircraft armament.

As a consequence of the London Naval Treaty, *Arkansas* became one of the oldest active battleships in the world. Unfortunately, apart from the Brazilian and Argentine battleships, some old French and Russian battleships, and the older Italian dreadnoughts prior to reconstruction, *Arkansas* was completely outclassed by any ship that she might conceivably meet in combat. The US Navy saw little point in further modernizing the ship, and for the rest of the 1930s *Arkansas* served in training duties. In 1937 she was placed in reduced commission.

Arkansas's operational tempo increased as the war in Europe heated up. She engaged in several more training cruises, including exercises with *New York* and *Texas*, which had also been withdrawn from the main battle line. She covered landings in Iceland in the summer of 1941, and served as an accommodation ship for a conference between FDR and Churchill. When war came in December 1941, no serious thought was given to transferring *Arkansas* to the Pacific. Along with *Texas* and *New York*,

she remained in the Atlantic and underwent an overhaul that further increased her AA armament and replaced her forward cage mast. Demonstrating that obsolescence is in the eye of the beholder, for the next three years she escorted convoys and carried out shore bombardment operations, including support for the D-Day landings in Normandy and Operation Anvil in southern France. In late 1944 she finally made for the Pacific, where she bombarded Japanese positions on Iwo Jima and Okinawa. The USN remained committed to keeping *Arkansas* as far away from Japanese ships as possible, and she was excluded from a group of older battleships detailed to defend against HIJMS *Yamato* in April 1945.

USS *Arkansas*'s final mission was to help determine the effect of atomic weapons on naval vessels. Anchored in Bikini Atoll, she survived the first blast but was in very close proximity to the second, which reportedly flipped her end over end and quickly sent her to the bottom. Three other US battleships (*Pennsylvania*, *Nevada*, and *New York*) survived the blasts only to be later sunk as targets. HIJMS *Nagato* joined *Arkansas* at the bottom along with dozens of other US, German, and Japanese ships.

Author's Note

Arkansas was a lovely old ship, and demonstrated that older vessels could still play important roles if limited to the appropriate missions. Fortunately, the USN had the luxury of using *Arkansas* in relatively safe areas. Other navies were not so lucky, and had to commit obsolescent ships to extremely dangerous missions.

Related Entries:

Preceded by... USS *Utah*
Served alongside... USS *New York*
Contemporary of... *Rivadavia*

Battleship Aviation

Battleships and aircraft don't mix, except when they do.

Not long after the flight of the first aircraft, it occurred to naval officers to wonder whether aircraft could be launched from a ship. Armies had long used balloons for reconnaissance and artillery spotting, tasks that were as useful at sea as on the land. The German navy had already launched into lighter-than-air aviation with a force of dirigibles that would eventually terrorize London, although it failed to have much of an impact on the war at sea.

The light cruiser USS *Birmingham* was the first warship to launch an aircraft. The first battleship to launch an aircraft was HMS *Africa*, a British pre-dreadnought equipped with a makeshift flight deck. By the end of the First World War, the first aircraft carriers and seaplane carriers were entering operational service. Several intended battleships provided the hulls for the first aircraft carriers; the Chilean *Almirante Cochrane* became HMS *Eagle*, and *Lexington*, *Saratoga*, *Akagi*, and *Kaga* all began construction as battleships or battlecruisers.

Bitter conflict between sailors, soldiers, and aviators roiled the interwar period. In navies that pursued aircraft carrier construction, divides emerged between naval aviators and surface warfare communities. Even the most dedicated battleship admirals, however, realized that the big ships needed some aviation support, if only for reconnaissance and artillery spotting.

Consequently, most of the World War I battleships that survived the Washington Treaty received catapults during the interwar period, often as part of a broader reconstruction. Cranes would recover the floatplanes after landing. Generally, the floatplanes did not compare favorably with carrier- or land-based aircraft, but most types had some provision for guns and small bombs.

These aircraft were only very rarely used for attack missions. Most often, they acted as the eyes of the fleet, complementing the work of any attached aircraft carriers. An aircraft launched by HMS *Warspite* proved a major exception, as it led an attack on *U-64* during the Norway campaign, destroying the submarine.

Larger battleships, naturally, carried larger complements of aircraft. HIJMS *Yamato* carried six scout planes, while the *Iowa* class battleships each carried three. Different navies arranged the aircraft in different ways, with some launching from the top of turrets, some from positions amidships, and some from the stern.

The Japanese grew so desperate for flight deck space late in World War II that they removed the aft turrets of two of their battleships. *Hyuga* and *Ise* could each have carried about a dozen aircraft after modification, but Japan lacked sufficient pilots to staff its frontline carriers, much less a pair of hybrids.

The development of the helicopter made the traditional floatplane obsolete. Of course, most battleships became obsolete around the same time, and the few remaining ships required no serious modifications. The *Iowa* class ships carried helicopters in Korea, Vietnam, and after modernization in the 1980s.

More imaginative planners considered several alternative plans for modification of the *Iowas*. One of the more compelling involved removing the aft turret and expanding the flight deck to accommodate additional helicopters and, potentially, Harrier jumpjets. However, all of these modifications proved too expensive for the projected benefits gained.

In the Gulf War, an RQ-2 Pioneer drone launched from USS *Wisconsin* "accepted" the surrender of a contingent of Iraqi troops, providing a fitting end to the era of battleship aviation.

SMS Friedrich der Grosse

Laid Down: 1910

Launched: 1911

Completed: October, 1912

Displacement: 24,700 tons

Main Armament: ten 12" guns, five twin turrets

Secondary Armament: fourteen 5.9" guns (casemates)

Speed: 22 knots

Major Actions: Battle of Jutland

Treaty: Pre-Washington Naval Treaty

Fate: Scuttled at Scapa Flow, June 21, 1919

Friedrich der Grosse was the second ship of the *Kaiser* class, commissioned in October 1912. The first eight German dreadnoughts followed the naming convention previously adopted for pre-dreadnoughts. Similar to US naval practice, battleships were named after states, cities, or regions. This changed with the construction of the *Kaisers*, the third class of German dreadnoughts. They, and their successors the *Königs*, were named after general or specific monarchs. After nine ships the Kaiserliche Marine reverted to the practice of naming battleships after states with the *Bayern* class of super-dreadnoughts. Although one might suspect that the decision to name battleships after monarchs was designed to please William II, he had always been an ardent supporter of the naval program and no such flattery was necessary. The battleship *Friedrich der Grosse* replaced an ironclad frigate of the same name, representing the evolution of German seapower from nearly nothing in the mid-nineteenth century to the world's second most powerful fleet in 1910. With the *Kaisers*, The Germans abandoned the wasteful hexagonal turret distribution that they had used in the *Nassau* and *Helgoland* classes, instead carrying one twin turret forward, two turrets rear, and two wing turrets. Theoretically, the wing turrets could fire on either broadside, but such use put enormous strain on the hull and the superstructure. The arrangement was mildly better than that of her predecessors, but the Germans wouldn't achieve a truly efficient tur-

SMS Friedrich der Grosse. Cay Jacob Arthur Renard.

ret arrangement until the completion of the *König* class. The *Kaisers* were also the first class of German dreadnoughts to use turbines.

At one point during the war, Austrian naval engineers visited Kiel and discussed the relative merits of different turret designs. The Austrians, correctly, argued that the German turret distribution was wasteful. The Germans insisted that the triple turrets preferred by the Austrians were too complex, and could not survive the rigors of sustained combat. The Austrians had a much better case; *Szent Istvan* could easily outgun *Friedrich der Grosse*, despite being 20 percent smaller. On the other hand, the German ships enjoyed far more stability than their Austrian counterparts.

The *Kaisers* did not compare favorably with the British super-dreadnoughts coming into service at the same time. The British ships carried ten 14" guns in center-line turrets, although the German ships did have good armor protection and damage absorption capability. In any case, by the time the *Kaisers* entered service, the Kaiserliche Marine had effectively lost the dreadnought race to the Royal Navy.

Friedrich der Grosse became flagship of the High Seas Fleet from roughly the date of her commissioning. The German strategic problem lay in the geographic advantage of British naval bases, and in the significant numerical superiority of the Grand Fleet. German operations, consequently, focused on harassment and deception designed to lure out a portion of the Grand Fleet. When, in May 1916, the Germans would succeed in drawing out the entirety of the Grand Fleet, *Friedrich der Grosse* would carry the flag of Admiral Reinhard Scheer at the Battle of Jutland.

Scheer's flagship operated at the midpoint of the German line, and thus missed much of the early part of the battle. As the battle devolved into managed chaos, *Friedrich der Grosse* managed to engage HMS *Warspite* (during the latter's uncontrolled turn in front of the German line), and the armored cruiser *Black Prince*, but it is unclear how many hits she managed.

Frederick the Great engraving, 1808. Meno Haas.

As the day wore on, the superiority of the Grand Fleet became apparent, and Scheer attempted a variety of maneuvers to disengage. For a time the German line found itself on the wrong side of the British fleet, but during the night the High Seas Fleet took advantage of poor British communications to cross the British line and escape toward Germany. Although many of the German dreadnoughts suffered heavy damage, *Friedrich der Grosse* escaped unscathed, and the Germans lost no battleships.

The rest of *Friedrich der Grosse*'s career was uneventful. She operated in the Baltic against the Russian Navy, and was interned by the Allies at Scapa Flow. On June 21, 1919 she was scuttled along with the rest of the High Seas

Internment of the High Seas Fleet at Scapa Flow

Fleet. In 1937 the hulk was raised and scrapped by a British entrepreneur.

Author's Note

It's not entirely clear why the Germans remained committed to inefficient designs with wing turrets while the rest of the world adopted much more sensible center-line turret distributions. Concern about superfiring turrets may have played a role. Nevertheless, German battleships remained quite dangerous, and many of them took an enormous beating at Jutland. Had *Friedrich der Grosse* survived the war, however, she could not long have contributed to a modern battleship squadron.

Aesthetically, the early German dreadnoughts were quite dull, when none of the majesty achieved by the British ships (with their tripod masts), or the quirkiness of the American (with cage masts). Their simple pole masts contributed an unappealing utilitarian look, without much in the way of character.

Related Entries:

Preceded by... SMS *Ostfriesland*
Contemporary of... HMS *Iron Duke*
Fought at... Jutland

HMS New Zealand

Laid Down: 1910
Launched: 1911
Completed: November, 1912
Displacement: 18,500 tons
Main Armament: eight 12" guns, four twin turrets
Secondary Armament: sixteen 4" guns (individual mounts)
Speed: 25 knots
Major Actions: Battle of Heligoland Bight, Battle of Dogger Bank, Battle of Jutland
Treaty: Pre-Washington Naval Treaty
Fate: Scrapped, 1922

The United Kingdom built an enormous number of gigantic capital ships between 1905 and 1915, and consequently had to develop innovative ways of paying for those ships. One way was to approach the Dominions. Australia purchased a battlecruiser for its own navy, on the understanding that HMAS *Australia* would support British objectives in time of war. Malaya would eventually contribute a *Queen Elizabeth* class battleship, and Winston Churchill struggled, without success, to secure funding from Canada for three more. The British had more success with New Zealand; out of duty, prestige, and a desire to match Australia, the Kiwi government contributed 1.7 million pounds, and three years later the battlecruiser HMS *New Zealand* joined the Royal Navy. She was New Zealand's second contribution of the decade; the pre-dreadnought *New Zealand* was renamed HMS *Zealandia* in order to free up the name for the new battlecruiser.

Like all battlecruisers, *New Zealand* could make a good speed (25–26 knots), but lacked the heavy armor of dreadnought battleships. *New Zealand* and other battlecruisers were designed to hunt and kill armored cruisers and to act as forceful scouts for the main battlefleet. Along with *Australia*, *New Zealand* filled out the *Indefatigable* class, the Royal Navy's second group of battlecruisers. The Royal Navy dispatched HMS *New Zealand* on a goodwill visit to New Zealand in 1913, where

HMS New Zealand. Courtesy of Australian War Memorial.

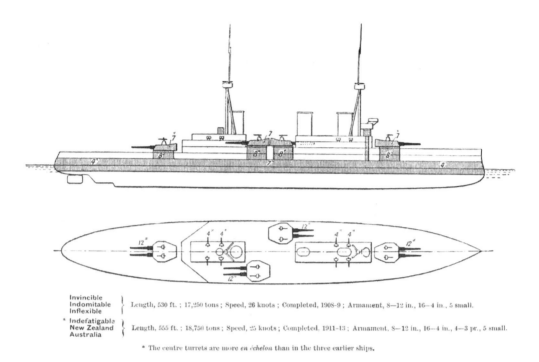

| Invincible Indomitable Inflexible | Length, 530 ft. ; 17,250 tons ; Speed, 26 knots ; Completed, 1908-9 ; Armament, 8—12 in., 16—4 in., 5 small. |
| * Indefatigable New Zealand Australia | Length, 555 ft. ; 18,750 tons ; Speed, 25 knots ; Completed, 1911-13 ; Armament, 8—12 in., 16—4 in., 4—3 pr., 5 small. |

* The centre turrets are more *en échelon* than in the three earlier ships.

HMS New Zealand. Brassey's Naval Annual 1915.

New Zealand fought in most of the major battlecruiser engagements of the Grand Fleet in the First World War, including the Battle of Heligoland Bight, the Battle of Dogger Bank and the Battle of Jutland. Because of their speed, and because the Royal Navy decided to deploy the battlecruisers at Rosyth instead of Scapa Flow, New Zealand and her kin were often active. At Heligoland Bight, fought in August, 1914, several Royal Navy battlecruisers ambushed a group of German light cruisers and destroyers on patrol, inflicting serious damage before the Germans could withdraw. At the Battle of Dogger Bank, New Zealand contributed to destruction of the German armored cruiser *Blücher*, and served as the flagship of Vice Admiral David Beatty after he transferred his command from the damaged *Lion*.

New Zealand escaped significant damage in either of these engagements. On maneuvers in April 1916, however, HMS New Zealand collided with HMAS Australia twice, severely

damaging the latter. New Zealand fortunately avoided significant damage, and was able to participate in the Battle of Jutland.

New Zealand's experience at the Battle of Jutland began with the Run to the South on the afternoon of May 31, 1916. Beatty's squadron of six battlecruisers intercepted Hipper's five, with the latter trying to draw the former into the teeth of the High Seas Fleet. New Zealand led Indefatigable in line, and followed Queen Mary. Indefatigable was the first to explode and sink. A short time later Queen Mary, ahead of New Zealand in line, also exploded and sank, inspiring Admiral Beatty to remark, "There seems to be something wrong with our bloody ships today."

Despite participating in every phase of the Battle of Jutland, including the Run to the South, New Zealand took almost no damage. New Zealand fired more shells than any other British dreadnought in the battle, and scored hits on several German ships.

The rest of the war was uneventful for New Zealand. In 1919, after the war, Admiral Jellicoe chose New Zealand as his

HMS New Zealand in Vancouver Harbor, 1919. British Museum.

flagship for a tour of the Dominions, and she once again visited her namesake country. Jellicoe would later serve as Governor-General of New Zealand. In 1922 *New Zealand* was decommissioned, and in 1924 she was scrapped in accordance with the Washington Naval Treaty.

Author's Note

Great Britain's approach to the Dominions feels a bit "Hey, that sounds like a great idea! Can we also purchase the optional all weather primer? And do you offer any kind of extended warranty or service plan?" Still, New Zealand depended for its security on the goodwill of the Royal Navy, and felt that the prestige of empire was sufficient to justify the contribution of funds to the United Kingdom. Unlike Canada or Australia, New Zealand could not hope to maintain a ship as large and powerful as a battlecruiser. Of course, any threat to New Zealand would also have been a threat to Australia and Great Britain, making it possible to free ride.

Related Entries:

Sister of... HMS *Australia*
Inspired by... HMS *Invincible*
Fought at... Jutland

HMS New Zealand. Allan C. Green. Courtesy of State Library of Victoria.

HMAS Australia

Laid Down: 1910

Launched: 1911

Completed: June, 1913

Displacement: 18,500 tons

Main Armament: eight 12" guns, four twin
turrets

Secondary Armament: sixteen 4" guns (individual mounts)

Speed: 25 knots

Major Actions: None

Treaty: Pre-Washington Naval Treaty

Fate: Scuttled, April 12, 1924

The Royal Navy effort to outpace the Germans in dreadnought numbers severely taxed the Royal Treasury. The Admiralty reasoned that since it fell to the Royal Navy to protect the Dominions, the Dominions ought to pay their fair share. Accordingly, Australia, New Zealand, and Malaya all coughed up the dough for new battleships. Canada initially offered to fund three *Queen Elizabeth*–type battleships, but the deal fell through on the collision of the Canadian domestic politics with an intransigent Winston Churchill.

HMAS *Australia* was the only of the three ships built to formally become a part of her dominion's navy. The second battlecruiser of

HMAS Australia. Allan C. Green. Courtesy of State Library of Victoria

HMAS Australia. Courtesy of State Library of Victoria

the *Indefatigable* class, she largely replicated the virtues and sins of the Royal Navy battle-cruisers of the period. Like her brethren, she carried inexcusably light armor protection (*Indefatigable* would sink from a magazine explosion at Jutland). Indeed, the armor scheme was, if anything, somewhat less effective than that of the preceding *Invincibles*.

Commissioned in June 1913, *Australia* arrived down under in late 1913 and immediately became the flagship of the Royal Australian Navy. Her early service reflected Australia's national independence, and efforts to create an Australian national identity. She visited ports across the country, showing the flag and demonstrating the power sophistication of the RAN. This impetus was hardly limited to Australia: Argentina, Brazil, Chile, the Ottoman Empire, and others acquired battleships for similar reasons.

Australia's first mission at the beginning of the war was pursuit of German raiders in the Pacific. She tried to find the German East Asia Squadron, which at the time was wreaking havoc across the Pacific, but failed to engage. However, her presence, and Admiral Graf von

Spee's evaluation of her likely effectiveness (he believed that HMAS *Australia* could destroy his entire squadron) undoubtedly affected German decisionmaking, driving the East Asia squadron around the Cape of Good Hope.

With the destruction of the East Asia Squadron at the Battle of Falkland Islands, and with the dominance of a friendly Japanese Navy in the region, *Australia*'s presence in the east was no longer required. In 1915 she returned to Great Britain and joined the Second Battlecruiser Squadron at Rosyth. *Australia* narrowly missed the Battle of Dogger Bank. In April, 1916, the bad signaling endemic to ships commanded by Admiral David Beatty led to two collisions during maneuvers between HMS *New Zealand* and HMAS *Australia*. *Australia* received serious damage, and did not return to service until early June. This prevented her from participating in the Battle of Jutland. This might have been for the best, given the poor performance of British battlecruisers in the line of battle.

The rest of *Australia*'s career was uneventful, although she served as a platform for a catapult-launched aircraft in 1918 and was pres-

HMAS Australia in Sydney. Photo by Samuel J. Hood. Courtesy of Australian National Maritime Museum.

ent at the surrender of the High Seas Fleet. HMAS *Australia* returned to Australia in 1919, again becoming the flagship of the Australian Navy. In 1921 she was placed in reserve. The framers of the Washington Naval Treaty understood that Australia would probably again join the Royal Navy in the event of hostilities (especially in the Far East), and thus included her in the Royal Navy count. Larger and newer ships were chosen to be kept ahead of her, and *Australia* was scuttled off Sydney in 1924.

air attack, a 24" "Long Lance" torpedo, or the guns of the one of the far larger and more powerful *Kongo* class battlecruisers.

Related Entries:

Sister of... HMS *New Zealand*
Contemporary of... HIJMS *Kongo*
Inspired by... HMS *Invincible*

Author's Note

Had *Australia* been retained in service (and presumably modernized in the interwar period), she might have been able to play some role in the defense of the Dutch East Indies in the early months of 1942. Her 12" guns would have been welcome at the Battle of Java Sea, for example. Navies often overstate "obsolescence"; HMAS *Australia* had virtues (speed, firepower) that could have maintained her usefulness well beyond 1924.

Still, it's hard to imagine that she could have played a decisive role in the battles of the Dutch East Indies. She would have represented an appetizing target for Japanese carriers, and most likely she would have fallen victim to

HMAS Australia in the process of scuttling, April 12, 1924. Photo by Allan C. Green. Courtesy of State Library of Victoria.

RN Giulio Cesare
Novorossiysk

Laid Down: 1910

Launched: 1911

Completed: May, 1914

Displacement: 23,000 tons

Main Armament: thirteen 12" guns, two twin
    and three triple turrets

Secondary Armament: eighteen 4.7" guns
    (casemates)

Speed: 21 knots

Reconstructions: 1933–37

Major Actions: Calabria, Taranto

Treaty: Pre-Washington Naval Treaty

Fate: Sank after underwater explosion,
    October 28, 1955

Giulio Cesare (Julius Caesar) was the third battleship commissioned by the Regia Marina. Like most Italian battleships, *Giulio Cesare* had decent speed but relatively light armor. Italian warship design in the first half of the twentieth century was characterized by innovation and experimentation, with some results more successful than others. The *Conti Cavour* class (of which *Giulio Cesare* was the second ship) was the first class of battleships in the world to use both twin and triple turrets. At the time, the Regia Marina named its battleships after famous figures from Italian history, with Julius Caesar serving as the representative of the Roman Empire.

The job of the Italian Navy in World War I was to counter the Austrian Navy. The Regina Marina did this job very well; the Austrian Navy rarely left port, and lost a battleship on one brief foray. The job of watching a fleet that never leaves port is not an exciting one, however, and *Giulio Cesare* had an uneventful war. Her sister, *Leonardo Da Vinci*, blew up in 1916; the Italians blamed Austrian frogmen, but the causes remain uncertain. *Giulio Cesare*'s sole mission before World War II was to bombard the Greek island of Corfu during a diplomatic dispute.

The Washington Naval Treaty prevented most of the great powers from building new battleships during the interwar period. So, instead of new construction, most countries rebuilt old ships. In some cases the changes were minor; most US battleships lost their cage masts, for example, and many ships

Giulio Cesare in original condition, 1915.

RN Giulio Cesare after reconstruction

exchanged casemates for turreted secondary armaments. The Japanese, never quite satisfied, reconstructed many of their battleships twice. The British put off the reconstruction too long, and went into the war with several ships (such as the battlecruiser *Hood*) unmodified from their original form.

Giulio Cesare went through a process that was less reconstruction than full transformation. After a four year modernization process, she emerged as a 29,000 ton unit, carrying ten 13" guns in two twin and two triple turrets, and capable of making 28 knots. The speed increase in particularly turned *Giulio Cesare* into a useful and dangerous unit, although her light armor continued to make confrontations with enemy battleships a dangerous proposition.

On July 9, 1940 the Regia Marina was tested against the Royal Navy. The Italians brought two battleships (including *Giulio Cesare*), fourteen cruisers and sixteen destroyers, while the British fielded a carrier, three battleships, five cruisers, and sixteen destroyers. Effectively, the distant escort groups of two convoys had collided with one another. *Giulio Cesare* engage an advancing HMS *Warspite*, but was hit by a 15" shell at 26,000 yards, which damaged her propulsion system. Fortunately, *Warspite* turned away, and the Italians retired successfully.

The problem of the Italian Navy in World War II had less to do with the ships than with their management. While the Italians could have challenged the Royal Navy for control of the Mediterranean (especially given British commitments in the Atlantic and the Pacific), the fleet rarely left port—a fact that the Royal Navy took advantage of on November 11, 1940, when the aircraft of a single light carrier

RN Giulio Cesare visiting Malta, 1938

devastated the Italian naval anchorage at Taranto. *Giulio Cesare* escaped damage, but her sister *Cavour* was sunk, and several other ships were damaged.

Giulio Cesare ran convoy escort missions until 1942, when the Italian Navy withdrew her from active operations because of increasing Allied dominance in the Mediterranean, along with a lack of fuel. Greater pressure in the Med could have helped the Axis war effort in other areas, but Italy lacked the resources for full commitment. Following the Italian surrender in September of 1943, *Giulio Cesare* and most of the rest of the Italian fleet surrendered to the Royal Navy at Malta, where the ships remained until the end of the war.

Giulio Cesare returned to Allied-controlled Italy as the war wound down, but the terms of surrender required the transfer of most of the remaining Italian heavy units to

the Allies. The Soviets sought one of the newer *Littorio* class battleships, but in a drawing of lots received *Giulio Cesare*. In 1948 Italy transferred *Giulio Cesare* (in relatively poor repair) to the Soviet Union. In a few short months she went from being the obsolete relic of a defeated second-rate navy to being the flagship of the Soviet Black Sea Fleet. *Giulio Cesare* became *Novorossiysk*, the most powerful Russian ship in the Black Sea since World War I. Although the presence of *Novorossiysk* may have delighted the commanders of the Black Sea Fleet, it bedeviled maintenance and repair crews, who could not speak Italian and had little guidance in putting the aging warship back into service. Nevertheless, *Novorossiysk* had an immediate effect on the balance of naval strength in the Black Sea, as the only other major units available were *Sevastopol* and the Turkish *Yavuz*.

Novorossiysk (Giulio Cesare under Soviet flag) in Sevastopol in 1950. Courtesy ofnavsource.narod.ru.

In late October 1955, *Novorossiysk* exploded and sank at anchor in Sevastopol. The cause remains unclear. Most likely, a left-over magnetic mine dropped by Germany during World War II attached itself to the bottom of her hull and exploded. 608 Russian crewmen died, largely because of the ineptitude of the Soviet captain who thought that she would settle on the bottom rather than capsize. Other theories of *Novorossiysk*'s end persist, however. One suggests that an Italian special forces team attached explosives to the ship and blew it up out of revenge. (It is rumored that several Italian frogmen received high decorations for mysterious reasons in the late 1950s.) Another theory suggests that the Italians planted explosives in the ship upon the transfer. Finally, one theory suggests that Soviet intelligence blew the ship up with the purpose of blaming Turkey for the tragedy and sparking a war. That the Soviets failed to go to war, and indeed concealed the sinking for some time, puts this theory into serious question.

Author's Note

Faced with the constraints created by the Washington Naval Treaty, the Italians did a better job than anyone (except perhaps the Japanese) at turning old dreadnoughts into modern, effective units. *Giulio Cesare* and her sisters lacked great protection, but they had the speed to operate with the fast, modern units of the Regia Marina.

Giulio Cesare's end is a truly remarkable story. The delivery of the Italian warship helped sate the Soviet appetite for battleships, and give them some experience with heavy, modern vessels. It also, eventually, revealed deep incompetence in the Soviet Navy. Nevertheless, it's interesting to imagine how long the Soviets might have tried to keep one of the *Littorio* class in service, if they'd won the draw.

Related Entries:

Fought against… HMS *Warspite*
Served alongside… *Sevastopol*
Contemporary of… *Bretagne*

Wreck of Novorossiysk, 1957. Courtesy of navsource.narod.ru.

SMS Viribus Unitis

Laid Down: 1910

Launched: 1911

Completed: December, 1912

Displacement: 20,000 tons

Main Armament: twelve 12" guns (four triple turrets)

Secondary Armament: twelve 6" guns (casemates)

Speed: 20 knots

Treaty: Pre-Washington Naval Treaty

Major Engagements: None

Fate: Sunk by Italian human torpedoes, November 1, 1918

SMS *Viribus Unitis* was the first Austrian dreadnought, commissioned in December 1912. *Viribus Unitis* meant "Joint Forces," the motto of Emperor Franz Joseph and a call for unity in service to the Empire, which faced nationalist pressures for most of Franz Joseph's reign. Like her sister SMS *Szent Istvan*, *Viribus Unitis* attempted a great deal on a small displacement, sacrificing stability for hitting power.

The four battleships of the *Tegetthoff* class presented a major problem for Italy and France as long as they remained afloat. They played the role of a classic "fleet in being," tying down larger forces than themselves simply by threatening to sortie. Consequently, any actual engagement with the heavy forces of the French or Italians represented an unacceptable risk.

The best opportunity for Austria to make a real naval impact came in the first days of the war. As *Goeben* attempted to elude her pursuers, Germany requested assistance from the Kaiserliche and Königliche Marine. At the time, *Viribus Unitis* led a squadron of three dreadnoughts and three *Radetzky* class "semi-dreadnoughts," more than a match for local British forces. However, still hoping to contain the conflict, the Austrians declined to assist the Germans. Had *Viribus Unitis* and her sisters successfully forced battle against either the armored cruisers of Admiral Troubridge, or the battlecruisers *Inflexible* and *Indefatigable*, a sortie would have been well worth the risk. However, it was difficult at the time to appreciate the contours of the future war.

The entry of Italy into the war further stacked the odds against the Austrians, and meant that *Viribus Unitis* would lead an

SMS Viribus Unitis

Emperor Franz Joseph I. Photo by Carl Pietzner.

uneventful career. In May 1915, she bombard-ed the Italian port city Ancona. In 1918, she and her three sisters sortied to attack the Otranto Barrage, a set of defenses designed to seal the Adriatic off and trap the Austrian Navy. The operation resulted in the loss of *Szent Istvan*. *Viribis Unitis* returned to port, where she sat while Austria-Hungary disinte-grated.

In late October 1918, Croatia and Slovenia severed their connection to the Hapsburg crown. Emperor Karl I (the successor of Franz Josef) turned over the entire Austrian navy to the state that would (eventually) become Yugoslavia. Italy had designs on some of the Austrian territory that might be turned over to the Croats, and didn't like the idea of an Austrian successor state taking possession of three modern dreadnoughts. Although the nascent Yugoslavia declared that it was no longer at war with the Allies, this declaration was not immediately recognized by the Italians. Accordingly, on November 1, 1918 Italy dispatched a pair of young men named Raffaele—one a Lieutenant Paolucci, and the other a Major Rossetti—to infiltrate Pula Harbor on a modified torpedo and attach a bomb to the hull of SMS *Viribus Unitis*. This

the Raffaeles succeeded in doing, but they were captured while escaping, and brought on board the battleship.

The ticking time bomb scenario has been of use to torture advocates because it purports to produce a "best case" for the use of torture. The features of the scenario are reasonably well known. A terrorist or individual of similar occupation has been captured. Authorities know, somehow, that a bomb will go off in the very near future in a target of great value. Authorities don't know exactly when or where the bomb will go off, but they know that the captured terrorist does know where the bomb is, and could supply that information if proper-ly motivated. In this scenario it is argued, by Alan Dershowitz among others, that torturing the terrorist into giving up the location of the bomb is legitimate and appropriate behavior.

Critiques of this scenario have hammered at the details. How precisely do authorities know that a bomb will go off, and that it will go off in a high value target? How do they know that the terrorist we have in custody actually has knowledge of the location of the bomb? How can they determine the veracity of the information acquired under torture? Except for the last, these questions suggest that the "ticking time bomb" scenario, while commonly

SMS Viribus Unitis painted by Alexander Kircher

SMS Viribus Unitis and two of her sisters at Pula.

found on television, isn't something that actually happens in real life. The last attacks the scenario in another way, suggesting that the proposed solution (torture) is unlikely to have the desired effect (finding the bomb).

The experience on *Viribus Unitis* was an almost classic ticking time bomb scenario. When the Raffaeles were brought on board, they told Admiral Vuckovich (the new commander of the dreadnought) that they had affixed a bomb to the hull and that the ship should be evacuated. This put the admiral in an awkward position. He could evacuate, but that would ensure the loss of the battleship when the mine exploded. The decision to concentrate on armament at the expense of stability left the ship vulnerable to underwater attack, making the threat of the bomb particularly potent. While it could be argued that the admiral should have evacuated *Viribus Unitis* anyway, thus saving the lives of his men, the ship was an extraordinarily expensive piece of state property. The men onboard the ship expected that they might have to die or kill in its defense. It was reasonable at the time to believe that the ship might be used to fight or deter the Italians. As such, evacuation didn't present a very compelling option. Instead, the admiral decided to keep enough sailors on board to allow the best possible response to the damage that the bomb would cause. Inevitably, it risked the deaths of many sailors, but at the same time held out the best chance for saving the ship.

But what of the Raffaeles? The Italian officers had already admitted that a bomb was attached to the hull, and that it would explode in a relatively short period of time. They begged Admiral Vuckovich to be allowed to leave the ship, and he agreed to let them go. However, when they reached the water they were assailed by angry sailors, and then dragged back onto *Viribus Unitis*. Fearing prosecution (and potentially execution) for what amounted to a legally questionable attack on what its owners presumed to be a neutral vessel, the Italians demanded to be treated as prisoners of war. Admiral Vuckovich made no determination at the time, but ordered the crew not to harm the Italians. Twenty-five minutes later the bomb exploded. Fifteen minutes after that Viribus Unitis rolled over and sank with 300 men, including Admiral Vuckovich but not including the Raffaeles, who were allowed by Admiral Vuckovich to abandon ship, and who spent about a week as

SMS Viribus Unitis carrying the body of Archduke Franz Ferdinand

prisoners of war.

Does this represent a genuine historical case of a classic ticking time bomb scenario? The Croats didn't have a lot of time to torture the Italians, but they could be fairly certain that the bomb existed and that the Italians knew where it was. If they had discovered the location, the Croats might have been able to either disable the bomb or to prepare damage control around the area of the explosion. Moreover, they may even have had enough time to confirm or disconfirm statements made under torture by the Italians.

Would the torture have worked? The Italians clearly wanted to stay alive, but they didn't give up the location of the bomb even when it seemed certain that they would fall victim to it. Whether they would have given up the information under threat of severe pain in addition to death is unclear. Had they given up the location of the bomb and survived, the Raffaeles would have probably have been made the object of scorn and derision in Italy, rather than receiving treatment as heroes.

How much weight should be placed on the behavior of Admiral Vuckovich? Charged with the defense of the ship, which entailed a willingness to see his sailors die and to kill the sailors of the enemy, Vuckovich decided that the information wasn't worth torturing the Italians. His decision likely depended upon a combination of utilitarian calculus, professional honor, and perhaps a revulsion against torture. It's possible that he made a mistake, but his evaluation of the situation should weigh heavily on the historical ledger.

Most of the wreck of Viribus Unitis remains at the bottom of Pula Harbor.

Author's Note

The Tegetthoffs were compact, innovative warships, despite their significant flaws. Austria-Hungary's geographic position made it virtually impossible for the ships to play a larger role in the war than they did. Even had Italy remained neutral, the Austrians would have struggled to deploy effectively in the presence of the Marine Nationale.

Nevertheless, the most interesting part of

Viribus Unitis's career is most certainly her loss. In World War II, the Italians used frogmen to good effect against British warships in the Med. A similar experience in December 1941 left two *Queen Elizabeth* class battleships on the bottom of Alexandria harbor. That frogmen (the forerunner of modern special forces operators) could lay low steel castles remains one of the great ironies of the battleship age.

Related Entries:

Sister of... SMS *Szent Istvan*

Meant to fight... *Giulio Cesare*

Contemporary of... SMS *Friederich der Grosse*

ARA Rivadavia

Laid Down: 1910

Launched: 1911

Completed: August, 1914

Displacement: 27,500 tons

Main Armament: twelve 12" guns (six twin turrets)

Secondary Armament: twelve 6" guns (casemates)

Speed: 22.5 knots

Major Actions: None

Treaty: Pre-Washington Naval Treaty

Fate: Sold for scrap, 1957

The Southern Cone dreadnought race began with the Brazilian order of *Minas Gerais* and *São Paulo* from British yards. Not to be outdone, Argentina and Chile soon ordered battleships of their own. The supply-side race was nearly as competitive as the demand side. Germany, Britain, and the United States all struggled to win the Argentine contract (Britain appeared to have the Chilean contact sewn up, as well as an additional Brazilian ship). The United States in particular leaned very heavily on the Argentine government, believing that it deserved a chunk of the naval contracts in its own backyard.

Eventually, and not without controversy, the Argentines decided to go with an American supplier. From the point of view of delivery, this turned out to be an excellent choice. At the beginning of World War I, Great Britain seized both Chilean battleships and two Turkish battleships for incorporation into the Royal Navy.

ARA Rivadavia, finishing construction in Boston Harbor. Boston Public Library.

ARA Rivadavia or ARA Moreno, nearing completion

A Greek dreadnought, *Salamis*, under construction in Germany was never completed as the Germans decided to work on their own ships (the Germans did not to complete and seize the ship out of fear of offending Greece). HIJMS *Kongo*, the most formidable warship under foreign construction at the time, escaped British seizure by a few months.

Rivadavia was completed in late 1914, making her and her sister rough contemporaries of the US *New York* class. The design of *Rivadavia* was, in some ways, more advanced than that of the *New Yorks*. *Rivadavia* had a similar displacement (27,000 tons), was powered by steam turbines, and could make almost 2 knots faster than the US ships. However, *Rivadavia* carried 12" guns to *New York*'s ten 14", and had somewhat lighter armor. *Rivadavia*'s armament was arranged in two superfiring turrets each fore and aft and two wing turrets, making her and *Moreno* the only battleships built in the United States to carry wing turrets. *Rivadavia* carried a single cage mast forward, making the ARA the only navy

besides the USN to operate dreadnoughts with cage masts.

The acquisition of *Rivadavia* and *Moreno* remained controversial in Argentina. The government in Buenos Aires, regretting the contracts on the advent of a major recession in 1910, considered selling them to several foreign buyers. The United States worried that Argentina would export them to Japan, and another scheme involved a French purchase and transfer to Greece. The United States Navy didn't want them, as they did not fit in well with the new "standard type" battleship squadron the USN was building. Argentina eventually bowed to the pressure and agreed to accept the ships it had purchased.

Upon their delivery to the ARA, *Rivadavia* and *Moreno* became the most powerful ships in South America, an indication of how rapidly battleship technology advanced in the first twenty years of the twentieth century. Whereas *São Paulo* and *Minas Gerais* had been among the most powerful ships in the world upon their completion in 1910, they were complete-

ARGENTINE BATTLESHIP.
DEC. 2. 1912

ARA Rivadavia under construction in Quincy, Massachusetts. Library of Congress.

ly outclassed by the Argentine ships in 1915. *Rivadavia* was not nearly the equal of *Almirante Latorre*, finally delivered to Chile after World War I, but the two Argentine ships made up the most powerful squadron in the area. *Rivadavia* also seems to have been better taken care of than the Brazilian ships. She received oil-fired boilers during a major refit in the 1920s, and remained fairly active in the 1920s and 1930s.

World War II brought only mild tensions to South America. Brazil leaned very heavily toward the Allies, eventually joining the war (and making a significant contribution both on land and at sea) in 1942. Chile and Argentina were less forthcoming, both having significant Axis sympathies. Both Argentina and Chile would eventually declare war on Germany and Japan, but neither lent any meaningful contribution to the Allied cause. *Rivadavia* embarked on her last long cruise in 1946, visiting a number of South American ports before being placed in reserve. By 1952 *Rivadavia*

was disarmed, and was struck from the ARA List in 1957. *Rivadavia* and *Moreno* were replaced by the US light cruisers *Boise* and *Phoenix*, which became *Nueve de Julio* and *General Belgrano*, respectively.

Author's Note

Rivadavia and *Moreno* were the only non-US dreadnoughts to carry cage masts, but they weren't the last battleships to do so. *Colorado* and *Maryland* both retained their cage masts until scrapping in 1959. *Rivadavia* and *Moreno* were also the fastest battleships built in the United States until USS *North Carolina*, an outcome that stemmed from the US decision to focus on armor and firepower over speed.

Related Entries:

Contemporary of... USS *New York*
Meant to fight... *São Paulo*
Meant to fight... *Almirante Latorre*

Imperator Aleksandr III (Imperial Russia)
Volya (Provisional Government)
Wolga (Imperial Germany)
General Alekseev (Whites)

Laid Down: 1911
Launched: 1913
Completed: 1918
Displacement: 24,000 tons
Main Armament: twelve 12" guns (four triple turrets)
Secondary Armament: eighteen 5.1" guns (casemates)
Speed: 22 knots
Major Actions: Crimea
Treaty: Pre-Washington Naval Treaty
Fate: Scrapped, 1924–36

Imperator Aleksandr III was the third of the *Imperatritsa Mariya* class, a group of dreadnoughts built in the Black Sea and designed to fight the Turkish Navy. The warship was initially named for Emperor Aleksandr III, who had succeeded to the throne of Russia upon the assassination of his brother in 1881. Although also the target of several assassination plots, Alexander III died of natural causes in 1894. A conservative, he helped roll back the reforms initiated by his father, and contributed in his own way to the revolutionary upheavals in Russia in the early twentieth century.

The design was similar to but a moderate improvement upon the *Gangut* class, carrying much heavier armor. Because of an obdurate Turkish government, the Black Sea Fleet was the only Russian fleet, following the Russo-Japanese War, to still possess ships. The Turkish purchases of the dreadnoughts *Sultan Osman I* and *Reshadiye* (later *Agincourt* and *Erin*) would have given the Turks decisive superiority over the five remaining Russian pre-dreadnoughts. *Imperator Aleksandr III* and her two sisters were designed to remedy this problem. With war came the seizure of the

Volya on high speed trials, April 29, 1917

two Turkish battleships by the British government, and the later transfer of the German battlecruiser *Goeben* to Turkish control.

This meant that the situation differed dramatically from what the Russians had expected. Laid down in 1911, problems with machinery and Russian industry delayed *Aleksandr's* completion. Moreover, in order to match the Turks, Russian officials accelerated the construction of *Aleksandr's* two sisters at *Aleksandr's* expense. The completion of the two battleships briefly gave the Russian Navy superiority in the Black Sea, at least until the accidental explosion of *Imperatritsa Mariya*, in October 1916, evened the ledger.

The February 1917, Revolution resulted in further chaos. *Imperator Aleksandr III* was taken over by the Provisional Government and renamed *Volya* (Freedom). Although still incomplete, she began to take her sea trials. Neither the Provisional Government nor the Bolsheviks were able to exert authority over southern Ukraine, however, and a few months later *Volya* was appropriated by one of the several independent Ukrainian governments that emerged in the wake of the Revolution. A few months after that, the inexorable advance of the Reichswehr gave Germany control of much of the Black Sea. The Treaty of Brest ceded control of *Volya* and her remaining sister to the Germans. The revolutionary crew of *Svobodnaja Rossija* (Free Russia, as *Imperatritsa Ekaterina* had been renamed) arranged the scuttling of their ship, but *Volya* was seized by the Germans, renamed *Wolga*, and commissioned (still incomplete) into the German Navy on October 15, 1918.

Germany surrendered on November 11, 1918, and ceded the ship to British control. The British did not want the Bolsheviks to have access to *Wolga*, and so transferred her (under Royal Navy flag) to Izmir, which had come under Allied control.

In 1919, the UK, US, France, and Japan all sought to strangle the Bolshevik Revolution in its crib, through a combination of direct action

Tsar Alexander III of Russia.

and support of White Russian forces. The British turned *Wolga* over to White Russians, who put the ship into working order and renamed her *General Alekseev*, after the Imperial and counter-revolutionary Russian General Mikhail Alekseev. *General Alekseev* conducted shore bombardments against Bolshevik forces along the Black Sea until mid 1920, when Red forces crushed White resistance in the Crimea. In November 1920, fleeing Bolshevik tyranny, *General Alekseev* led a ragtag fleet away from Crimea and out of the Black Sea. Dubbed Wrangel's Fleet (after the

Volya in Sevastopol, 1918.

Volya in Novorossiysk, 1918.

General Mikhail Alekseev, 1915. Le Miroir

final White commander in the region), it include *Alekseev*, a pre-dreadnought battleship, two cruisers, ten destroyers, four submarines, and a few smaller vessels. The fleet carried 4,500 civilian refugees in addition to the crews.

General Alekseev made its way to Bizerta, in the French colony of Tunisia. *Alekseev* was interned there by the French until 1924, when France officially gave up on its policy of isolating the Soviet Union and recognized the Bolshevik government. The French and the Soviets couldn't come to an agreement with respect to repatriation of the ship, in part because of its poor condition, and in part because of French demands for back payment of docking fees. It's an open question as to whether *Alekseev* was in any worse shape than *Sevastopol* or any of the other old Russian battleships, and in the end the Soviets probably could have used her in the Black Sea. In any case, the French kept *General Alekseev*, and slowly scrapped her at Bizerta over the course of the next decade.

Strangely enough, the saga doesn't end there. France transferred *Alekseev*'s main battery to Finland in early 1940, to defend against the Soviet invasion. Eight of the guns made it through, while four were seized by the Germans in transit after the inva-

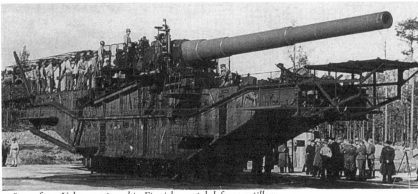

12" gun from Volya, equipped in Finnish coastal defense artillery.

sion of Norway. The Germans installed those four guns in coastal fortifications in occupied Guernsey. The Finns used six of the guns as coastal defense and railway artillery during the war, eventually surrendering two to the Soviet Union. The Soviets used these guns as coastal artillery into the 1990s. One turret and one gun remain on display at Finnish military museums.

Author's Note

General Alekseev's career was short, but as indicated by her history of name changes, remarkably interesting. She was owned or operated by at least seven different governments during her career, plus three more if you count the adventures of her guns. Her experience is symbolic of the disorder and chaos that seized Russia, and really all of Eastern Europe, in the wake of the Great War.

I also find fascinating the idea of an Imperial Russian battleship rotting away in Bizerta for more than a decade, abandoned and alone.

Still, the basic four-turret, flush deck design was a dead end, and produced some remarkably ugly battleships. Given that the Soviets failed to build any battleships in the inter-war period, it can't be argued that *Alekseev* and her cousins delayed or hindered Soviet battleship production. However, the process through which the Imperial Navy managed to produce hopelessly obsolete, outdated battleships is itself an indictment of the direction the empire was taking on the eve of the Revolution.

Related Entries:

Preceded by... *Sevastopol*
Meant to fight... SMS *Goeben*
Contemporary of... USS *New York*

USS New York

Laid Down: 1911

Launched: 1912

Completed: April, 1914

Displacement: 27,000 tons

Main Armament: ten 14" guns (five twin turrets)

Secondary Armament: twenty-one 5" guns (casemate)

Speed: 20 knots

Treaty: Pre-Washington Naval Treaty

Reconstruction: 1926–28

Major Engagements: Vera Cruz, Operation Torch, Okinawa

Fate: Sunk as target, July 8, 1948

USS *New York* (BB-34) was the ninth dreadnought battleship built for the US Navy. At the time of her commissioning, she carried one of the heaviest armaments on any battleship in the world, although she would soon be matched by HMS *Canada* (the former *Almirante Latorre*). German ships did not carry weapons of greater than 13", and the *Queen Elizabeth* class battleships, with their 15" guns, would not come into service for over a year.

Like several other US ships of the day, *New York*'s first action was against Mexico. She proceeded to Vera Cruz immediately after commissioning, without the typical extensive shake-down cruise. As World War I raged in Europe, *New York* acquired a reputation as a generous ship with a generous crew, and maintained a strong relationship with her home city and state.

New York served in various capacities off the East Coast until late 1917, when she became flagship of a squadron of USN battleships that joined the Grand Fleet at Scapa Flow. The addition of the US battleships only added to the overwhelming Royal Navy advantage over the German High Seas Fleet, although the experienced crews of the Grand Fleet viewed the American sailors with con-

USS New York in original condition, 1915

USS New York, second in line behind USS Arkansas, 1917. Library of Congress.

tempt, and did not highly value their fighting capability.

New York was modernized extensively in the late 1920s, acquiring new boilers, a new superstructure, heavier armor, and an enhanced anti-aircraft armament. This reconstruction did not bring her up to par with the "standard type" battleships, but it did make her a much more effective unit in her own right. After reconstruction, she joined the US Pacific Fleet.

In 1937, *New York* transferred from the Pacific Fleet to the Atlantic Fleet, representing the United States at the coronation of King George VI. Shortly thereafter, she served as a test-bed for some of the earliest shipborne radar systems. For the rest of the pre-war period she operated mostly in a training role, until joining her sister USS *Texas* and the older USS *Arkansas* in Atlantic convoy escort work.

When Pearl Harbor was attacked, *New York* was in the midst of an overhaul. She was quickly returned to service, but not dispatched to the Pacific; like all of the older USN battleships, she lacked the speed to keep up with fleet carriers, and it was believed that she could play a more important role in the Atlantic.

After additional convoy escort duty, *New York* carried out shore bombardment during Operation Torch, briefly serving as distant cover against the French battleship *Jean Bart*. From 1943 she served mostly as a training ship, finally deploying to the Pacific in December 1944. She conducted shore bombardment of Okinawa in the first half of 1945, leaving for a refit at Pearl Harbor before the end of the war.

New York eventually engaged in bombardment operations off of North Africa and Normandy, and deployed to the Pacific for similar operations in 1945.

By the end of the war, *New York* was quite obsolete. The USN decided that *New York* would be more useful as a target than as scrap. Along with *Arkansas*, *Nevada*, *Pennsylvania*, and the Japanese *Nagato*, *New York* helped the Navy figure out what happens when atomic bombs fall near large ships. One of the few ships to survive Operation Crossroads, New York was studied for the effects of radiation, and eventually sunk as a target off Oahu.

Author's Note

USS *New York* was laid down at Brooklyn Navy Yard on September 11, 1911. Unlike her sister *Texas*, it appears there was little interest in preserving the ship after the war. Had she survived, more than a few commentators would

USS New York as target ship and survivor of Bikini atom bomb tests, 1948. Elliot Elisofon, Life Magazine.

The pre-standard type dreadnoughts of the USN (everything before USS *Nevada*) made up a powerful squadron in their own right, likely the equal in quality (if not quantity) of the similar squadrons in Germany and the United Kingdom. Even for World War II, *New York* retained a respectable main armament, capable of inflicting very serious damage on modern foes. Her armor would have proven a problem in any encounter with a German raider, however, especially *Bismarck* or *Tirpitz*.

Related Entries:

Preceded by…USS *Arkansas*
Followed by… USS *Oklahoma*
Contemporary of… HMS *Iron Duke*

surely have noted the historical coincidence of her conception.

Standard Type Battleships

The "standard type" battleships refer to a group of twelve battleships constructed by the US Navy between 1914 and 1921. The *Nevada, Pennsylvania, New Mexico, Tennessee,* and *Colorado* classes comprised the standard types, along with the six canceled ships of the first *South Dakota* class.

The intention behind the standard type design was to plan a squadron of battleships that could operate together without major differences in speed or capability, while still being able to take advantage of technological innovations as they developed. All standard type battleships could make 21 knots, used oil-fired boilers, and carried their main armaments in four superfiring turrets split fore and aft. This avoided the problems suffered by the Royal Navy at Jutland, where ships of different speeds and different capabilities had trouble operating as a cohesive unit.

The standard type also pioneered the "all or nothing" armor scheme. This scheme concentrated the ship's armor in a box around the magazines and machinery. Tests and experience had shown that engagements were likely to take place at ranges that would make smaller secondary weapons useless. Thus, it was pointless to attempt to protect the less vital parts of the ship with light belts, as heavy shells could penetrate the light armor and probably the (consequently) lighter main belt as well. For example, whereas USS *Oklahoma* carried a 13.5" main belt and 4.5" deck armor concentrated around her middle, her immedi-

ate predecessor *New York* carried a 12" main belt, little deck armor, light fore and aft protection, and a 6" upper belt that protected from not much of anything. *Oklahoma* accomplished this on a displacement virtually identical to *New York*.

In service, the standard type battleships were notable for their ability to resist damage. The Japanese attack on Pearl Harbor damaged eight of the twelve ships, although all but six were eventually returned to service. The biggest problem with the standard type involved its lack of speed. Whereas the Royal Navy could use the fast *Queen Elizabeth* class battleships in a variety of tactical and operational situations, the USN struggled to find a role for the slow standards. The USN eschewed an increase in speed during the interwar period in order to maintain the integrity of the squadron. Indeed, the first designs for the post-London Naval Treaty battleships envisioned only a modest one or two knot increase over the standards, which would have left the USN with a far less useful inventory of ships.

Almirante Latorre
HMS Canada
Almirante Latorre

Laid Down: 1911

Launched: 1913

Completed: October, 1915

Displacement: 25,000 tons

Main Armament: ten 14" guns (five twin turrets)

Secondary Armament: sixteen 6" guns (casemates)

Speed: 22 knots

Reconstruction: 1929–1931

Major Actions: Jutland, Chilean Naval Mutiny

Treaty: Pre-Washington Naval Treaty

Fate: Scrapped, 1959

Chile was the final entrant into the Southern Cone battleship race. Although smaller than either Argentina or Brazil, Chile had maintained a respectable fleet and a strong martial tradition in the nineteenth century. When the other two ordered battleships, Chile felt compelled to follow suit, more for reasons of prestige than security. Chile ordered *Almirante Latorre* and *Almirante Cochrane* from Armstrong-Whitworth in 1911. The ships were very similar to the excellent British *Iron Duke* class, except with a heavier gun armament (borrowing the 14" gun from the Japanese *Kongo*). Unfortunately for Chile, World War I intervened, and both ships were purchased by the Royal Navy. *Almirante Latorre* was completed as HMS *Canada*, and joined the 4th Battle Squadron of the Grand Fleet.

Named after Admiral Juan Jose Latorre, a hero of the War of the Pacific, *Almirante Latorre* was a well-armed, well-designed ship. Her armament compared favorably with most foreign competitors, and (eventually) made *Latorre* the most powerful warship in South America. She could also outpace the battleships of Chile's neighbors. As HMS *Canada*, she participated in the Battle of Jutland and most of the other actions of the Grand Fleet, but did not play a decisive role in any engagement.

Following the war, *Almirante Latorre* was refit and sold back to Chile. The Chileans decided not to re-purchase *Almirante Cochrane*, which was renamed *Eagle*, converted into an air-

Almirante Latorre, 1921. Underwood and Underwood, United States Library of Congress.

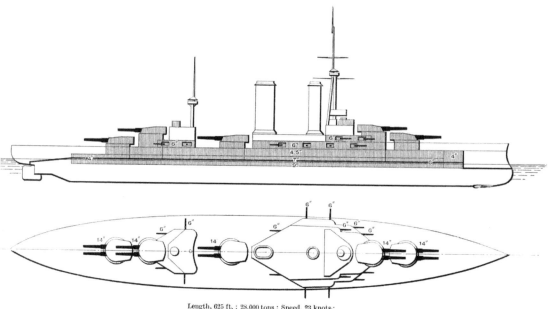

Length, 625 ft. ; 28,000 tons ; Speed, 23 knots ;
Armament, 10—14 in. ; 16—6 in. ; 4—3 in. and smaller.

HMS Canada in Royal Navy service, Brassey's Naval Annual 1915, and Almirante Latorre in Chilean service, Brassey's Naval Annual 1923.

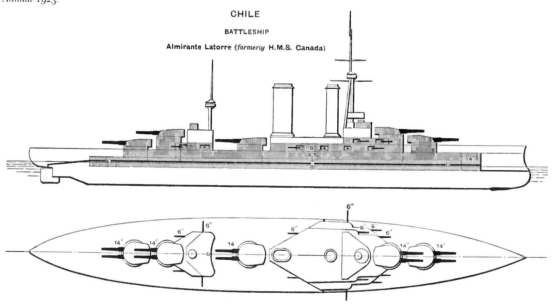

CHILE

BATTLESHIP

Almirante Latorre (*formerly* H.M.S. Canada)

Length, 625 ft. ; 28,000 tons ; Speed, 23 knots ;
Armament, 10—14 in. ; 14—6 in. ; 6—3 in., and smaller.

craft carrier, and enjoyed an eventful World War II career until she was sunk by a U-boat.

Almirante Latorre served as flagship of the Chilean Navy for most of the interwar period. In contrast to her Brazilian counterparts, *Almirante Latorre* was kept in good condition up until an engine room fire in 1951. In 1929 she underwent an extensive modernization in the United Kingdom.

The Great Depression struck Latin America hard, leaving the Chilean government with minimal resources for maintaining the fleet. In 1931, in protest over a pay cut, the crew mutinied. The mutiny was launched from belowdecks, with enlisted personnel leading the charge. The rebellion spread quickly from *Almirante Latorre* to the other ships in the fleet, and radicalized over the course of several days. A second flotilla joined the rebellion, as did groups of sailors ashore. For a while, the Chilean government feared that the rebellion would become a general revolt. Chile's leadership requested the transfer of bombs from the United States that could penetrate *Latorre's* armored deck, as well as submarines that could defeat the rebel squadron. Chilean Air Force planes, attempting to put down the mutiny, scored a near miss on the battleship, but failed to do any serious damage. However, a combination of internal division and government repression ended the rebellion with relatively little bloodshed.

Following the Pearl Harbor attack of December 7, 1941, the United States Navy offered to purchase *Almirante Latorre*. Talks did not go far, as the USN did not really suffer from a shortage of battleships. Three of the eight battleships at Pearl Harbor were returned to service in short order. In fact, the USN withdrew the *Tennessee*, only lightly damaged at Pearl Harbor, from service for an extensive two year refit. *West Virginia* and *California* also underwent much longer than necessary refits. The USN made no effort to bring *Wyoming*, demilitarized under the terms of the 1930 London Treaty, back to active service, although this probably would have been cheaper and quicker than buying the Chilean ship. *Almirante Latorre* would have been roughly equivalent to the USS *New York*, which served most of the war in shore bombardment and convoy escort duty. In any case, the Chileans declined to sell their flagship to the United States.

After the engine fire in 1951, *Almirante Latorre* spent its last few years inactive. In 1958, she was sold to a Japanese company for scrapping. In 1959, Admiral Chester Nimitz was supporting a project to refurbish the Japanese battleship *Mikasa*, last survivor of the Battle of Tsushima. *Mikasa* had suffered some damage in World War II and had generally been neglected since the end of the war. Nimitz provided financial and administrative support for the restoration of *Mikasa* to her original state. *Almirante Latorre*, being a rough contemporary of *Mikasa*, was cannibalized in the service of this restoration. Thus, parts of the last survivor of Jutland were used to restore the last survivor of Tsushima.

Author's Note

Almirante Latorre was, like most of the British super-dreadnoughts, a handsome vessel. The idea of her serving in both the Royal Navy and the USN is appealing, but it's hard to say what purpose the Americans would have put her to. The Southern Cone naval race remains one of the most curious interactions of the twentieth century, producing some fascinating battleship designs but also some absurdist politics. Eventually, the Southern Cone navies would replace their battleships with American light cruisers, one of which (USS *Phoenix*) remained in service until 1982, when it fell to a Royal Navy submarine during the Falklands war.

Related Entries:

Meant to fight... *Rivadavia*
Contemporary of... USS *New York*
Fought at... Jutland

Almirante Juan Jose Latorre Benavente, National Library of Congress of Chile.

HIJMS Kongo

Laid Down: 1911

Launched: 1912

Completed: August, 1913

Displacement: 27,000 tons

Main Armament: eight 14" guns (four twin turrets)

Secondary Armament: sixteen 6" guns (casemates)

Speed: 30 knots

Reconstructions: 1929–31, 1935–37

Major Actions: Midway, Guadalcanal, Philippine Sea, Leyte Gulf

Treaty: Pre-Washington Naval Treaty

Fate: Sunk by USN submarine *Sealion* on November 21, 1944

The Imperial Japanese Navy of Togo Heihachiro, including the fleet that destroyed the Tsar's armada at Tsushima, was primarily constructed in Great Britain. Although relations between Japan and the United Kingdom remained close, the Japanese understood the need for a domestic shipbuilding industry. The IJN built its next four units (*Satsuma*, *Aki*, *Kawachi*, and *Settsu*) in Japanese yards with varying percentages of British components.

The IJN also understood the different character of war in the Pacific. Because of the great distances, capital ships were less likely to find each other and fight. More common would be cruiser actions. The IJN found the battlecruisers of the Royal Navy very attractive, and decided to procure four battlecruisers to provide the basis for a new fleet. Finally, the Japanese decided that the first battlecruiser, *Kongo*, would be built in a British yard, although to a Japanese design. The British had experience with battlecruisers, and the Japanese wanted to take no chances with the first of these expensive warships.

Kongo was commissioned in August of 1913. She was a magnificent ship, the first battleship anywhere in the world to carry 14" guns. When commissioned, she was one of the most powerful warships in the world. Fortunately for the Japanese, Kongo was dispatched to Japan prior to the beginning of World War I. Had her construction been delayed a few months, it is possible that Winston Churchill would have been unable to give up the most powerful ship at his disposal, just as he was unable to give up Turkish and Chilean battleships under construction in 1914. Whether the Japanese, closely allied

HIJMS Kongo after first reconstruction

HIJMS Kongo prior to 1929–1931 reconstruction

with Great Britain in 1914, would have taken this lying down is an open question. When the Royal Navy attempted to lease the *Kongo* and her sisters during World War I, the IJN refused. The presence of *Kongo* and her sisters at Jutland might well have turned a draw into a rout, as their heavy weaponry would have made short work of Hipper's battlecruisers.

Kongo was rebuilt twice during the interwar period. The first reconstruction was designed to bring her up to the armor standards of contemporary battleships. It resulted in a slower, but better protected, warship. Unfortunately, it also resulted in a less useful unit. More sensible heads prevailed, and a second major reconstruction lengthened her hull, improved her machinery, and restored her speed to 31 knots. Even with the first reconstruction, *Kongo*'s protection remained inadequate to combat against other battleships, but her speed meant that she could perform carrier escort missions.

On December 7, 1941, *Kongo* and her sisters were, in spite of their age, and with the exception of HMS *Prince of Wales*, the most useful units in the Pacific theater.. While any American battleship could defeat *Kongo* in single combat, none of them could actually force that combat because of their slow speeds. While the experience of the British battlecruiser squadron at Jutland left a bad taste in the mouth of most major navies after World War I, it turned out that the superior speed of battlecruisers made them more useful units in World War II.

Kongo's first World War II duty was to counter the British battleships *Repulse* and *Prince of Wales*, both operating out of Singapore. Japanese aircraft dispatched both ships before they could meet *Kongo* and her sister *Haruna*. *Kongo* participated in almost every major action of World War II, including the Battle of Midway, the Guadalcanal Campaign, the Battle of Philippine Sea, and the Battle of Leyte Gulf. *Kongo* and *Haruna* served together in every engagement, up to and including Leyte Gulf. At Leyte Gulf *Kongo* was part of Admiral Kurita's main force, which included the battleships *Musashi* and *Yamato*. Kurita's force intended to attack and destroy the American invasion fleet off Leyte after the main US force had been drawn off by

Japanese decoy carriers. Shockingly enough, the decoy plan worked; Admiral Halsey and his battleships left their position off Leyte in a futile attempt to destroy the Japanese carriers.

Off the island of Samar, Admiral Kurita's force of four battleships, ten cruisers, and eleven destroyers met an American force that consisted of three destroyers and four destroyer escorts. The US force was covering a group of eighteen escort carriers—small, slow ships with almost no defensive armament. In desperation, the US destroyers attacked. Miraculously, they won. The American destroyers, along with aircraft launched by the escort carriers, managed to sink three Japanese cruisers and to disrupt the Japanese attack. The Japanese battleships, expecting to meet battleships, had armed themselves primarily with armor-piercing shells. These shells passed through the unarmored American ships, causing only minimal damage.

HIJMS Kongo in mid-1920s

Eventually, terrified that the American battleships would return and cut off his retreat, Kurita ordered his fleet to turn around and escape. *Kongo* suffered heavy damage from ensuing air attacks.

In mid-November 1944, *Kongo* and the rest of the fleet embarked for Kure for refits and repairs. On the night of November 21,

1944, off Formosa, *Kongo* was hit by three torpedoes from the US submarine *Sealion*. *Yamato* and *Nagato* were in line with Kongo, and the latter barely managed to avoid another set of torpedoes. Fires started by the torpedo hits spread to *Kongo's* magazines, and she exploded and sank. Had her captain not insisted on maintaining a high speed, the damage might have been contained, but he feared additional torpedo attacks. 1,250 sailors died when *Kongo* succumbed.

Author's Note

Fast, slim ships like *Kongo* played a major role in the Second World War, despite their great age. Despite the problems the type suffered in World War I, most of the battlecruisers that survived into World War II proved very useful vessels. The British almost certainly erred in disposing of the battlecruiser *Tiger*, in 1930, instead of one of the slow "R" class battleships. Had the United States decided in 1918 to press ahead with the construction of three *Lexington* class battlecruisers instead of the three *Colorado* class battleships, the United States might well have possessed two useful ships in the wake of Pearl Harbor, instead of two more old, slow battleships.

Related Entries:

Preceded... HIJMS *Fuso*
Inspired by... HMS *Lion*
Inspired... USS *Wisconsin*

USS Oklahoma

Laid Down: 1912

Launched: 1914

Completed: May 1916

Reconstruction: 1927–1929

Displacement: 27,500 tons

Main Armament: ten 14" guns (two twin turrets and two triple turrets)

Secondary Armament: twenty-one 5" guns (casemates)

Speed: 20 knots

Major Actions: Pearl Harbor

Treaty: Pre-Washington Naval Treaty

Fate: Sunk by Japanese carrier aircraft, December 7, 1941.

USS *Oklahoma* and her sister, USS *Nevada*, were the first of the "standard type" US battleships. *Oklahoma* entered service in May 1916. Unfortunately, because of problems with suppliers, *Oklahoma* was equipped with reciprocating engines, leading to vibration problems for her entire career. For this reason, she was the least popular battleship in the fleet.

During World War I she engaged in some convoy escort, but because of oil supply concerns did not deploy to the United Kingdom. Rebuilt between 1927 and 1929, Oklahoma had her cage masts replaced by twin tripods. Her interwar career was uneventful, apart from a visit to Spain in 1936, when she helped rescue American refugees of the Spanish Civil War.

USS *Oklahoma* was top of the list of first-line battleships to be replaced by new construction. On December 7, she was moored outboard of USS *Maryland*. At least five torpedoes hit *Oklahoma*'s port side. Although her torpedo protection was good for 1916, and had been improved in 1929, *Oklahoma* could not survive this kind of attack. She rolled over to port, stopping only when her masts became stuck in the mud. Some survivors of the attack described the turtle-turned *Oklahoma* as more psychologically devastating than the upright *Arizona*. Fortunately, about half of her crew escaped, many because of heroic efforts to cut open the underside of her hull. Her sister, USS *Nevada*, was the only battleship to get underway during the attack. *Nevada* eventually beached herself near the mouth of the entrance channel.

USS Oklahoma in original condition, 1917

USS Oklahoma after reconstruction, 1929

No serious effort was made to restore *Oklahoma* to service, as her advanced age and extraordinary damage would make the effort more trouble than it was worth. However, something had to be done with the hulk. Salvage efforts began in March 1943, involving a massive effort to roll the old battleship over and patch her hull. Her guns and upper works were removed to make the hulk more stable, and *Oklahoma* made it to drydock by December. Patched more fully, she spent the rest of her career as an abandoned hulk at Pearl. In 1947, on the way to being scrapped in San Francisco, she sank during a storm. Her sister *Nevada* was refloated, repaired, and modernized, participating in both the Atlantic and Pacific theaters during World War II.

Author's Note

Oklahoma had the misfortune, along with her sister *Nevada* and the sisters *Pennsylvania* and

USS Oklahoma salvage operation, 1943

Arizona, of being refit during the US Navy's aesthetic fallow period. Her cage masts were replaced by ungainly tripod masts, leaving a visual impression not unlike a gangly giraffe. The *New Yorks* enjoyed a much more balanced look with only tripod foremast, while the *New Mexico* class gained a solid, stacked forward superstructure. *Pennsylvania* and *Nevada*, refit after Pearl Harbor, would lose their aft tripods and gain much more substantial forward superstructures.

Had *Oklahoma* survived, her career would have been similar to that of USS *New York* and USS *Arkansas*, as her reciprocating engines likely would have precluded service with the battle squadron.

USS Oklahoma, capsized after Pearl Harbor attack. USN photo.

Related Entries:

Preceded by... USS *New York*
Contemporary of... HIJMS *Yamashiro*
Fought at... Pearl Harbor

HMS Iron Duke

Laid Down: 1912

Launched: 1912

Completed: March, 1914

Displacement: 25,000 tons

Main Armament: ten 13.5" guns (five twin turrets)

Secondary Armament: twelve 6" guns (casemates)

Speed: 21 knots

Major Actions: Battle of Jutland, Great Fire of Smyrna

Treaty: Pre-Washington Naval Treaty

Reconstruction: 1931–32

Fate: Scrapped, 1948

HMS *Iron Duke* was the second battleship named after the Duke of Wellington. The first, scrapped in 1906, had the distinction of ramming and sinking HMS *Victoria*. The second *Iron Duke* was the name ship of the last class of dreadnoughts to enter Royal Navy service prior to the beginning of World War I. She and her sisters were considered "super-dreadnoughts," an ill-defined term that distinguish-es the second generation of dreadnought battleships from the first. Generally speaking, super-dreadnoughts avoided wing turrets, carrying guns in the centerline with super-firing turrets. Most super-dreadnoughts carried weapons heavier than 12" (although this varied from country to country), and had more advanced armor schemes. However, no one has successfully established a clear definition for the distinction.

Iron Duke was a well-designed ship, capable of outgunning her German (if not her American) counterparts, and serving as the basis for the even more heavily armed Chilean battleship *Almirante Latorre*. The *Iron Dukes* were the third four-ship class of super-dreadnought (following the *Orions* and the *King George Vs*), and represented a staggering degree of peacetime construction on the part of the United Kingdom. The Royal Navy, mindful of its competition with Germany, would commission twenty-two super-dreadnoughts between 1912 and 1917, plus another half-dozen battlecruisers. Only US aircraft carrier construction in World War II can compare with this level of productivity.

HMS *Iron Duke* became flagship of the Grand Fleet upon its creation in August, 1914.

HMS Iron Duke after demilitarization.

Coat of Arms of the Duke of Wellington. CCA, Sodacan.

Iron Duke carried the flag of Admiral John Jellicoe, who had been promoted by Winston Churchill to command at the beginning of the war. Jellicoe's job was not to lose the war, and the way to do that was to avoid being destroyed by the German High Seas Fleet. Given that the German fleet was smaller than the Grand Fleet and was limited geographically, this was an achievable task. Jellicoe understood that numerical superiority was key to victory in modern naval engagements, and steadfastly refused to allow the Royal Navy to meet the High Seas Fleet in detail. Consequently, the Grand Fleet spent most of its time conducting gunnery and seamanship drills, punctuated by the occasional sortie to try to catch the High Seas Fleet in the open.

The only genuinely productive sortie of this sort came in late May 1916, when *Iron Duke* served as Jellicoe's flagship at the Battle of Jutland. At the head of the British line, she inflicted serious damage on SMS *König*, as well as several smaller ships. The German prey escaped in the night, however, and *Iron Duke* returned to Scapa Flow as the Navy became

mired in controversy. The failure to destroy the High Seas Fleet, despite obvious British advantages, took a severe toll on public and elite impressions of Admiral Jellicoe. Jellicoe was eventually "promoted" out of the command of the Grand Fleet, and replaced by David Beatty. The crew of *Iron Duke* didn't care for the new admiral, so Beatty moved his flag to *Queen Elizabeth*. The rest of *Iron Duke*'s World War I career was uneventful.

The battleships fleets of the world were constrained by the Washington Naval Treaty, but *Iron Duke* survived the first cut of 1922. She served in the Black Sea and in the Mediterranean, helping to manage the fallout of the Russian Civil War and the Greco-Turkish War. The London Naval Treaty of 1930 further reduced the battleships allowable to the three great naval powers, and *Iron Duke* was reclassified as an auxiliary.

Iron Duke served as an accommodation ship at the beginning of World War II. In October 1939, long-range German bombers struck Scapa Flow, and damaged her badly enough to force a grounding. A March 1940 raid inflicted additional damage, and *Iron Duke* would remain in place for the balance of the war. In 1948 *Iron Duke* was sent to the breakers.

Author's Note

From an aesthetic point of view, HMS *Iron Duke* and her sisters perfectly captured the

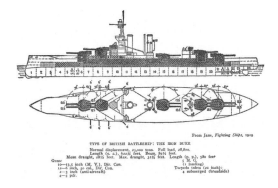

From Jane, *Fighting Ships*, 1919

TYPE OF BRITISH BATTLESHIP: THE IRON DUKE
Normal displacement, 25,000 tons. Full load, 28,800.
Length (o. a.), 622¾ feet. Beam, 89½ feet.
Mean draught, 28½ feet. Max. draught, 32¾ feet. Length (p. p.), 580 feet
Guns: 5 M. G.
   10—13.5 inch (M. V.), Dir. Con.   (1 landing)
   12—6 inch, 50 cal., Dir. Con.   Torpedo tubes (21 inch):
   2—3 inch (anti-aircraft)   4 submerged (broadside)
   4—3 pdr.

HMS Iron Duke. Jane's Fighting Ships, 1919.

HMS Iron Duke, 1912. Weltrundschau zu Reclams Universum 1913.

"super-dreadnought" concept; their large guns, tripod masts, and balanced appearance made them look both stout and deadly. *Iron Duke* seemed singularly well-named for her role as flagship of the Grand Fleet, although it is odd that the greatest collection of Royal Navy capital ships was led by a ship that took the name of a British Army commander. Her type was of so little use by World War II that the Royal Navy made no effort to restore her to front-line service, as she would have suffered badly under the guns of modern German, Japanese, and Italian warships.

Related Entries:

Contemporary of... USS *Oklahoma*
Preceded... HMS *Barham*
Fought at... Jutland

HMS Warspite

Laid Down: 1912

Launched: 1913

Completed: March, 1915

Displacement: 27,500 tons

Main Armament: eight 15" guns (four twin turrets)

Secondary Armament: fourteen 6" guns (casemates)

Speed: 24 knots

Major Actions: Battle of Jutland, Second Battle of Narvik, Battle of Calabria, Taranto, Battle of Cape Matapan, Sicily, Salerno, Normandy

Treaty: Pre-Washington Naval Treaty

Reconstructions: 1924–26, 1934–37

Fate: Ran aground April 19, 1947; scrapped in place

HMS *Warspite* was the second of the magnificent *Queen Elizabeth* class battleships. *Warspite* and her sisters outclassed every battleship in the world upon their commissioning, and remained useful and impressive ships until the end of World War II. Seventh ship of her name (accounts vary as to what exactly the name refers to), *Warspite* led the most distinguished career of any Royal Navy battleship in the twentieth century.

For the bulk of World War I, *Warspite* and her four sisters constituted the Fifth Battle Squadron of the Grand Fleet, a designation designed to take advantage of the ship's high speed. In ordinary operations, *Warspite* would have been part of the main battle line of the Grand Fleet, which would have limited her to a speed of about 20 knots. The necessities of maneuvering in formation limited the speed of a squadron to somewhat less than that of its slowest ship. *Warspite*, thus, had difficulty operating with the rest of the Grand Fleet. While the US Navy solved this problem by designing all of its battleships with a common (slow) speed, the Royal Navy accepted a speed differential and pursued an organizational solution. In early 1916, the Fifth Battle Squadron was detached from the Grand Fleet and placed under Admiral David Beatty, commander of the Royal Navy battlecruisers.

Due largely to Beatty's signaling problems, the Fifth Battle Squadron arrived late at the Battle of Jutland. Beatty's battlecruisers were being taken to the woodshed by the High Seas Fleet when *Warspite* and her sisters arrived, diverting fire from Beatty's wounded ships and

HMS Warspite in Scapa Flow during World War I.

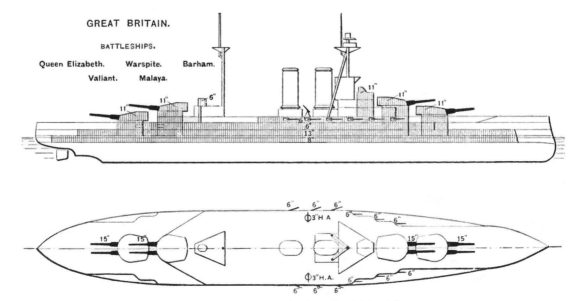

GREAT BRITAIN.

BATTLESHIPS.

Queen Elizabeth.   Warspite.   Barham.
        Valiant.   Malaya.

Length, 600 ft. ; 27,500 tons ; Speed, 25 knots : Completed, 1915-1916 ;
Armament, 8—15 in., 12—6 in. 2—3 in. H.A., 4—3 pr., 5 M.

HMS Warspite. Brassey's Naval Annual 1923.

inflicting serious damage on the already battered German battlecruisers. For a short period, the Fifth Squadron faced the whole of the High Seas Fleet. After turning away from the German fleet, *Warspite* suffered a mechanical "incident." Her steering jammed, and she sailed in two full circles in front of the High Seas Fleet, receiving fifteen hits from German heavy guns. *Warspite*'s accident saved the armored cruiser HMS *Warrior*, on the verge of sinking after taking heavy German fire. *Warpite* survived, and slowly made her way back to port, avoiding two German U-boat attacks along the way. The experience at Jutland helped *Warspite* acquire a reputation for poor luck; she also managed to ram her sisters *Barham* and *Valiant*, to run aground once, to suffer a boiler room fire, and was a close witness to the internal explosion that destroyed HMS *Vanguard*.

Warspite was modernized twice during the inter-war period. The second modernization was quite extensive, replacing the entire original superstructure and repairing some of the damage left over from Jutland. Because of the damage, *Warspite* was the first of the *Queen Elizabeths* to undergo this second reconstruction. In effect, this made her the most modern battleship available to the Royal Navy in September 1939. In particular the speed of *Warspite* and her sisters, a couple knots above most other World War I veterans, kept them useful in the Second World War.

Warspite claimed her first blood of the Second World War in the Norway campaign, where the Germans tried to make up for numerical shortcomings by attacking with surprise and air superiority. On April 13, 1940, a Swordfish floatplane launched from HMS *Warspite* dropped a bomb that sank *U-64*, a German Type IX submarine. *U-64* was the first U-boat of World War II lost solely to air attack, and the only submarine in either war sunk by an aircraft launched from a battleship. Later in the day, *Warspite* helped sink eight German destroyers which had found themselves trapped in a Norwegian fjord.

Following the failure of the Norway campaign, *Warspite* departed for the Med. Her first action came on July 9, 1940 at the Battle of Calabria, where she led a force of three battleships and several light cruisers against an Italian force of two battleships and several heavy cruisers. Fighting alone against both

Italian battleships early in the battle, *Warspite* hit *Giulio Cesare* at a range of 26,000 yards, thought to be the longest hit of one moving battleship against another.

In March 1941, *Warspite* participated in the Battle of Cape Matapan, helping *Valiant* and *Barham* to destroy three Italian heavy cruisers. Two months later, she helped defend Crete against German air assault, but took serious damage from German bombing attacks. Because of a shortage of shipyard space, she had to travel all the way to Bremerton, Washington for repairs, a trip which took two months and saw *Warspite* visit Manila, Pearl Harbor, and several other ports that would soon come under Japanese attack.

Repairs at Puget Naval Yard lasted until late December, by which point the United States was at war in both theaters. The Admiralty determined that *Warspite* would be of greatest immediate use in the Pacific, and she made her way to Australia, thence to Ceylon. The Eastern Fleet fought a few inconclusive actions with the Imperial Japanese Navy, but its aging battleships (*Warspite* and

several "R" class battleships) stood no chance against Kido Butai, the Japanese carrier battle group. The Japanese soon chased the Eastern Fleet to the coast of Africa. In 1943, *Warspite* was transferred back to the Mediterranean.

Warspite's service in 1943 focused mainly on support of British and American landings in Sicily and Italy. On September 15, 1943 a German Fritz X glider bomb hit *Warspite*, tearing through her superstructure, her main deck, and her hull. *Warpite* had to be towed to port, and was never fully repaired. She participated in shore bombardment at the Normandy landings, but hit a mine shortly afterward. Pieced together enough to deliver further shore bombardment in late 1944, she was retired in early 1945.

A campaign to preserve *Warspite* after World War II failed. Although the reluctance of the cash-strapped post-war British government to spend money on preserving a battered, aging battleship is understandable, it is nonetheless unfortunate that no British capital ships of the twentieth century survive. *Warspite*, the most active of Royal Navy bat-

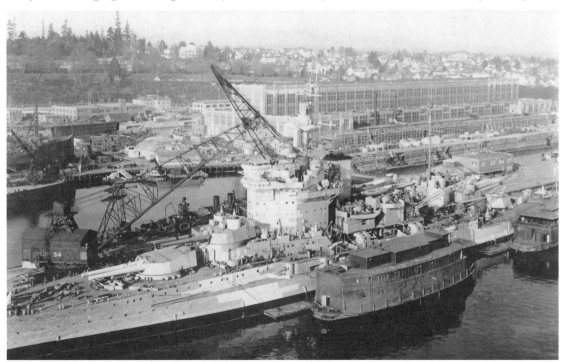

HMAS Warspite undergoing repairs at Puget Sound, 1941.

HMAS Warspite in France, 1944.

tleships and the most beloved of the British public, would undoubtedly have been the best choice for preservation. On the way to being scrapped in 1947, *Warpite* ran aground. She was taken apart over the course of the next three years.

of its warships means that we don't have any extant examples of the *Queen Elizabeth* class to visit today. *Warspite* was, HMS *Victory* notwithstanding, almost certainly the finest ship ever to serve in the Royal Navy, and it's a pity she met such an ignominious fate.

Author's Note

Very few combat ships could contribute decisively in 1916 and continue to fight usefully in 1945. Sadly, the reluctance of the Royal Navy to commit resources to the preservation of any

Related Entries:

Sister of... HMS *Barham*
Fought against... *Giulio Cesare*
Fought at... Jutland

SMS Lutzow

Laid Down: 1912

Launched: 1913

Completed: March, 1916

Displacement: 26,600 tons

Main Armament: eight 12" guns (four twin turrets)

Secondary Armament: fourteen 5.9" guns (casemates)

Speed: 26.5 knots

Major Actions: Battle of Jutland

Treaty: Pre-Washington Naval Treaty

Fate: Scuttled following Battle of Jutland, June 1, 1916

Although the debate between a cruiser navy and a battleship navy had largely been settled in the favor of battleships by 1906, Germany wanted to keep a respectable cruiser fleet in order to manage its possessions in the Pacific and threaten British trade. HMS *Invincible* was larger and faster than any extant armored cruisers, making it very difficult for the Germans to compete. German intelligence learned of the construction of *Invincible*, but unfortunately reported her armament as consisting of 9.2" guns. The German response was

the cruiser *Blücher*, a hybrid design that, because of her small guns and insufficient speed, was utterly outclassed by *Invincible*.

Nevertheless, as with battleships German battlecruiser design advanced quickly. Six German battlecruisers were complete by mid-1915, and most had advantages over their Royal Navy counterparts. In particular, they carried slightly heavier, better arranged armor, and had better internal subdivision. The *Derfflinger* class, of which *Lutzow* was the second ship, represented a major improvement on the earlier battlecruisers. Considerably larger than their predecessors, the *Derfflingers* carried 12" guns in four superfiring turrets, eliminating the wasteful practice of wing turrets.

Lutzow was named for Prussian Lieutenant General Ludwig von Lutzow, who had distinguished himself in the final campaigns of the Napoleonic Wars. Lacking a strong naval history, many ships of the Imperial German Navy took their names from Prussian generals, as well as other figures from German military history. The Kaiserliche Marine was cobbled together from several pre-unification German navies, but it its early years was virtually adjunct to the Reichswehr.

Only five battlecruisers were available to the High Seas Fleet at the beginning of World War I as the sixth, *Goeben*, had constituted the

SMS Lutzow. Journal of the United States Artillery, 1916.

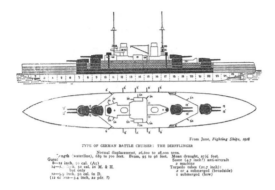

Derfflinger class battlecruiser. Jane's Fighting Ships, 1918.

bulk of the German Mediterranean squadron. The Germans learned at important lesson at the Battle of Dogger Bank (which did not include *Lutzow*) when *Seydlitz* almost exploded from a magazine fire. From that point forward, the Germans took extreme care with their magazine spaces, ensuring that no single hit could destroy a ship. The Royal Navy, sadly, would not learn this lesson until 1916.

SMS *Lutzow* entered service in early 1916, as wartime demands had slowed her construction. Her first action came in the Lowestoft Raid, an effort to keep the crews sharp and potentially draw out portions of the British fleet. In conjunction with zeppelins, the German battlecruiser squadron bombarded the towns of Lowestoft and Yarmouth, doing insignificant damage before withdrawing. The Lowestoft Raid also represented Germany's perfunctory effort to support the Irish Easter Rebellion.

A month and a half later, *Lutzow* carried the flag of Admiral Franz von Hipper. The German gambit, to draw out a portion of the Grand Fleet and expose it to Scheer's battleships, had worked; Hipper's squadron successful drew out both Beatty's battlecruisers and Evan-Thomas's battleships. The situation was ideal for the Germans, as the British battlecruiser squadron had been weakened by damage to HMS *Australia* and the temporary transfer of three older battlecruisers to Scapa Flow. The British would intercept Hipper's battlecruisers with six, instead of ten, ships.

The German advantage during the "Run to the South" was reinforced by tactical conditions, as the British ships were framed against the setting sun. *Lutzow* scored a devastating hit against Beatty's flagship, HMS *Lion*, with a shell that destroyed the latter's center turret and nearly detonated the entire ship. While the German ships suffered a battering, none exploded, and none were mortally crippled. *Lutzow*, Hipper's flagship, suffered from the most severe damage. When the British finally solved their signaling problem, the German battlecruisers came under devastating fire from the four *Queen Elizabeth* class battleships of the Fifth Battle Squadron. Nevertheless, all of Hipper's battlecruisers maintained their positions in line.

In the melee that developed following the Run to the South, *Lutzow* and several other German battleships found the armored cruiser HMS *Defence*, and quickly sent her to the bottom. But a much more formidable opponent was on the horizon. The lead ships in Grand Fleet were the Third Battlecruiser Squadron, consisting of three *Invincible* class battlecruisers. These ships had just undergone gunnery retraining, which paid off in extremely accurate fire against the Germans. HMS *Invincible* struck *Lutzow* with eight heavy shells. In reply, *Lutzow* and his sibling *Derfflinger* hit *Invincible* with several salvos, the last resulting in a magazine explosion.

At this point *Lutzow* was too badly damaged to continue the battle. *Lutzow* had fired nearly 400 shells and contributed to the sinking of two British ships and the crippling of another, but had received 24 heavy shell hits (including at least four from 15" guns) in return. Admiral Hipper transferred his flag to a destroyer, and *Lutzow* attempted to withdraw under cover of fog and darkness.

Unfortunately, the damage proved mortal. *Lutzow*'s crew could not contain the flooding, and the ship began to sink bow first. An effort to reverse the engines and pull the ship backward did not prevent additional flooding.

Eventually, in order to avoid either a grounding (that might have given the Royal Navy an opportunity to seize the ship) or a capsizing (which would have threatened the loss of the entire crew), *Lutzow* was abandoned and scuttled.

Author's Note

The *Derfflingers* were handsome vessels, much better organized than the first generation of German battlecruisers. *Lutzow* and *Derfflinger*, like all the ships of Hipper's squadron, absorbed enormous punishment at Jutland, but more or less kept on ticking. Had *Lutzow* survived, she certainly would have been scuttled with the rest of the High Seas Fleet at Scapa Flow. As it was, in *Lutzow*'s very short career she accounted for more enemy ships than most battleships ever had the opportunity to fight.

Related Entries:

Preceded by…SMS *Goeben*
Contemporary of… HMS *Lion*
Fought at… Jutland

Why did the Battlecruisers Explode?

The United Kingdom constructed thirteen battlecruisers (if we include HMS *Hood*). The Imperial Japanese Navy built or acquired four, and the Kaiserliche Marine built seven. Six American battlecruisers were canceled by the Washington Naval Treaty, along with several British and Japanese ships.

Of the twenty-four battlecruisers built, four were lost to gunfire at Jutland. HMS *Hood* was sunk by *Bismarck* at the Battle of Denmark Straits, and HIJMS *Kirishima* and *Haruna* were lost at Guadalcanal. *Kongo* and *Hiei* were lost later in the war, to submarine and air attack respectively. HMS *Repulse* was sunk by Japanese aircraft off the coast of Malaya.

Ten ships out of twenty-four is a high rate of attrition. Why were they lost at such a higher rate than their battleship cousins?

The three British battlecruisers lost at Jutland all suffered catastrophic explosions. The reason for these explosions most likely lies with a combination of their paper-thin armor and powder handling procedures aboard the ships. The Royal Navy altered both after the battle, increasing armor on HMS *Hood* and revising the ways in which powder was stored and transferred. SMS *Lutzow* nearly survived a brutal bludgeoning at the guns of the Royal Navy, as did the other German battlecruisers.

Several of the ships were lost for reasons unrelated to their status as battlecruisers. HMS *Repulse* demonstrated nearly as much staying power in the face of air attack as *Prince of Wales*, a fast battleship. Similarly, the loss of *Kongo* and *Haruna* had little to do with their battlecruiser characteristics. The loss of HMS *Hood* depended more on her age than her class. An unmodified *Queen Elizabeth* would have been just as likely to fall to *Bismarck*'s salvo.

The Japanese battlecruisers lost at Guadalcanal certainly could have performed more effectively. *Hiei* was crippled by shellfire from American cruisers and destroyers, and *Kirishima* crumpled under the guns of USS *Washington*. In both cases, we can expect that battleships might have performed better (although HIJMS *Fuso* was lost to destroyers at Leyte Gulf). Still, *Hiei* and *Kirishima* were operating off Savo primarily because of their high speed.

And indeed, the key factor in nearly all the losses is that the high speed of the battlecruisers placed them into situations where they faced enemy gunfire. Few dreadnoughts enjoyed so much action. And so in many cases, the battlecruisers were lost simply because they were more useful than their slower kin. That the saw more extensive action, and often were lost in the course of that action, should hardly be interpreted as a condemnation of the type. Rather, the battlecruisers were lost while doing things that battleships could not do.

SMS Szent Istvan

Laid Down: 1912

Launched: 1914

Completed: December, 1915

Displacement: 20,000 tons

Main Armament: twelve 12" guns (four triple turrets)

Secondary Armament: twelve 6" guns (casemates)

Speed: 20 knots

Treaty: Pre-Washington Naval Treaty

Major Engagements: None

Fate: Sunk by Italian torpedo boats, June 10, 1918

The Compromise of 1867 had created a dual administrative structure in the Austro-Hungarian Empire, giving the Hungarian nobility substantial control over their own lands, and making Franz Joseph both King of Hungary and Emperor of Austria. This arrangement created a variety of problems in foreign and security policy, as the military serv-ices of the empire needed to adjust in order to serve the various nationalities. In the army, this resulted in dedicated units for particular nationalities. For the navy, it involved compromises with respect to construction and employment. When the empire sought to build its first squadron of dreadnoughts, the government had to make allowance for the interests of both Austria and Hungary. As a precondition of incurring the expense, Hungary demanded that one of the ships be built in a Hungarian yard and be manned by a Hungarian crew. Of course, Hungary today has no major naval shipyard (neither does Austria, of course), but the jurisdiction of the Hungarian half of the Empire extended to Fiume, now known as Rijeka in modern Croatia.

Szent Istvan, fourth ship of the *Tegetthoff* class, was the only dreadnought battleship constructed by Hungary. Befitting her unique status, *Szent Istvan* was named after King Stephen I, the first Christian king of the Magyar people, who lived between 975 and 1038. Saint Stephen is regarded as the founder of the Hungarian state, and a critical figure in

SMS Szent Istvan

the Hungarian national imagination.

SMS *Szent Istvan* carried twelve 12" guns in four triple turrets, an extremely heavy armament for a ship of her size. The guns were disposed in the modern fashion, with two superfiring turrets at either end. This meant that *Szent Istvan* and her sisters combined a very heavy broadside with excellent end-on fire. The dreadnoughts were very well arranged, with respectable armor for their time period. The major flaw in the design was an almost complete lack of underwater protection; combined with the top heavy armament, this made them very vulnerable to torpedoes. Early on in the design process, German engineers recommended that the top two turrets be reduced from three to two guns, and that the weight saving be used to shore up her compartmentation. Unfortunately, this advice was rejected.

Sadly, the shipyard at Fiume lacked experience with a ship as large as *Szent Istvan*. While her Austrian sisters entered service between 1912 and early 1914, Szent Istvan was not completed until late 1915. The quality of construction wasn't quite up to par, and *Szent Istvan* couldn't make the same speed as her sisters. This was not a great handicap for most of the war. The Austro-Hungarian Navy rarely left port, instead serving as a "fleet in being" designed to tie down Allied naval forces. In practice, this meant that the French and Italian navies spent most of their time waiting for the Austro-Hungarian Navy to sortie, freeing the Royal Navy up for confrontation with the German High Seas Fleet. This made for a boring war in both theaters of operation.

In February 1918, Emperor Karl I appointed a career naval officer named Miklos Horthy Commander-in-Chief of the Austro-Hungarian Navy. Admiral Horthy, a Hungarian, believed in a more aggressive use of the fleet. He authorized the battleships to sortie from Pula in an effort to attack a line of mixed naval defenses known as the Otranto Barrage, which was impeding the deployment of U-boats into the Med. *Szent Istvan* and her

King Stephen I of Hungary executing a rebel. Miniature, 1360.

sister left Pula on June 9. Unfortunately, poor workmanship on *Szent Istvan* meant that the ship began to vibrate violently when she exceeded 16 knots. The effort to make that speed also produced an inordinate amount of smoke, which attracted a pair of Italian torpedo boats. The torpedo boats attacked, evading the escorts and the secondary armament of the battleships. *Szent Istvan* was struck by two torpedoes and capsized, although most of her crew was rescued. A film crew on her sister, *Tegetthoff*, witnessed and recorded the destruction of the ship.

Thus ended the sole major sortie of the Austro-Hungarian Navy in World War I, and Hungarian naval power more generally. Miklos Horthy returned to Hungary a war hero, and played an important role in crushing the 1919 Communist revolution. Horthy was named Regent of the Kingdom of Hungary (Karl was not recalled), and ruled until 1944. He helped lead Hungary into World War II on the side of Nazi Germany but, to his credit, resisted German demands to deport Hungarian Jews. He died in Portugal in 1957.

SMS Szent Istvan sinking after torpedo hit

Author's Note

Horthy's sortie was aggressive, but given the circumstances at the time it is hard to find fault in using the resources that Austria-Hungary had available for fighting. *Szent Istvan* remains the only dreadnought ever sunk by torpedo boats, although HIJMS *Fuso* suffered at least one hit from American patrol torpedo boats before sinking at the hands of American destroyers.

The naming of *Szent Istvan* is particularly interesting, because Hungary never had another opportunity to name a capital ship. The name speaks to a particular moment in Hungarian history, but also to a larger vision of what Hungarian nationalism meant. We rarely get such a clear sense of symbolic national preference. The unfortunate fate of *Szent Istvan* also puts into sharp relief why navies often take great care in avoiding names of symbolic national import.

Related Entries:

Sister of... SMS *Viribus Unitis*
Meant to fight... *Dante Alighieri*
Contemporary of... SMS *Friederich der Grosse*

SMS Szent Istvan in some distress after receiving torpedo hit from Italian motorboat, June 10, 1918. Photographed from SMS Tegetthoff.

Bretagne

Laid Down: 1912

Launched: 1913

Completed: September, 1915

Displacement: 24,000 tons

Main Armament: ten 13.4" guns (five twin turrets)

Secondary Armament: twenty-two 5.4" guns (casemates)

Speed: 20 knots

Treaty: Pre-Washington Naval Treaty

Major Engagements: Mers El Kebir

Fate: Sunk by gunfire from British battleships, July 3, 1940

Dreadnought created a problem for the French Navy. The French had begun construction of a class of six *Dantons* almost simultaneous with *Dreadnought*. These ships occupied all of the large French construction slips, meaning that the French arrived very late to the dreadnought game. The first French effort, the *Courbet* class, turned out well enough for a series of ships built in 1910.

Unfortunately, they were not completed until 1914. *Bretagne*, an improvement on the *Courbets*, was named for the region of Brittany. The French never achieved any consistency with respect to naming conventions.

Slowed by the outbreak of World War I, *Bretagne* was completed in late 1915 and entered service in early 1916. Like her immediate predecessors, *Bretagne* suffered in comparison with the ships emerging from British, Japanese, and American yards. The *Nevada* class carried heavier guns, more (and better arranged) armor, and could make a higher speed. The British *Queen Elizabeths* could easily outgun and outrun the French ships, as could the Japanese *Fusos*. *Bretagne*'s armor scheme was also relatively light. At the time of construction, *Bretagne* would probably have proven more than a match for the Italian *Giulio Cesare*, but after the radical reconstruction of the latter in the 1930s, Giulio Cesare was clearly the superior unit.

Bretagne's career was relatively uneventful. She spent most of World War I in the Mediterranean, preparing for the possible break out of the Austrian Navy. During the interwar period, the French undertook only

Bretagne during World War I

middling efforts to modernize their battlefleet. While the British, Americans, Japanese, and Italians all engaged in major rebuilds of their existing units (a policy forced by the Washington Naval Treaty), the French left the *Courbets* and the *Bretagnes* relatively intact, with only a few incremental changes (addition of rangefinders, conversion to oil-fired boilers, increase in anti-aircraft armament). This policy undoubtedly saved France money, but it also meant that existing French battleships were far less useful than their counterparts in other navies.

In World War II *Bretagne* escorted some Mediterranean convoys from North Africa to France, but Italy did not enter the war until just before France's surrender. Following the capitulation, *Bretagne* found herself with a French naval squadron at the port Mers El Kebir, not too far from Oran in what is now Algeria. The French fleet had, by and large, escaped the fall of France unscathed. The world, and especially London, now wondered what the disposition of the fleet would be. Shortly after the armistice, Winston Churchill decided to stop waiting.

On July 3, 1940, a Royal Navy task force paid a visit to Mers El Kebir. The task force consisted of the battleships HMS *Valiant*, HMS *Resolution*, and HMS *Hood*, along with the aircraft carrier HMS *Ark Royal* and several smaller ships. The visit was not friendly. Winston Churchill had determined that the French fleet was a threat to the United Kingdom. Two Royal Navy admirals bitterly disagreed with Churchill on this point; they felt that destroying the French fleet would be a political disaster. French ships in other locations were forcibly seized, but this was not an option at Mers El Kebir.

The French fleet consisted of *Provence*, *Bretagne*, *Strasbourg*, *Dunkerque*, and six modern destroyers. *Provence* and *Bretagne* were old, slow battleships that could contribute little to either side; they lacked the speed to operate with the main battle line of the Italian navy, and the British already had an excess of old, slow battleships. The British ultimatum was simple. The French could join the British and continue the war against Germany. They could sail their ships to British ports and allow them to be taken over by the Royal Navy

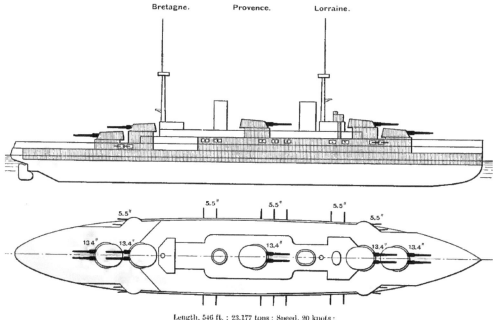

Length, 546 ft. ; 23,177 tons ; Speed, 20 knots ;
Armament, 10—13·4 in., 22—5·5 in., 8 small.

Bretagne. Brassey's Naval Annual 1915.

Bretagne in 1916. La Guerra.

until the end of the war. Finally, they could sail their ships to the West Indies where they would be demilitarized or turned over to the care of the United States. The French response to this ultimatum was, more or less, "Can't we all just get along?" The British reply came in the form of salvos of 15" shells.

The French fleet was not prepared for combat. *Provence* and *Dunkerque* were each struck by several 15" shells, but managed to beach themselves and escape serious damage. *Bretagne* was not so fortunate. Her armor was not up to modern standards, and one of the 15" shells apparently penetrated a magazine before exploding. *Bretagne* exploded and rolled over thirteen minutes into the engagement. *Strasbourg* and five destroyers escaped the harbor with only minor damage, making their way eventually to Toulon. The British fleet attacked *Dunkerque* later that week, inflicting minor damage but not preventing *Dunkerque* from also moving to Toulon under her own power.

Author's Note

The attack at Mers El Kebir must be seen as a political and operational disaster of the highest order for Great Britain. Having decided to attack its erstwhile ally, the British brought insufficient force to do the job, and allowed the most powerful French ships to escape with minimal damage. Moreover, the deaths of 1,300 French sailors (roughly 1,100 on *Bretagne*) were a massive propaganda victory for the Germans, and undoubtedly made the job of Charles De Gaulle and the Free French much more difficult. Much of the blame must lie with Winston Churchill, who fundamentally misunderstood the French political situation in 1940. Even after Mers El Kebir, the French did not hand their fleet over to the Axis, and in fact scuttled most of their ships at Toulon in 1942, in order to avoid German capture. Had Mers El Kebir not happened, those ships might have found their way to Gibraltar or Malta, instead of to the bottom.

Related Entries:

Preceded by... *Danton*
Contemporary of... USS *Oklahoma*
Sunk by... HMS *Hood*

HMS Barham

Laid Down: 1913

Launched: 1914

Completed: October, 1915

Displacement: 27,500 tons

Main Armament: eight 15" guns (four twin turrets)

Secondary Armament: fourteen 6" guns (casemates)

Speed: 24 knots

Major Actions: Battle of Jutland, Dakar, Battle of Cape Matapan

Treaty: Pre-Washington Naval Treaty

Reconstruction: 1930–34

Fate: Sunk by U-331, November 25, 1941

While First Lord of the Admiralty, Winston Churchill repeatedly tried to name a battleship in honor of Oliver Cromwell. Churchill settled on one of the *Queen Elizabeth* class, a squadron of powerful new fast battleships that would be commissioned in 1915. King George V didn't like the idea of having one of his most powerful ships named after Britain's most famous regicide, and prevailed upon Churchill to choose a more suitable name.

The names finally decided upon for the class were *Queen Elizabeth*, *Valiant*, *Warspite*, *Barham*, and *Malaya*. *Barham* was the third ship to carry the name of Admiral Charles Middleton, First Baron Barham. In addition to serving in the American Revolution, in the Napoleonic Wars, and as the First Lord of the Admiralty, Middleton had played an important role in the abolition of slavery in the British Empire.

The five ships of this class were the finest battleships ever built for the Royal Navy. The *Queen Elizabeth* class represented a leap forward in battleship design almost equivalent in degree to that of *Dreadnought*. Following the construction of *Iron Duke*, the Admiralty decided to pursue a class of ships that would be larger, more heavily armed, and faster than any predecessor or any foreign competitor. Churchill pushed the development of the 15" weapon, a move that would give the *Queen Elizabeths* a major gunnery advantage over the battleships of Germany, Japan, and the US. The heavier guns gave the *Queen Elizabeths* a broadside heavier and with more penetrative capability than the preceding *Iron Dukes* in spite of carrying one fewer turret. The initial design provided for an armament of ten 15" guns in five twin turrets, but the Admiralty decided to sacrifice one turret in favor of a higher speed. This decision would be critical for the future of the class.

Perhaps of greatest consequence, a study by Jackie Fisher suggested that oil propulsion would be both possible and desirable. The

HMS Barham in final condition, 1940s. Arthur Conry,

Queen Elizabeths were the first battleships equipped with oil-fired boilers, which carried several advantages. Oil was less labor-intensive as a fuel than coal, and did not require the employment of a large number of stokers to maintain speed. While human endurance and difficulties associated with the transportation of coal around the ship had limited the duration at which a ship could maintain its highest speed, oil could be transported automatically and stored more efficiently. Oil produced less smoke, helping a ship avoid engagements and perform better during combat (smoke tended to obscure firing positions). Finally, oil burned more efficiently, allowing a higher speed. This higher speed put *Queen Elizabeth* in between battlecruisers and traditional battleships.

A sixth ship was planned, but canceled at the start of the war in favor of smaller, simpler ships. The Royal Canadian Navy seriously considered ordering three of the ships in 1913. The ships would have been assigned to the Royal Navy, but crewed with Canadians and flying under a Canadian flag. Needless to say, this would have made Canada a player in naval affairs of similar stature to Austria-Hungary, Italy, and even France. However, Churchill thought the notion of a Canadian squadron serving in the Royal Navy on a permanent basis absurd, although he wanted the ships. The Canadian Parliament turned the proposal down, making Canada virtually the only country of its size to sensibly eschew the dreadnought fantasy.

Barham and her sisters were attached as a fast battleship squadron to Admiral David Beatty's battlecruisers at the Battle of Jutland. *Barham*, *Valiant*, *Malaya*, and *Warspite* closed with the engaged German battlecruisers and covered the retreat of Beatty's remaining ships. They drove off Hipper's ships, but in doing so became engaged with the vanguard of the High Seas Fleet. All of the ships took hits, but all dealt a great deal of damage, and all four made it back to port.

The rest of the war passed uneventfully for

HMS Barham with HMS Malaya and HMS Argus, 1920s. Royal Navy photographer.

Barham, as the Grand Fleet and High Seas Fleet never met again. All of the *Queen Elizabeths* survived the Washington Naval Treaty and both London Naval Treaties, and all went through a major modernization in the early 1930s. *Warspite*, *Valiant*, and *Queen Elizabeth* went through an additional modernization in the late 1930s, but *Barham* missed out because of the onset of war.

Although she retained many features of her World War I configuration, battleships that could make a decent speed were at a premium in World War II, so *Barham* proved very useful in the early part of the war. She took a torpedo while on patrol in December 1939, but made it back to port without difficulty. In September 1940 she tangled with the French battleship *Richelieu* at Dakar in a failed attempt to support a Free French invasion.

Barham spent the remainder of her war in the Med. In March 1941, the Regia Marina sent a task force to disrupt British convoys engaging in an ill-considered effort to support Greece in the wake of Italy's equally ill-considered invasion. The Italians had misjudged the strength of both the Greeks, and of the Royal Navy in the Med. The British hoped to catch the Italian flagship, the *Vittorio Vento*, with *Barham*, *Warspite*, and *Valiant* (all veterans of Jutland), as well as the aircraft carrier *Formidable*.

HMS Barham following modernization in the 1930s.

Despite suffering a torpedo hit, *Vittorio Vento* escaped. Her escort of heavy cruisers was less lucky. In an effort to take one of their number (damaged by a torpedo) under tow, three heavy cruisers failed to notice the approach of the three British battleships until they had closed to point blank range. *Barham* and her sisters opened up at 3,800 yards, and quickly crippled or sank the three Italian cruisers.

On April 21, 1941, *Barham* participated in the bombardment of Tripoli harbor, an operation designed to destroy Italian port facilities and limit the amount of material the Axis powers could send to Africa. Churchill had initially proposed using *Barham* in suicidal fashion, sinking her as a blockship in order to disrupt the port for an extended period of time. Royal Navy authorities found the proposal, which would leave them short a heavy unit and result in the loss of most of *Barham's* crew, rather less to their liking. Nevertheless, *Barham* and her sisters conducted the bombardment, causing negligible damage.

On November 25, 1941, *U-331* happened upon a Royal Navy squadron on its way to attack Italian convoys to Libya. The German captain fired four torpedoes at the center ship in the British line, then dove to 820 feet, roughly 2.5 times the recommended maximum depth for a submarine of that class. The Germans heard, but did not see, three torpedoes hit *Barham*, which sank in eight minutes with about 800 men.

U-331 was sunk by British aircraft a year later. Its captain, Freiherr Hans-Diedrich von Tiesenhausen, managed to survive and lived the rest of the war in a prison camp. In 1951 he moved to Vancouver, Canada, where he became an interior designer and nature photographer before passing away in August 2000.

Author's Note

With their big 15" guns, the *Queen Elizabeths* had a powerful look to them. They were well known to the Germans, even in World War I, and constituted the bulk of the Royal Navy's battleship strength in the interwar period. Very few classes of ships could contribute so effectively in both World Wars. Of course, *Barham* and her sisters owed this relevance to the naval treaties, which prevented the timely replacement of the older battleships.

I find the story of *Barham* sinking (you can find the video on Youtube) extremely interesting because of the German captain. I lived in the Northwest for several years while he was still alive, and it would have been a delight to interview him.

Related Entries:

Sister of… HMS *Warspite*
Inspired… HIJMS *Nagato*
Fought at… Jutland

Naval Rifling

Battleships carry big guns. Indeed, big guns separated the earliest battleships from their cousins the armored cruisers. Gun size was one of the key legal determinants of what constituted a battleship under the interwar naval treaties.

Early battleships carried a variety of big guns (HMS *Victoria* had a single twin 16" turret), but these early weapons do not compare easily with the guns that became standard in the 1890s. By the time the pre-dreadnought type emerged, 12" weapons had become standard. Although HMS *Dreadnought* carried the same guns as her predecessors, the embrace of the all-big-gun ship made an increase in gun size almost inevitable.

Bigger guns had several advantages. Larger caliber could hurl heavier shells farther, with more penetrating power when they hit their target. Smaller guns could (in theory) fire more rapidly, but in practice the hitting power of heavy guns tended to carry the day.

The British upped the ante with the *Orion* class super-dreadnoughts, which carried 13.5" weapons. Japan, ever sensitive to the power of individual ships, consistently escalated the firepower race. The battle-cruiser HIJMS *Kongo* was the first ship to carry 14" guns. *Kongo* was soon followed by HMS *Queen Elizabeth*, the first of fourteen British battleships to carry the 15"/38 gun. Five years later, the Japanese again jumped ahead with the 16" guns of HIJMS *Nagato*. The Washington Naval Treaty then froze the competition for another twenty years.

Most of the interwar modification increased the elevation capacity of the main guns, so that they could take advantage of improved spotting and range finding to fire longer distances. Italian battleships received a complete makeover, including bored out guns that increased the power of the main armament.

Of all the major powers, the Germans displayed the least interest in rifle size. The first German dreadnoughts (in keeping with their pre-dreadnought predecessors) carried 11" guns, and German warships kept updated versions of 11" guns throughout the Second World War. These guns could hurl a #1,250 shell over 25 kilometers, a throw weight that exceeded any of the guns carried by heavy cruisers in World War II.

When HIJMS *Yamato* entered service, her guns could fire shells of roughly 3,300# to a distance of 42 kilometers. *Yamato* and her sisters carried the heaviest broadside, followed by the American *Iowas*. Although never tested in battle, many Americans argue that the *Iowas*, with more penetrating power despite the smaller size, and with advanced gunnery radar, would have carried the day against their Japanese counterparts.

In any case, the Age of the Gun yielded, shortly after World War II, to the Age of the Missile. Few ships built after World War II carry guns larger than 5", although a few US heavy cruisers with quick-firing 8" guns remained in service for quite some time. The Soviets, always well behind their Western counterparts, constructed a class of gun-armed light cruisers in the 1950s. Today, the Zumwalt class destroyer carries of pair of long-range, hyper-accurate 6" guns, and represents the zenith of gun development.

HIJMS Yamashiro

Laid Down: 1913
Launched: 1915
Completed: March, 1917
Displacement: 29,300 tons
Main Armament: ten 14" guns (three triple turrets)
Secondary Armament: sixteen 6" guns (casemates)
Speed: 22.5 knots
Reconstruction: 1930–1935
Treaty: Pre-Washington Naval Treaty
Major Engagements: Battle of Leyte Gulf
Fate: Sunk by gunfire and torpedoes, October 25, 1944.

Yamashiro and her sister *Fuso* were the first super-dreadnoughts built by the Imperial Japanese Navy. Constructed at the same time as the *Kongo* class battlecruisers, they represented Japan's effort to match the American standard-type battleships, as well as the big 14" gunned ships of the Royal Navy. In terms of speed and broadside, *Yamashiro* was compara-

ble to the British *Queen Elizabeth* class. She entered service in March 1917, but World War I was effectively over in Asia, and plans to transfer a portion of the IJN's battlefleet to Europe never came to fruition.

Yamashiro (the name referenced a type of mountain castle, as well as a medieval Japanese province) was modernized between 1930 and 1935, acquiring new boilers, additional armor, a "pagoda" mast, and some extra speed. Although fast and powerful, *Yamashiro* was not as well-protected as her American contemporaries. The experience of World War II demonstrated that this was a good tradeoff, as speedy ships proved themselves far more useful than their slow, well-armored kin. *Yamashiro* and her sister both participated in the Sino-Japanese War, conducting patrols in support of Japanese Army units.

In spite of her high speed relative to other battleships of her era, *Yamashiro* was not used to much effect in the early part of the Second World War. She and her sister pursued the American carriers *Hornet* and *Enterprise* after the Doolittle Raid, but succeeded in catching only a Russian merchant ship. In the Midway operation, *Yamashiro* supported the decoy

HIJMS Yamashiro in original condition

HIJMS Yamashiro with HIJMS Kaga, October 1930. Kure Maritime Museum.

Aleutian landings. *Yamashiro*'s moment would not come until 1944, when the IJN's options ran short in face of the advancing United States Navy.

In October 1944, the USN prepared a fleet of enormous size to protect and support the invasion of Leyte Island in the Phillipines. The US fleet included six fast battleships, six slow battleships, a dozen fleet carriers, and hundreds of other vessels. The IJN by 1944 was simply incapable of defeating this force in open battle, so the Japanese high command developed a plan designed to decoy the main US fleet away from Leyte, allowing Japanese battleships to destroy the invasion vessels. A force consisting of two battleships and four aircraft carriers would provide bait for Admiral Halsey's Third Fleet, which included the six fast battleships. In the absence of protection from Halsey, a force of five battleships under Admiral Kurita would attack the Leyte armada

from the north, while a force of two battleships and four cruisers would attack from the south. *Yamashiro* was flagship of Admiral Nishimura, commander of the southern force.

The plan demanded a degree of coordination and communication that the IJN could not provide. Little allowance was made for the squadron of six slow US battleships, which remained close to the invasion beach. Utter air supremacy on the part of the USN meant that the Japanese ships would suffer devastating air attacks on their way to Leyte. Finally, while outright victory would delay the invasion of the Philippines for a time, it would probably result in the destruction of most of the strength of the IJN. The IJN was desperate, however, and decided to gamble.

The operation began poorly. Massive air attacks on the US fleet by land-based Japanese air sank only a single American carrier. Attacks by US carriers destroyed one of Kurita's most

HIJMS Yamashiro

HIJMS Yamashiro or HIJMS Fuso underway to Surigao Strait, October 24, 1944. USN photo.

powerful battleships, *Musashi*, and three of the carriers in the decoy force before they could lure Halsey away. Shockingly, however, the basic ruse worked, and Halsey moved his six new battleships away from Leyte, allowing Kurita access to the invasion fleet.

Things did not go so well for *Yamashiro*. Nishimura's force was expected to reach Leyte through the Surigao Strait, a narrow body of water between Leyte and Dingnat. American forces, alerted to Nishimura's presence by air recon, were well prepared. Squadrons of destroyers and PT boats lined either side of the strait, which was capped by Admiral Oldendorf's battle squadron. Around 3:00 AM, American PT boats began to attack the advancing Japanese column. *Yamashiro*'s sister, *Fuso*, took a hit amidships and fell out of the battleline, slowing and eventually reversing course. Destroyer attacks began around 3:30 AM, and *Yamashiro* received between two and four torpedo hits. The first hit slowed *Yamashiro* to five knots, although she soon increased her speed back to eighteen.

At the end of Surigao Strait lay the battleships and cruisers of the American Seventh Fleet. Five of the six battleships (*Pennsylvania, Maryland, West Virginia, California,* and *Tennessee*) had survived Pearl Harbor. *West Virginia, California,* and *Tennessee* had been radically reconstructed since 1942, making their fire and fire control systems state of the art. On the best of days, *Yamashiro* might have been expected to tangle with *Pennsylvania* or *Mississippi* with some chance of success. The other four American ships were out of her league. This was not, however, the best of days. The battleships were accompanied by eight cruisers and numerous destroyers. Moreover, the American squadron had accomplished the apogee of twentieth-century battleship tactics, the "crossing of the T." The American ships were capable of firing full broadsides against *Yamashiro*, while the Japanese ship could only reply with its forward turrets.

At 3:53 AM, the American ships opened fire. With advanced targeting radars, *Tennessee, California,* and *West Virginia* were able to find *Yamashiro* with several salvos each. *Maryland* also successfully engaged *Yamashiro*, and *Mississippi* was able to fire one salvo. *Yamashiro*, with no targeting radar and under heavy assault, responded with uncoordinated fire. Admiral Nishimura ordered *Fuso* to support *Yamashiro*, but *Fuso* had unfortunately exploded twenty minutes earlier. (*Fuso* broke in half but did not sink, leaving the survivors of her crew of 1,400 to contemplate the uselessness of a broken-in-half battleship.) Just after 4:00 AM Admiral Oldendorf ordered a cease fire, because American shells were hitting American ships close to *Yamashiro*. Miraculously, *Yamashiro* was still capable of maneuvering, and managed to turn away from the American ships at nineteen knots. As she was moving away, however, she was caught by two additional torpedoes, and quickly capsized.

Three survivors from *Yamashiro* were picked up by US destroyers. The US record indicates that the remaining survivors did not want to be picked up. The crew of the *Fuso*, according to the USN, also refused rescue. There is good reason to be suspicious of this account. The Pacific War was a nasty conflict, and it was not uncommon for either side to treat surrendering enemy forces brutally. The Imperial Japanese Navy did not condone surrender, and a "cult of suicide" existed even before the Kamikaze, but it is by no means clear whether the refusal to rescue was on the part of the Japanese or the Americans.

The destruction of *Yamashiro* was the last clash of battleships in the twentieth century.

Author's Note

The *Fusos* were genuinely odd-looking, with the central turrets contributing to a rickety appearance. Nevertheless, they would have been among the most powerful ships at Jutland, had the IJN chosen to deploy them

HIJMS Yamashiro (background) with HIJMS Fuso, 1935. Kure Maritime Museum.

with the Grand Fleet. The follow-on *Ise* class modified many aspects of the design, although the basic framework remained similar.

Admiral Nishimura's decision to push forward with his squadron is alternately heroism or suicide. Aerial recon prior to the battle indicated how difficult penetrating Surigao Strait might be. Whether Nishimura believed that his force had a chance, or thought that distracting Oldendorf from Kurita was worth the sacrifice, remains unknown. The sacrifice did give Kurita the opportunity to destroy the larger part of American landing forces, although

Kurita blundered that opportunity away. Alternatively, Nishimura might have envisioned a holding operation that would have kept Oldendorf's attention without engaging in a suicidal frontal assault against a massive enemy force.

Related Entries:

Inspired by... HMS *Barham*
Preceded... HIJMS *Hyuga*
Fought against... USS *Maryland*

SMS Baden

SMS Baden

Laid Down: 1913

Launched: 1915

Completed: March, 1917

Reconstruction: None

Displacement: 32,000 tons

Main Armament: eight 15" guns (4 twin turrets)

Secondary Armament: sixteen 5.9" guns (casemates)

Speed: 22 knots

Major Actions: Scapa Flow

Treaty: Pre-Washington Naval Treaty

Fate: Scuttled, 1919; refloated and sunk as target, 1921

Two characteristics distinguished the dreadnoughts of the High Seas Fleet. First, they were well armored and had excellent survivability characteristics, such as extensive compartmentalization. These qualities extended to the battlecruisers, most of which survived brutal damage at Jutland. On the downside, the Germans undergunned their battleships relative to foreign competitors. The first German dreadnoughts, the *Nassaus*, carried twelve 11" guns in an extremely wasteful hexagon pattern that allowed a broadside of only eight guns. Later German dreadnoughts adopted the 12" gun, but the Germans continued to arrange the turrets poorly, not adopting a full centerline plan until the *König* class of 1913.

To some degree these choices involved a value trade-off. The Germans focused on survivability more than did the British, although probably less than the Americans. The Germans also believed that battles in the North Atlantic would be fought at short ranges, and that at these short ranges lighter guns, with their increased rate-of-fire, would prove superior to heavy guns.

On the other hand, heavy guns did more damage when they hit, and were more likely to penetrate a ship's main armor belt and do

SMS Baden in 1916. Courtesy of German Federal Archive

severe damage to the vitals. Heavier guns did not necessarily require a larger frame or sacrifices in speed or protection. The eight 15" guns of *Queen Elizabeth* weighed no more than the ten 13.5" guns of Iron Duke. Correctly arranged, larger guns could actually save weight while maintaining strength of broadside and increasing effective range.

The Royal Navy steadily increased the size of its guns, from 12" on *Dreadnought* to 13.5" on *Orion* to 15" on *Queen Elizabeth*. The Imperial Japanese Navy designed *Kongo* with 14" guns, and the USN followed suit with the 14" gunned *New York*. The otherwise quite modern *König*, a contemporary of these ships, carried only ten 12" guns. The German Navy, upon discovering that the British had decided to arm *Orion* with 13.5" weapons, finally authorized the use of a larger gun. The next class would add tonnage, and carry eight 15" guns. These ships would become *Bayern* and *Baden*, and would be the only German battleships, in either war, to be sufficiently armed for their size.

Baden was built to a well-balanced design. She displaced 32,000 tons and could make 22 knots, slower but better armored than the *Queen Elizabeth* class. *Baden* had a mixed propulsion system that used both oil and coal. Unfortunately for the Germans, neither *Baden* nor *Bayern* commissioned in time for the Battle of Jutland. No single ship (other perhaps than the USS *New Jersey*) could have transformed the outcome at Jutland, but there's little doubt that the presence of *Baden* would have allowed the Germans to inflict much more damage. In particular, the battleships of the Fifth Battle Squadron, including *Barham* and *Warspite*, would have suffered under the heavier German guns. *Warspite* only barely escaped after being hit by fifteen 12" shells. The 15" guns of *Baden* might well have sent her to the bottom.

Upon commissioning, *Baden* became the flagship of the High Seas Fleet. However, the Kaiserliche Marine made only a few brief sor-

ties after Jutland, and *Baden* had a relatively uneventful career. German sailors refused a suicidal order to engage the Grand Fleet in late 1918, and at the end of the war the Allies demanded the internment of the most powerful German ships. The German squadron (disheveled after poor maintenance in the last year of the war) was escorted from Wilhelmshaven to Scapa Flow by a huge fleet of British, French, and American battleships. The situation remained tense, and the Allies were careful to keep their guns trained on the German battleships as they left port. *Baden* was not originally slated for internment, but another ship, *Mackensen*, was not complete and the Allies took *Baden* as substitute.

The German fleet remained, with skeletal crews, at Scapa Flow as peace talks dragged on. Several of the ships would have made significant prizes for the Allies, including *Baden* and *Bayern*. France in particular would have liked to incorporate some of the German ships into her fleet. The Royal Navy was content to let the ships rust. The British were reluctant to seize the ships while peace talks continued, and they believed, in any case, that the German crews would react to an attempt at seizure by scuttling the ships.

On June 21, 1919, acting on what may have been an erroneous report about the negotiations, Admiral Ludwig von Reuter ordered the High Seas Fleet to scuttle itself. Eleven battleships, five battlecruisers, and dozens of smaller ships opened up their hulls and sank. The Royal Navy, out on maneuvers, was unable to stop the Germans, although a few German sailors were shot in the confusion. Deeply annoyed, the British imprisoned the crews for some time before allowing a repatriation to Germany. Only the *Baden* could be saved, as the British towed her into shallow water before she sank.

Over the next two years, the Royal Navy tested, prodded, poked, and disassembled *Baden* in order to figure out how she compared to British ships. Their conclusions, which should be viewed with some skepticism, were that *Baden* was definitely inferior to her Royal Navy contemporaries. On 16 August 1921, *Baden* was mercifully sent to the bottom by fire from Royal Navy battleships. The wrecks of eight German battleships and battle-cruisers remain at the bottom of Scapa Flow, and have become an attraction for adventurous SCUBA divers.

Author's Note

The *Bayerns* were the zenith of World War I German battleship design, and on paper compared favorably with the best British ships. However, their relatively slow construction was emblematic of Germany's inability to match British shipbuilding.

Had the *Bayerns* survived, either in German or foreign hands, it would have been interesting to see how they would have fared in World War II. A reconstruction could have made them even more formidable, especially if (as was Italian practice), the rebuild increased their speed.

Related Entries:

Contemporary of... HMS *Warspite*
Preceded... *Tirpitz*
Served alongside... SMS *Friedrich der Grosse*

HMS Royal Sovereign
Arkhangelsk

Laid Down: 1914
Launched: 1915
Completed: May, 1916
Displacement: 29,900 tons
Main Armament: eight 15" guns (four twin turrets)
Secondary Armament: fourteen 6" guns (casemates)
Speed: 22 knots
Treaty: Pre-Washington Naval Treaty
Major Engagements: None
Fate: Scrapped, 1949

The Royal Navy followed up its outstanding *Queen Elizabeth* class battleships with five *Revenges* (commonly known as the "R" class). Slightly smaller, slower, and powered by coal, the *Revenges* represented an intentional step back, an effort to check the increasing cost of the super-dreadnought competition with Germany. *Royal Sovereign* took her name from a long line of British front-line battleships; one of her predecessors served at Trafalgar.

Royal Sovereign commissioned just before Jutland, but missed the battle as her crew had not yet fully worked up. She served with the Grand Fleet for the rest of World War I, participating in a few abortive sorties against the High Seas Fleet.

Royal Sovereign and her sisters were retained under the terms of the London Naval Treaty, but, unlike most other battleships of the interwar period, were not subjected to an extensive modernization. The vessels had three major design flaws that limited their expected future effectiveness. First, their slow speed, while also characteristic of American battleships, left them incapable of performing many of the missions that would be necessary in the Second World War. The "R" class would rarely conduct a mission other than shore bombardment or convoy escort. Second, the armor scheme was obsolete almost as soon as the ships were completed, as it left the ships

HMS Royal Sovereign at sea

HMS Royal Sovereign fires her guns during World War I. Peter Hodges, The Big Gun: Battleship Main Armament 1860-1945, 1981.,

vulnerable to long range plunging shells. Winston Churchill referred to the R class as "coffin ships," and the Admiralty strove to keep them as far away from enemy ships as possible. Finally, the ships were designed with reduced stability in order to induce a rolling motion conducive to good gunnery. Unfortunately, this made reconstructing them almost impossible.

Royal Sovereign had a remarkably dull career for a ship that survived both world wars. The early part of her war was taken up with convoy escort, and the closest she came to real combat came at the Battle of Calabria, where her slow speed prevented her from closing with Italian battleships. In late 1941 she deployed to the Far East with her surviving sisters (*Royal Oak* was lost to *U-47* in September 1939), but the presumptive superiority of the Japanese carrier battle group meant that she never came close to seeing action.

From 1942 on, one of the major duties of the Royal Navy was to escort convoys to Murmansk against German surface ships and submarines. After the destruction of *Tirpitz* in 1944, the surface fleet of the Kriegsmarine could pose little threat to the convoys. Some of the older battleships were placed in reserve even before the war ended because of a man-power crisis. Instead of retiring *Royal Sovereign*, it was decided to transfer her to the Soviet Navy in an effort to give the Russians some responsibility for protection of the northern convoys. She represented a down payment on Italian war reparations, as the Soviets had won the rights to a battleship during the surrender negotiations.

Royal Sovereign was renamed *Arkhangelsk*, assigned to the Northern Fleet, and served in the Red Navy until 1949. The Soviets had little experience with warships as modern as *Royal Sovereign* (the battleships that had survived the Revolution were even older), and could not maintain the ship in good condition. In 1949, when the Soviets took possession of the Italian *Giulio Cesare*, *Arkhangelsk*'s turrets were so badly corroded that they couldn't rotate, and there was some question as to whether she was seaworthy enough to return to the United Kingdom. The Royal Navy successfully repossessed her, however, and she was scrapped beginning in 1949.

Author's Note

I haven't found any account of why *Royal Sovereign* specifically was chosen for transfer, but I would like to think that Churchill or

Arkhangelsk, ex-Royal Sovereign in Soviet service.

HMS Royal Sovereign. Malcolm William Burgess Warships To-day, 1936.

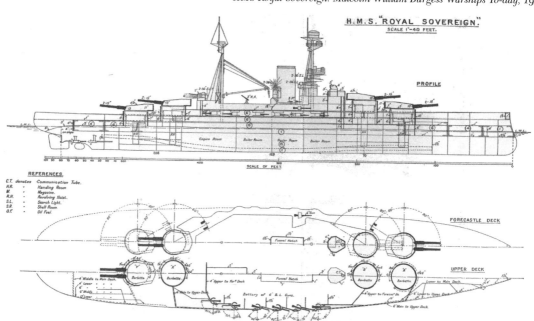

someone in the Admiralty, evincing a particularly dark sense of humor, thought that there was some amusement to be had in the transfer of a ship named *Royal Sovereign* to a nation that had massacred its last monarch and his family.

As I've argued in other places, I suspect that the Royal Navy would have been much better served by disposing of one of the R class in favor of the battlecruiser HMS *Tiger*, which at least could have hunted raiders and escorted fast carriers.

Related Entries:

Filled in for... *Giulio Cesare*
Contemporary of... USS *Arizona*
Preceded by... HMS *Warspite*

USS Arizona

Laid Down: 1914

Launched: 1915

Completed: October 1916

Reconstruction: 1929–1931

Displacement: 29,000 tons

Main Armament: twelve 14" guns (four triple turrets)

Secondary Armament: twenty-two 5" guns (casemates)

Speed: 21 knots

Major Actions: Pearl Harbor

Treaty: Pre-Washington Naval Treaty

Fate: Sunk by Japanese carrier aircraft, December 7, 1941. Wreck preserved as museum.

USS *Arizona*, second ship of the *Pennsylvania* class and fourth "standard type" American battleship, was commissioned in October 1916. She shared with the other standard types excellent armor protection, a heavy armament, and a uniform speed. Along with most oil-fired American battleships, *Arizona* saw very limited action in World War I. Although larger, more heavily armed, and better protected than the most modern Royal Navy battleships, the threat the U-boat campaign posed to British oil supplies meant that only the older, coal-fired American ships would deploy with the Grand Fleet.

Arizona sailed to Europe after main hostilities ceased, participating in a variety of commemorations and victory celebrations before deploying to the Mediterranean to monitor tensions between Greece and Italy. Neither state was particularly satisfied by the distribution of spoils after World War I, or by the disposition of Turkish possessions. The presence of US fleet units helped ensure that no conflict would break into the open. After returning to the United States for a brief refit, Arizona transited the Panama Canal, joining the Pacific Fleet in 1922. A reconstruction from 1929–1931 replaced Arizona's cage masts with tripods, improved her fire control, and increased and repositioned her secondary and anti-aircraft armaments.

Apart from modernization, Arizona remained in the Pacific for the rest of her career. In April 1940, USS *Arizona* deployed to Pearl Harbor, along with the rest of the battleships of the Pacific Fleet. On the morning of December 7, 1941, *Arizona* sat second in the inner line of Battleship Row, ahead of *Tennessee* and behind

USS Arizona in 1930s, after reconstruction

USS Arizona in the East River, New York, December 24, 1916.

Nevada. The supply ship *Vestal* sat alongside, protecting *Arizona*'s flank. *Arizona* was attacked by a flight of "Kate" bombers launched from HIJMS *Kaga* and HIJMS *Hiryu*. At 8:06 AM, a bomber flown by Tadashi Kusumi, with bombardier Noburu Kanai, dropped an 800 kg bomb (a modified 16" shell) that penetrated the deck between *Arizona*'s forward two turrets. The bomb detonated *Arizona*'s forward magazine, blowing out *Arizona*'s bottom and quickly sinking the ship. 1,177 of *Arizona*'s crew died in the blast and ensuing flooding.

Because of the great damage, no thought was given to salvaging *Arizona*. The main guns and the masts were cut from the wreck later in the war, the former being used in coast defense fortifications on Oahu. Noburu Kanai died two weeks later at the Battle of Wake Island, Tadashi Kusumi at the Battle of Midway.

After the war, USS *Arizona*'s wreck was designated a national shrine, complete with the construction of a memorial above the hulk. Today, USS *Missouri* is permanently berthed next to *Arizona* on Battleship Row. Every year, thousands of tourists visit the memorial, which still leaks oil stored in the battleship's tanks.

Author's Note

USS *Arizona* is almost more interesting as sociological event than as piece of military technology. She represented, until September 11, 2001, the greatest intelligence and military failure in American history. Her wreck also served as a physical manifestation of the World War II generation. Had she survived, *Arizona* would likely have had a career much like the other standard types, including modernization, shore bombardment, and convoy escort.

Related Entries:

Preceded... USS *Mississippi*
Contemporary of... SMS *Baden*
Fought at... Pearl Harbor

USS Arizona shortly after December 7, 1941

USS Mississippi

Laid Down: 1914
Launched: 1915
Completed: December, 1917
Displacement: 32,000 tons
Main Armament: twelve 14" guns (four triple turrets)
Secondary Armament: fourteen 5" guns (six single mounts, eight casemates)
Speed: 21 knots
Treaty: Pre-Washington Naval Treaty
Reconstruction: 1931–34
Major Engagements: Battle of Surigao Strait
Fate: Scrapped, 1956

In 1904, the United States laid down USS *Mississippi* (BB-23), second of her name and the first of a class of two pre-dreadnoughts intended to stem the growth in naval construction costs. Embittered by the cost of the six *Connecticut* class battleships, Congress limited the *Mississippis* to 13,000 tons, nearly a quarter smaller than their predecessors. This resulted in a lighter secondary armament, lower speed, and shorter range—characteristics which only enhanced their obsolescence when HMS *Dreadnought* entered service

before they commissioned. The USN sought to discard these unusable ships as quickly as possible (they could not even operate with the pre-dreadnought squadrons that then constituted the Atlantic Fleet), and in 1914 succeeded in selling both to Greece. Both ships were sunk by German aircraft in 1941.

This freed up the name USS *Mississippi* (BB-41) for one of twelve "standard type" battleships, designed with a common armor scheme, speed, and main armament in order to operate together. She differed from her immediate predecessors, the *Pennsylvania* class, by having a clipper bow and a better arranged secondary armament. Because of the fortuitous sale of the preceding USS *Mississippi*, the United States government could afford to buy three ships of the class, rather than the standard two.

Commissioned in late 1917, *Mississippi* was not deployed with the Grand Fleet because of oil shortages created by the German U-boat campaign. In any case, the Grand Fleet then held presumptive dominance over the High Seas Fleet, a situation which would hold until the end of the war.

Mississippi and her sisters survived the Washington Naval Treaty. Like most US battleships, *Mississippi* was heavily modernized

USS Mississippi, 1919

during the interwar period. Unlike the preceding classes, *Mississippi* and her sisters were rebuilt with a citadel superstructure. This arrangement was more useful (and aesthetically pleasing) than the tripod mast reconstructions adopted in earlier ships. War tension in the Europe prompted the USN to transfer *Mississippi* and her two sisters to the Atlantic in early 1941, and she was escorting convoys during the Pearl Harbor attack. After the attack *Mississippi* rejoined the Pacific Fleet, first undergoing an overhaul that increased her anti-aircraft armament.

Mississippi's war record was similar to that of other battleships of her vintage. She escorted convoys, acted as a reserve force, and bombarded islands in preparation for Marine assaults. The most exciting part of her service came on the morning of October 24 when she, along with five other battleships, participated in the destruction of HIJMS *Yamashiro*. *Mississippi*, lacking the most modern radar (she was equipped with Mark 3 radar, the same type used by USS *Washington* at Guadalcanal), fired only one salvo at *Yamashiro*, less than a minute before Admiral Oldendorf issued a cease-fire order. *Yamashiro* quickly sank from torpedo and gun damage.

Hit by a kamikaze in January 1945,

USS Mississippi transiting Panama Canal.

Mississippi still participated in most of the actions at the close of the Pacific War. After the war she was converted into a gunnery training ship and given a new designation, AG-128. *Mississippi* was more fortunate than her sisters and half-sisters, who found themselves either at the bottom of Bikini Atoll, at the scrapping yard, or in reserve. In late 1952 she was equipped with Terrier surface-to-air missiles for testing purposes. For the next four years she carried out tests of missiles, before decommissioning in 1956. She was sold for scrap in November of that year.

USS Mississippi with her two sisters, USS Idaho and USS New Mexico, December 1943

USS Mississippi firing Terrier surface-to-air missile, March 28, 1955. USN photo.

USS Mississippi, April 12, 1945.

Author's Note

Mississippi was a "bad luck" ship; she suffered turret explosions in 1924 and 1943 that each killed dozens of men.

The USN floated a variety of schemes in the postwar era to convert battleships into missile ships. Apart from *Mississippi* and the four *Iowa* ships (which eventually sported Tomahawk and Harpoon missiles), the plans came to naught. Several heavy cruisers underwent conversion to SAM missiles ships, intended to protect carrier battlegroups from Soviet bombers carrying long-range cruise missiles. The last of these ships left service in 1980.

Related Entries:

Fought against... HIJMS *Yamashiro*
Preceded... USS *Maryland*
Contemporary of... HMS *Royal Sovereign*

HMS Renown

Laid Down: 1915

Launched: 1916

Completed: September, 1916

Displacement: 27,600 tons

Main Armament: six 15" guns (three twin turrets)

Secondary Armament: seventeen 4" guns (five triple mounts, two single mounts)

Speed: 32 knots

Treaty: Pre-Washington Naval Treaty

Reconstructions: 1922–26, 1936–39

Major Engagements: Norway, Cape Spartivento

Fate: Scrapped, 1948

HMS *Renown* was to be the sixth "R" class battleship, but the Admiralty suspended construction in favor of smaller vessels that might have a more immediate impact. The return to service of Lord Jackie Fisher and the victories of Royal Navy battlecruisers at the Falkland Islands and Heligoland Bight changed this calculation, however, and the Admiralty decided to complete *Renown* and her sister *Repulse* as battlecruisers. *Renown* was a well-worn Royal Navy name, having identified at least a half a dozen ships since the seventeenth century. The *Renowns* traded speed for protection and armament, dropping a 15" turret and considerable armor in return for an eleven knot advantage over the *Revenge* class battleships.

Commissioned in September 1916, *Renown* fortunately missed the Battle of Jutland. The loss of three battlecruisers convinced the Admiralty that *Renown*'s protection was too light, resulting in the addition of extra armor. *Renown* participated in the rest of World War I but never engaged the High Seas Fleet. *Renown* and her sister *Repulse* were never popular ships in the Royal Navy, suffering from constant teething problems, and enjoying the nicknames "Refit" and "Repair." However, the RN decided to retain both ships under the terms of the London Naval Treaty (a third battlecruiser, HMS *Tiger*, was discarded). *Renown* underwent a major reconstruction along the same lines as the *Queen Elizabeth* class battleships between 1937 and 1939, resulting in a new superstructure, better fire control, and a greatly enhanced anti-aircraft armament. She rejoined

HMS Renown after reconstruction. National Archives and Records Administration.

the fleet in September 1939, just in time for the Second World War.

Although an older unit, *Renown's* high speed made her useful for operations that other old battleships could not undertake. *Renown* could hunt German raiders (such as the pocket battleships, or the *Scharnhorst* class battleships), escort fast carriers, and support cruiser flotillas. Her weak armor was a handicap, but used appropriately *Renown* could make a significant contribution to the war effort. One of *Renown's* first operations involved convoy escort and support of British operations in Norway. In service off the latter, *Renown* encountered the German battleships *Scharnhorst* and *Gneisenau* in April 1940. *Renown* scored two hits on *Gneisenau* before the Germans broke off.

The German decision to break off contact was probably fortunate for the British, as the destruction of *Renown* was well within the capabilities of either German ship, much less both. The *Scharnhorst's* 11" guns could easily penetrate *Renown's* light armor, and with their high rate of fire and large number of guns, *Scharnhorst* and *Gneisenau* could each fire 27 shells per minute to *Renown's* 12. Better German fire control and damage absorption capability should have made the fight no con-

test (although *Scharnhorst's* fire control malfunctioned during the battle), but the Germans failed to press their advantage. In fairness, the German commanders worried that even moderate damage could mean a death sentence in seas that remained under Royal Navy control.

Renown participated in operations in the Atlantic and the Med for the next two years, including pursuit of the battleship *Bismarck* in 1941. In November 1941, she participated in the Battle of Cape Spartivento, where she briefly tangled with the Italian fast battleship *Vittorio Veneto*. In 1944 *Renown* shifted to the Pacific, operating out of Ceylon and escorting carrier attacks on Japanese bases in Southeast Asia. By mid-1945 *Renown* was simply worn out, and massive Allied naval superiority meant that she could be placed in reserve before the war ended. After use as a training ship for a couple years, *Renown* was sold for scrap in 1948.

Author's Note

Like most of the British battlecruisers, *Renown* was a very attractive ship, with sleek lines and a well-proportioned superstructure. The reconstruction added a bulky forecastle

HMS Renown prior to reconstruction

HMS Renown entering the Panama Canal

which, however practical it may have been, significantly reduced *Renown*'s aesthetic appeal. As with nearly all the battlecruisers that survived into World War II, she had an eventful career relative to her slower comrades. It's worth considering just how far down this could apply; would it have made sense for the Royal Navy to keep *Lion*, *Princess Royal*, and *Tiger* instead of three of the *Revenges*? Given how

sparingly the Royal Navy used the R class, it seems quite likely.

Related Entries:

Preceded... HMS *Hood*
Fought against... *Scharnhorst*
Contemporary of... HIJMS *Kongo*

Interlude

Jutland

Context

When the First World War opened, the Royal Navy enjoyed a huge advantage in battlecruisers and battleships over the Kaiserliche Marine. On August 1, 1914, the Royal Navy could boast twenty dreadnoughts, including ten *Orion*, *King George V*, and *Iron Duke* class ships that compared favorably with anything the Germans could offer. Within three months, four more dreadnoughts would enter service (two *Iron Dukes*, and two ships seized from Turkey). The British also possessed eight battlecruisers, with HMS *Tiger* about to enter service and HMAS *Australia* in transit from the Pacific.

By contrast, the Germans owned thirteen dreadnoughts, with another three entering service in the first three months of the war. The High Seas Fleet operated three battlecruisers (another, *Goeben*, was stuck in the Med), and would receive a fourth shortly after the war began.

The Royal Navy had greater global responsibilities, of course, but outside of Germany Austria-Hungary was the only Central Power which possessed battleships, and the Marine Nationale easily outclassed the Imperial fleet. Thus, the Royal Navy could freely concentrate on the North Sea, which it quickly did through the creation of the Grand Fleet. Indeed, the Allies had a sufficient number of pre-dreadnoughts in reserve to use them for a variety of less critical tasks, such as the effort to force the Dardanelles.

Time would exacerbate these challenges for the Central Powers. The entry of Italy and her six battleships into the war, and the pace of Russian, French, and British construction widened the gap with the Germans. Three French and six Russian battleships entered service between August, 1914 and Jutland. The Royal Navy itself added nine new battleships, eight of which carried 15" guns.

Theoretically, German and British positions were asymmetrical. The High Seas Fleet was pretty, but Germany did not strictly need it in order to win the war. The capture of Paris or the collapse of Russia would result in German victory notwithstanding the destruction of the German battleship flotilla. The Allies, on the other hand, needed naval power in order to secure their supply lines with each other, and with the United States. On paper, this resulted in a situation where Germany should have accepted large risks for the chance of a decisive victory over the British.

Of course, a host of other considerations worked to curb Germany's risk-acceptance. Even if Germany might survive a catastrophic defeat, the Kaiserliche Marine saw no benefit in the destruction of its best ships and the death of its best men. No commander wanted to play the part of Villenueve (the French admiral at Trafalgar, who later committed suicide), however the strategic balance might have fallen out. The crews themselves had little interest in suicidal overtures.

And so the Germans needed to take great care. German naval authorities planned to force an engagement against a portion of the Royal Navy, thereby weakening the whole. Contemporary naval theory suggested (correctly) that material advantage in a naval battle was exponential, rather than additive. In other words, a larger force could be expected to perform much better than a small force; numerical superiority was more important than usual. The High Seas Fleet, under Reinhard Scheer, could never defeat John Jellicoe's Grand Fleet in open battle, but could hope to destroy a portion of it without significant cost.

Setting

Many of the early operations of the High Seas Fleet involved efforts to lure part of the Grand Fleet under the guns of the High Seas Fleet. German battlecruisers could raid the English coast and make it back to safety before the

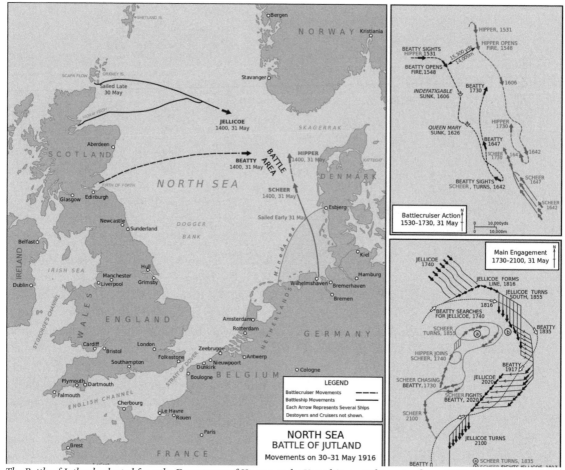

The Battle of Jutland, adapted from the Department of History at the United States Military Academy. CCA, Grandiose.

Grand Fleet, deploying from Scapa Flow, could catch them. In deference to public and political opinion, the Royal Navy needed to respond to these raids in some fashion, which led to the deployment of the Grand Fleet's battlecruisers to Rosyth, under the command of Admiral David Beatty. The battlecruisers were joined by the five fast battleships of the Fifth Battle Squadron, serving under Admiral Hugh Evan-Thomas.

In early 1916, the Germans decided on a more elaborate operation to cut into the growing British advantage. German battlecruisers would try to lure out the British battlecruisers by threatening to raid the British coast. The Royal Navy battlecruiser squadron would then be attacked with the whole of the High Seas Fleet. The Grand Fleet (including 24 of the 31

British dreadnoughts) was based at Scapa Flow, in the far north of Great Britain, and could not arrive in time to save the British battlecruisers. The Grand Fleet would be further hampered by pre-positioned U-boats.

After several weeks of delay, Admiral Franz Hipper's battlecruiser squadron sortied into the North Sea in order to draw out the British. Beatty's battlecruisers took the bait, supported by the four *Queen Elizabeth* class battleships of the Fifth Battle Squadron. Hipper would hook Beatty, then reel him into the jaws of Reinhard Scheer's High Seas Fleet.

The Run to the South

The two fleets made contact at 3:30 PM on the afternoon of May 31, 1916. When they first met, the Germans had five battlecruisers and the British six, along with a variety of support craft on either side. The sun favored the Germans, illuminating the British while shading Hipper's ships. The Germans also had much better fire control than the British, and quickly scored hits on three of the British ships, including Beatty's flagship *Lion*. The effectiveness of the German fire was enhanced by the fact that damage control aboard the British battlecruisers was wholly inadequate.

The German advantage soon paid dividends. At 4:02 PM, a salvo from SMS *Von der Tann* set off a magazine explosion in HMS *Indefatigable*. 1,017 of her crew of 1,019 died. At 4:25, HMS *Queen Mary* suffered the same fate. By that time, however, the Fifth Battle Squadron had arrived on the scene. HMS *Barham*, HMS *Valiant*, HMS *Malaya*, and HMS *Warspite* were the four most powerful battleships in the world, carrying eight 15" guns and capable of 23.5 knots. However, the battleships trailed the battlecruisers by a considerable distance, and would not join Beatty as quickly as possible due to signaling problems. When they arrived the pressure on Beatty's battlecruisers eased considerably.

At 4:40 PM, Beatty received word that the van of the High Seas Fleet was coming into range. At that point the Run to the South became the Run to the North. Beatty turned his ships around, although poor signaling meant that the Fifth Battle Squadron received word late and had to undergo several minutes of concentrated fire from the German battleships. The first trap had closed, and it seemed that the only question was how much damage the Germans could inflict on the fleeing British.

The Main Engagement

Unfortunately for the Germans, the British had received signals intelligence indicating that the High Seas Fleet was preparing to deploy. The Grand Fleet, led by Admiral John

Admiral John Jellicoe. Library of Congress.

Jellicoe aboard HMS *Iron Duke*, left Scapa Flow before the High Seas Fleet left Kiel. The pre-positioned U-boats, because of the delays, had reached the limits of their endurance, and failed to find any targets. The British had taken the bait, but with too much force. The trap set by the Germans had become a trap for the Germans.

The High Seas Fleet continued to plug north in pursuit of Beatty's ships, encountering the advance elements of the Grand Fleet in a squadron of four armored cruisers and another squadron of three battlecruisers. The Germans savaged the armored cruisers, destroying HMS *Defence* and crippling HMS *Warrior*. The crew of *Warrior* was saved by a mechanical problem on board *Warspite*. Her rudder damaged, *Warspite* made two full turns in front of the German Navy, taking fifteen hits in the process but eventually limping away. As

Admiral Franz Hipper, center. Erich Raeder, commander of the Kriegsmarine in World War II, is second from the left. German Federal Archives.

Warspite sailed out of reach, the three battle-cruisers of Rear Admiral Horace Hood engaged the battered German battlecruiser squadron. HMS *Invincible* poured fire into SMS *Lutzow* before succumbing to a salvo from SMS *Derfflinger*, exploding and sinking with all hands.

And then the smoke cleared, and the twenty-four dreadnoughts of the Grand Fleet became visible to the German van.

Beatty had kept in intermittent contact with Jellicoe during the Run to the North, but had not kept his superior fully apprised of the disposition of the German fleet. Nevertheless, Jellicoe ordered the Grand Fleet to deploy in line-of-battle to the east, in hopes of crossing Scheer's "T" and cutting the Germans off from home. When the Grand Fleet came into view, it became apparent that Jellicoe had succeed-ed, and the lead elements of the German line began to come under fire from the broadsides

of the British ships.

Scheer knew that he couldn't fight the Grand Fleet, and did the sensible thing. He ordered the High Seas Fleet to make a 180 degree turn in line; a very difficult maneuver that required a great deal of practice. Essentially, each ship turned simultaneously, rather than in line formation. At the end of the turn, the trailing ship was in the lead, and Scheer's fleet was moving to the southwest, away from the British fleet but also away from the German bases.

This left the Germans on the wrong side of the Grand Fleet, however, and Admiral Scheer soon ordered another 180 degree turn. This took the Germans directly into the center of the British line, with potentially disastrous consequences for the lead ships. Finally, Scheer ordered a third 180 degree turn to escape from the British. To cover the German escape, he ordered the destroyers and battlecruisers to launch an attack against the Grand Fleet.

This move may have saved the High Seas Fleet from destruction. The battered battlecruisers took another beating, but eventually turned away and rejoined the German line. The destroyers conducted a torpedo attack, which left Jellicoe with a critical decision. Faced with the German destroyers, Jellicoe had to decide whether or not to turn into the torpedoes or turn away from them. By turning in, the British line might have suffered some losses, but could have stayed in contact with the Germans. By turning away, the British risked losing the Germans.

Jellicoe, in accordance with normal practice of the day, turned away. The Grand Fleet struggled to regain contact with the Germans before nightfall. Poor communications continued to afflict the British effort, and in the darkness Scheer's battleships crossed the rear of the Royal Navy's line. Several British ships noted the German movement, but none reported in to Jellicoe. In the final engagements, the Germans lost a pre-dreadnought to torpedo attack, and the British another armored cruiser. The Germans scuttled SMS *Lutzow* in the early morning, after rescuing nearly her entire crew.

Aftermath

The battle is counted as a tactical German victory and a strategic British victory. British losses (3 battlecruisers, 3 armored cruisers, 8 destroyers, and 6,097 sailors) were heavier than German (1 battlecruiser, 1 pre-dreadnought, 4 light cruisers, 5 destroyers, and 2,551 sailors), but several German ships were very badly damaged, and the High Seas Fleet did not play a significant role in the rest of the war. Allied surface naval dominance would continue to increase, and the Germans would turn to the submarine to win the naval war. Moreover, while it's easy to imagine scenarios in which the British inflict much more damage

on the High Seas Fleet, it's hard to see how the Germans could have done much better than they did.

Why did the Grand Fleet fail to destroy the High Seas Fleet at Jutland, in spite of a massive advantage in material and a devastating tactical position? There was no single decisive moment at Jutland; the tactical and operational situations resulted from the accretion of a tremendous number of decisions large and small.

British command at the Battle of Jutland featured what historian Andrew Gordon has referred to as a doctrinaire officer (Admiral John Jellicoe), and a ratcatcher (Admiral David Beatty). Of course, these are ideal types that can never quite catch the complexities of particularly individuals; Jellicoe would not have risen to command if he had not found himself among fellow doctrinaire officers, and Beatty tamed his rebellious streak enough to move up the Royal Navy hierarchy.

The case against David Beatty is complex, but compelling. His audacity made him a capable commander, but he lacked a sense for detail. His evaluation of subordinates was suspect, and in any case he did not communicate well with his senior officers. These shortcomings may well have had an impact in the early stages of the Battle of Jutland. Had Beatty taken more care to coordinate with the Fifth Battle Squadron, more damage might have been inflicted on Hipper's battlecruisers, and *Queen Mary* just might have been saved. Later, poor communications with his subordinate created a zone of vulnerability for the Fifth Battle Squadron, which could have but did not lead to the loss of one or more of the most valuable units in the Royal Navy.

The initial reaction to Jutland in the United Kingdom was to blame Jellicoe; he had failed to destroy the Germans, and in fact the Grand Fleet ended up suffering greater losses than the High Seas Fleet. Jellicoe was "promoted" out of command of the Grand Fleet, and Beatty was promoted into command.

Admiral David Beatty.

Beatty, in spite of all the mistakes he made, did his job; he drew the High Seas Fleet into a hopeless tactical position against a vastly superior enemy force. The loss of a battlecruiser or two would hardly be remembered if Jellicoe's Grand Fleet had proceeded to destroy the Germans, as it clearly was capable of doing. Put differently, the loss of a battlecruiser may be attributable to Beatty's mistakes, but the escape of the High Seas Fleet is on Jellicoe.

And some of Jellicoe's decisions surely deserve scrutiny. After the war, Jellicoe's decision to turn away in the face of the German torpedo attack attracted a great deal of attention. In Jellicoe's favor, it was noted that he had a reasonable expectation that it would be possible to maintain contact with the German fleet and to prevent it from returning to its bases. The German torpedo attack might have

cost several dreadnoughts, it was argued, and given the widespread belief that the Germans had ship-to-ship superiority, this could have nullified the British advantage. Finally, it was argued that Jellicoe's job was not to destroy the German fleet, but to prevent the destruction of the Royal Navy.

On the other hand, the communications struggles afflicting the Grand Fleet were of no surprise to Jellicoe. He could have worked more vigorously to solve Royal Navy communications problems before the battle, and he must have appreciated the possibility of a German mistake. Moreover, the British had 27 dreadnoughts and 6 battlecruisers at the time of the turn. The Germans had 16 battleships and 4 battlecruisers, and the German fleet had suffered a much more severe battering than the British. Even accepting the loss of several ships, the Grand Fleet had a commanding superiority over the High Seas Fleet.

Was Jellicoe thinking at a level above his paygrade? Jellicoe seems to have agonized over his position as the only man who could lose the war in an afternoon. The architects of the greatest victories in modern naval history (Horatio Nelson, Heihachiro Togo, William Halsey) rarely seem to have dwelt on strategic problems. They were given a job (destruction of the enemy), and a set of tools with which to do that job, and both of them undertook as expediently as possible to bring the enemy under their sights and destroy him.

And such a mindset might have led the commander not to turn away from the destroyer attack, but rather to maintain contact with the Germans. Had contact been maintained, the outcome of the battle could not have been in doubt; the British had more ships, better ships, and a tactically advantageous situation. The Grand Fleet, even accepting a few torpedo hits, would have utterly destroyed the High Seas Fleet with relatively light losses.

However, it is surely worth noting that Beatty, Jellicoe, and most of the other officers of the Grand Fleet successfully accomplished the tremendous number of very difficult tasks that were necessary to bring the High Seas Fleet to the point of destruction; they shifted formation and maintained station, avoided submarines, avoided collision, and in general did all of the tasks that are expected by professional naval officers.

The Germans faced a less ambiguous situation. Even had the High Seas Fleet suffered complete annihilation, the British would have struggled to turn victory into long-term strategic advantage. Trafalgar, it should be noted, did not lead to the defeat of Napoleon. It would have been very difficult for the Royal Navy to enter the Baltic in any force, and Germany was not dependent on foreign trade. On this point, Jellicoe was quite correct to avoid a risky situation. The British public and the British government, however, did not want a calm and judicious decision. They wanted Nelson and Trafalgar.

By the time of the torpedo attack, the Germans stood no chance of victory; the best they could do was escape. In later years, however, Reinhard Scheer suggested that more vigorous action during the Grand Fleet's deployment for battle might have turned the tide. The credibility of this belief aside, what could a German victory have meant? Theoretically, the German navy could have raided the British coast, could have attacked British trade on the surface, and could have threatened the supply lines to France. What if Scheer had pulled off a "Nelson at Trafalgar"?

Imagine that the High Seas Fleet managed to destroy twenty of the twenty-eight British dreadnoughts and six of the nine battlecruisers, while only suffering losses of one battleship and one battlecruiser. This is wildly implausible given the technology of the day, but helpful as grist for the thought-exercise. The Germans had one dreadnought in reserve, bringing their total to 16 dreadnoughts and four battlecruisers. The British had two dreadnoughts and one battlecruiser in reserve, giving them ten dreadnoughts and four battle-cruisers. This would seem to leave the Germans with a substantial, and potentially war-winning, advantage.

But not so fast. France had seven dreadnoughts that weren't doing anything particularly vital in the Mediterranean, and that could have been immediately incorporated in the Grand Fleet. The six Italian dreadnoughts could easily counter four Austrian ships, leaving the Allies in control of the Med. British construction was also more advanced than German. Two battlecruisers and three battleships would enter the Royal Navy in 1916, compared with one battlecruiser and two battleships for the German fleet. By the end of 1916, assuming no further losses on either side, the Grand Fleet would have consisted of twenty dreadnoughts and six battlecruisers, while the High Seas Fleet would have had eighteen dreadnoughts and five battlecruisers.

In short, having won one Trafalgar, Scheer would have had to win another Trafalgar to achieve a decisive superiority over the Royal Navy. He would have had to do this before the United States' entry into the war (which might well have been accelerated by a German victory at Jutland), and the commitment of twelve additional dreadnoughts (not including the slow *Michigan* and *South Carolina*) to the Allied cause. Also, in desperate need the Allies might have made concessions necessary to accelerate Brazil's entry into the war (along with its two dreadnoughts), and gain access to the four battlecruisers and six dreadnoughts of the Imperial Japanese Navy, which would eventually commit a squadron to the Mediterranean.

Of course, this doesn't include the effect on British morale, which might have suffered dramatically from a decisive German victory. Then again, British morale didn't collapse at the height of the U-boat campaign. The fall of France in 1940 might be counted as a reasonably similar event, and it didn't result in a British collapse. The Allies still had plenty of buttons to push in the naval war. It is possible that a German victory could have driven Britain from the war, but unlikely.

Legacy

It's strange that a battle of this caliber, representing so much investment from both sides, had so little impact on the course of the war and involved so little damage to the belligerents. Jutland would be the only major conflict in either war between fleets of dreadnought battleships. Battleship combat in World War II would rarely involve more than one or two ships on either side, and the aircraft carrier, especially in the Pacific, would come to dominate naval warfare. It is surely worth noting that a Tsushima-esque battle of annihilation would likely not have shortened the war by a day, but would have killed some 20,000 German (and no small number of British) sailors who, in the real world, survived the war.

Twelve of the twenty surviving German capital ships to serve at Jutland were interned at Scapa Flow at the end of the war. The eventual disposition of these ships was open to debate, as returning them to Germany was out of the question. Several countries, including Italy and France, sought to seize some of these ships in the post-war settlement. On June 21, 1919, in anticipation of a final peace treaty that would disperse the ships among the victors, the heart of the Kaiserliche Marine scuttled itself. Fifteen dreadnoughts and battlecruisers in total were lost, the greatest single daily loss in the history of the battleship. The remaining German battleships were dispatched to the Allies, and either sunk as targets or sold for scrap.

The vast bulk of the British ships were scrapped in accordance with the requirements of the Washington Naval Treaty, or the London Naval Treaty. Only eight of the battleships made contributions in World War II; in two cases (HMS *Iron Duke* and HMS *Centurion*), these contributions came as auxiliaries. Two (HMS *Barham* and HMS *Royal Oak*) suc-

cumbed to submarine attack, although the rest survived the war. The last battleship remaining in Jutland was HMS *Canada*, a super-dreadnought that the Royal Navy had borrowed from Chile at the outbreak of the war. As *Almirante Latorre*, HMS *Canada* survived into the 1950s, although she played no role in the Second World War.

Admiral Hipper was well regarded for his command of the German battlecruisers at Jutland. While the other three admirals (Beatty, Jellicoe, and Scheer) made identifiable mistakes, Hipper handled his ships very well against superior numbers. He was eventually promoted to command of the High Seas Fleet, although he failed in his effort to put down the Kiel Mutiny. He died in 1932, fourteen years into retirement.

David Beatty assumed command of the Grand Fleet in November 1916, a position that he held through the rest of the war. He took HMS *Queen Elizabeth* as his flagship, a fast battleship altogether more suited to his temperament than HMS *Iron Duke*. Beatty managed the surrender of the High Seas Fleet to generally poor reviews (at least from the German perspective), and became First Sea Lord in 1919. He retired in 1927, and died in January 1936, three months after serving as a pallbearer for Jellicoe, his old commander.

Scheer earned some credit for preventing the destruction of the High Seas Fleet, and continued to use his ships aggressively. Eventually, however, he committed to the idea that only U-boats could win the war for Germany. In June 1918 he became the Chief of Staff of the Kaiserliche Marine, which allowed him to preside over its effective dissolution. He died in 1928, just before a trip to visit John Jellicoe.

John Jellicoe became First Sea Lord in November, 1916, a promotion which obscured discontent with his command decisions at Jutland. Jellicoe resisted, but eventually implemented, the installation of a convoy system to protect Allied merchant shipping against unrestricted submarine warfare. He was dismissed from his position in late 1917, as a result of squabbling in the British high command. He later served as Governor-General of New Zealand, and died in 1935.

The Royal Navy originally intended to name the last two battleships of the *King George V* class after Jellicoe and Beatty, but renamed them *Anson* and *Howe*, respectively. The Kriegsmarine, which took Jutland and the scuttling at Scapa as its founding myths, named a Deutschland class "pocket battleship" after Reinhard Scheer, and a heavy cruiser after Franz Hipper. Both ships were lost in the final days of World War II.

The last survivor of Jutland was Henry Allingham, who served on a naval trawler that trailed and supported the Grand Fleet. He passed away in July 2009, at the age of 113. The last ship remaining from Jutland is HMS *Caroline*, a light cruiser that served as a headquarters and accommodation ship in Belfast for most of her career. After much dispute and consternation, the British government has determined that *Caroline* will remain in Belfast and become a national museum.

HIJMS Hyuga

Laid Down: 1915

Launched: 1917

Completed: April 1918

Displacement: 31,000 tons

Main Armament: twelve 14" guns (six twin turrets)

Secondary Armament: twenty 5.5" guns (eighteen casemates, two single mounts)

Speed: 23 knots

Major Actions: Aleutians, Leyte Gulf, Kure Raid

Treaty: Pre-Washington Naval Treaty

Reconstruction: 1926–28, 1934–36, 1943

Fate: Sunk by US carrier aircraft, July 24, 1945. Wreck scrapped 1946–47.

The Imperial Japanese Navy was not completely satisfied with the *Fusos*, its first effort at super-dreadnoughts. For the last two ships of the class (*Ise* and *Hyuga*), Japan's naval architects slightly modified the design to rectify the odd distribution of turrets, which allowed them to include more protection and a higher speed.

Even with the modifications, the six turret arrangement resulted in less extensive protection (armor spread across a larger area) than American contemporaries, but the Japanese found the increase in speed worth the trade.

Hyuga and her sister *Ise* were effective ships, with a heavier armament than *Queen Elizabeth* and more speed than the American "standard types." Like most Japanese battleships, *Hyuga* underwent two inter-war constructions that increased her speed, size, armament, and protection. She participated in several actions off China prior to and during the Sino-Japanese War.

In spite of her relatively high speed for an old battleship, *Hyuga* was not employed during the initial Japanese offensive of 1941 and 1942. *Hyuga*'s first action came in April 1942. An American carrier task force, led by Admiral William "Bull" Halsey and including the USS *Enterprise* and the USS *Hornet*, launched sixteen B-25 medium bombers in an operation intended to bring the war to the Japanese home islands. *Hyuga*, *Ise*, *Fuso*, and *Yamashiro* were detailed to intercept the American task force, but found only a Russian freighter traveling from San Francisco to Vladivostok.

HIJMS Hyuga under attack, Battle of Leyte Gulf

Disappointed, the Japanese ships returned to port. A month later *Hyuga* suffered an explosion during gunnery practice that killed fifty-one sailors and nearly resulted in the loss of the ship. *Hyuga*'s #5 turret, now inoperable, was removed and replaced with anti-aircraft guns. In June, again in concert with her sister *Ise*, *Hyuga* participated in the invasion of the Aleutian Islands. Unfortunately for the IJN, the concurrent operation to invade Midway Island resulted in disaster and the loss of four aircraft carriers.

HIJMS Hyuga after conversion to hybrid carrier.

The devastating losses at Midway left the IJN searching for ideas to increase carrier deck space. The first plans envisioned a full conversion of the older battleships, leaving no main armament and a deck capable of operating 54 conventional aircraft. The IJN decided that this would take too long, and instead opted for a half-measure in which the aft two turrets of *Hyuga* and *Ise* would be removed and replaced with a flight deck, hangar, and catapults. While *Hyuga* and *Ise* could not equal a fleet or even a light carrier, and were not expected to carry the most modern aircraft, it was hoped that they would ease the load of the surviving carriers, especially in regards to recon aircraft. Because the flight deck was short, the 22 aircraft that *Hyuga* could launch would need to land on either a normal carrier or a land base. The Japanese also converted the incomplete *Yamato* class battleship *Shinano* into an aircraft carrier support vessel, designed to carry only about 50 aircraft but with enough space for fuel, ammunition, and machine shops to support a full carrier task force. *Hyuga* began her conversion in late 1942 and re-commissioned in late 1943. Heavy concrete was added to the flight deck in order to compensate for the loss of weight and to increase structural stability.

Although *Hyuga* launched aircraft in various tests, in practice there were simply not enough trained pilots to fill the deck space of the existing Japanese carriers. Thus, the flight deck was not used as intended during opera-

tions. Instead, rockets and additional anti-aircraft weapons were installed. In October 1944, *Hyuga*, her sister *Ise*, and four remaining Japanese carriers were deployed, under the command of Admiral Ozawa, as a decoy force intended to draw Halsey's Third Fleet away from Leyte Island and allow Admiral Kurita's surface force to destroy the American transports. The first part of this operation was more or less successful, as American aircraft attacked Ozawa's force, destroying the four carriers and lightly damaging *Hyuga*. *Hyuga* retired, avoiding attacks from at least four different USN submarines along the way.

Following Leyte Gulf, *Hyuga* was deployed to Southeast Asia. In February 1945, narrowly avoiding multiple air and submarine attacks, she and her sister *Ise* returned to Japan. No fuel and no ammunition meant that *Hyuga* would not play an active role in the rest of the war. On July 24, 1945 American aircraft

HIJMS Hyuga, sunk in shallow water. USN photo.

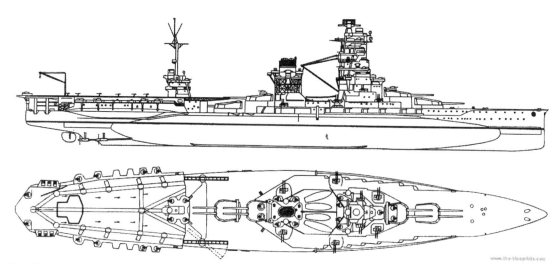

Office of Naval Intelligence recognition drawing of Hyuga and Ise.

attacked *Hyuga* and sank her in shallow water. She was scrapped over the course of the next two years.

Author's Note

From an aesthetic point of view, the pagoda mast worked best with a relatively balanced design, as with the *Nagatos* and the *Kongos*. *Hyuga* and her sister simply looked odd, although not as odd as *Fuso* and *Yamashiro*. Nevertheless, the Japanese decision to opt for speed left them with more useful heavy units than the Americans or the British.

This was not the first carrier conversion idea. The Japanese themselves had converted the incomplete *Akagi* and *Kaga*, and would later complete *Shinano*. Apart from *Furious*, *Courageous*, and *Glorious*, no complete heavy ship was ever successfully converted to a carrier. The half conversion idea spoke, like many similar projects, to the lack of a full appreciation of the gravity of Japan's situation on the part of the IJN's strategic thinkers.

Related Entries:

Preceded by... HIJMS *Yamashiro*
Contemporary of... USS *Mississippi*
Preceded... HIJMS *Nagato*

HMS Hood

Laid Down: 1916

Launched: 1918

Completed: May, 1920

Displacement: 46,700 tons

Main Armament: eight 15" guns (four twin turrets)

Secondary Armament: twelve 5.5" guns (individual mounts)

Speed: 31 knots

Treaty: Pre-Washington Naval Treaty

Major Engagements: Mers El Kebir, Battle of Denmark Straits

Fate: Sunk by gunfire from German battleship *Bismarck*, May 24, 1941

Hood was the name ship of the Admiral class, a group of four superdreadnoughts ordered near the close of World War I. *Hood* was named after Admiral Samuel Hood, who served in the Seven Years War, the American Revolution, and the French Revolutionary Wars. Famous for his own exploits, Hood's mentoring relationship with Admiral Horatio Nelson served to further enhance his reputation. Hood's brother, cousin, and great-great grandson were also Royal Navy admirals. The last, Admiral Horace Hood, was killed in the explosion of the battlecruiser HMS *Invincible* at the Battle of Jutland. Horace Hood's widow attended the launch of HMS *Hood* in 1918

The Royal Navy classified the Admirals as battlecruisers, but even before modification they had much heavier protection schemes than most British battlecruisers, effectively making them the first fast battleships. Shortly before *Hood* was laid down, three British battlecruisers exploded and sank at the Battle of Jutland. The Royal Navy re-worked *Hood's* design to improve her protection, an effort which roughly made her protection equivalent to that of the *Queen Elizabeth* class battleships. Unfortunately, the redesign was haphazard, resulting in some serious weight distribution problems. The Royal Navy decided to start over, and *Hood's* three sisters were scrapped in favor of a new class of postwar battlecruisers.

Nevertheless, *Hood* was an impressive warship. The restrictions imposed by the Washington Naval Treaty made her, by a fair margin, the largest warship in the world. *Hood* could make 31 knots, which meant she was also the fastest battleship afloat. In addition to being the fastest and the largest, the Mighty *Hood* was probably the most famous battleship of the interwar period. She made several cruises to various ports to "show the flag" and demonstrate the power of the Royal Navy.

HMS Hood during visit to Australia, March 17, 1924. Courtesy of State Library of Victoria.

Samuel Hood, 1st Viscount Hood. Antoine Maurin.

Hood was an impressive looking ship, although true naval aesthetes tended to prefer the smaller, more balanced HMS *Tiger*. *Hood* was one of three battlecruisers retained by the Royal Navy under the terms of the 1930 London Naval Treaty.

Hood was such a valuable unit that the Royal Navy, in the interwar period, could not bear to be without her. This was unfortunate. *Hood* was scheduled for a major overhaul in 1941, but the onset of war made this impossible. The Royal Navy simply lacked the fast ships to spare *Hood* for an extended period of time. *Hood* spent 1939 and most of 1940 patrolling for German raiders, although she did not encounter either a pocket battleship or *Scharnhorst* and *Gneisenau*. This was probably fortunate for the Germans, for while *Hood* was old, she was still large enough and powerful enough to deal with most of the new German ships. In July 1940, *Hood* led the force that attacked the French fleet at Mers El Kebir, destroying *Bretagne* and damaging *Dunkerque* and *Provence*. *Hood* stripped a turbine chasing the French battlecruiser *Strasbourg*.

By 1940 the "naval holiday" imposed by the Washington Naval Treaty was clearly over. New battleships were coming into service, and these new ships took advantage of twenty years of technological developments. Most of the new ships carried heavy guns and armor, and

could make high speeds. Largest of these new ships (at least until the commissioning of *Yamato* in late 1941) was the German battleship *Bismarck*. *Bismarck* left Kiel in May 1941 for a raiding cruise in the Atlantic. By the time the Royal Navy had usable intelligence regarding *Bismarck*'s intended course, only *Hood* and the new battleship *Prince of Wales* were available for interception. The rest of the fleet was too slow, in refit, or deployed in other areas.

Hood and *Prince of Wales* found *Bismarck* on May 24 in the Denmark Straits, between Greenland and Iceland. Rear Admiral Lancelot Holland knew that *Hood*'s old armor scheme was vulnerable to *Bismarck*'s guns, especially at long range, and decided to close as quickly as possible. This gave *Bismarck* time to fire full broadsides against *Hood* and *Prince of Wales* during the approach. The crew of *Bismarck*, like most naval aficionados around the world, was well acquainted with *Hood*. The attitude on board *Bismarck* grew grim when it became known that *Hood* had found them, as even in the Kriegsmarine, *Hood* was widely believed to be the most powerful ship in the world. *Bismarck* was accompanied by the heavy cruiser *Prinz Eugen*, and Admiral Holland unfortunately mistook the latter for the former, ordering fire to be concentrated against the cruiser. This allowed *Bismarck* to fire without interference. *Hood* was struck early by an 8" shell, setting fire to her deck but not seriously threatening the ship.

At about 6:00 AM, *Hood* turned to bring her aft guns into play against *Bismarck*. A salvo from *Bismarck* struck her amidships, and she exploded. The exact cause of the explosion has never been ascertained, although multiple theories persist. *Hood* sank very, very quickly. A fair number of crew members reportedly escaped the immediate destruction of the ship only to be pulled into the vortex that accompanied her sinking. Only three sailors, from a crew of 1,418, escaped the wreck. It is thought that an enormous air bubble escaped from the engine room and buoyed the three survivors to

HMS Hood

the surface where they were rescued by the destroyer *Elektra*. The last, Ted Briggs, died in October, 2008.

Author's Note

We often talk about aesthetically pleasing battleships, but there's nearly unanimous agreement among those who care that HMS *Hood* was a beautiful warship. Long and lean, she seemed to carry the weight of British empire effortlessly. The ability of HMS *Hood* to "show the flag" as the largest, fastest, most powerful, most beautiful battleship in world eventually worked to her detriment, as the Royal Navy delayed her reconstruction until it was too late.

We're accustomed to thinking of HMS *Hood* as a doomed vessel, her great size and prestige contributing ironically to the legend of her loss. However, as with most explosive resolutions to naval battles, the sinking of *Hood* at Denmark Straits depended as much on chance as anything else. In most realities, *Hood* and *Prince of Wales* either sink or fatally damage *Bismarck*, notwithstanding the latter's modern design.

The magnitude of *Hood*'s loss was brought into sharp, if symbolic, relief by the impact on her crew. Three survivors from a crew of 1,418 on the most powerful battleship in the world is a remarkable statistic. Ted Briggs hosted HMS *Hood* crew gatherings for much of his life, although he struggled to compartmentalize that part of his identity.

Related Entries:

Fought alongside… *Prince of Wales*
Inspired… USS *Lexington*
Fought… *Strasbourg*

USS California

Laid Down: 1916

Launched: 1919

Completed: August, 1921

Reconstruction: 1942–1944

Displacement: 32,300 tons

Main Armament: twelve 14" guns (four triple turrets)

Secondary Armament: fourteen 5" guns (individual mounts)

Speed: 21 knots

Major Actions: Pearl Harbor, Leyte Gulf, Okinawa

Treaty: Pre-Washington Naval Treaty

Fate: Scrapped, 1959

The first American battleship built on the West Coast was USS *Oregon*, commissioned in 1896. USS *Virginia*, USS *Massachusetts*, and USS *New York* were built in their nominal states. The first and only battleship built in its own state on the West Coast was USS *California*, second ship of the *Tennessee* class, and second of the "Big Five," the last five of the twelve ships built to the standard type. The Big Five adopted a new underwater protection system, a more modern secondary armament,

a more extensive superstructure, and reinforced cage masts capable of supporting heavier conning towers. The first two ships carried twelve 14" guns, while the next three carried eight 16" guns.

As a member of the Big Five, USS *California* carried the honor of being one of the most powerful battleships in the world during the interwar period, but suffered from the decision of the USN to delay reconstruction as long as possible. Having decided to build its next generation of battleships with 28 knot speeds, the USN struggled to sort out what to do with its still-capable standard type ships, a problem that would extend into World War II. Unlike Italy and Japan, the United States did not attempt to increase the speeds of its battleships during reconstruction, meaning that the "old" squadron could never operate with the "new" squadron.

On December 7, 1941, USS *California* was sitting at anchor somewhat south of Battleship Row. Prepared for inspection, *California* was not ready for underwater attack. Struck by two bombs and two torpedoes, *California* was abandoned prematurely in fear of a burning oil slick advancing off of the other damaged battleships. Upon their return, the crew could not control the flooding and she settled onto the harbor floor. She was refloated in March 1942

USS California, 1921

Two views of USS California passing under Golden Gate Bridge, October 11, 1936. National Archives and Records Administration.

US fleet in 1940, Lahaina, Maui.

and sent, in June of the same year, to Puget Sound Naval Yard for reconstruction. Instead of returning USS *California* to service as soon as possible, which might have taken three months or so, the USN decided to rebuild *California* and two of her sisters (*Tennessee* and *West Virginia*) completely, such that they visually resembled the *South Dakota* class rather than their erstwhile sisters USS *Maryland* and USS *Colorado*. USS *California* emerged with a modern superstructure, an advanced anti-aircraft armament, new radar, and a wider beam (chubby enough that she could not advance through the Panama Canal).

California reactivated in early 1944 and deployed to the Pacific in a shore bombardment capacity until October. She was present at the Battle of Surigao Strait, where the pur-

USS California on December 7, 1941. USN photo.

pose of the American task force was to seal off the area around Leyte from any Japanese naval forces coming from the south. The northern approaches were supposed to be covered by the fast battleships attached to Admiral Halsey's carrier task forces. *California* and the other two "Big Three" members (*West Virginia* and *Tennessee*) detected and opened fire on the Japanese battleship *Yamashiro* well before their unmodified comrades.

Admiral Oldendorf's battleships and cruisers easily overwhelmed the squadrons of IJN Admirals Nishurima and Shima. If, however, the larger force led by Admiral Kurita had taken the southern route, the situation might have become more interesting. American air and submarine attacks sank or turned away a battleship, three cruisers, and two destroyers, but Kurita still had a respectable force. Had Kurita's force met Oldendorf's, the balance would have been six battleships, twelve cruisers, and twenty-nine destroyers on the American side against four battleships, nine cruisers, and eleven destroyers on the Japanese. Assuming that the lighter ships canceled each other out (although the American advantage would have weighed over time), the encounter would have come down to the confrontation of battle lines. The Japanese had the most powerful ship in either fleet (*Yamato*), but the next three most powerful were the Big Three. USS *Maryland* was probably roughly equivalent

to *Nagato*, and *Mississippi* and *Pennsylvania* were clearly superior to the battlecruisers *Kongo* and *Haruna*. The American line had a substantial advantage in guns and armor, especially as the Japanese battlecruisers could not have expected to last long under accurate fire. However, the Japanese line had 5–6 knots on the Americans, which might have allowed them to pull off a replay of Tsushima, where a faster Japanese line twice crossed the Russian T.

Given local US air superiority and the need for the Japanese to escape before the return of Halsey's battleships, that encounter would have been fairly brief. The Japanese might well have lost one or both of the battlecruisers, but *Nagato* and *Yamato* probably would have escaped, although not before heavily damaging several of the American ships. Had *Musashi* survived the air attacks prior to the battle, the story might have been different.

California participated in several other shore bombardment operations before the end of the war, although a kamikaze attack delayed her arrival at Okinawa. After the end of the war, she supported occupation landings in Japan and elsewhere before returning to the United States. Placed in reserve in 1946, *California* and the rest of the Big Five were retained for thirteen years in case of a need for shore bombardment ships. As the Korean War did not even justify the activation of the much newer *North Carolina* and *South Dakota* class-

USS California after reconstruction, January 1944

USS California mothballed with her sister, USS Tennessee, in 1946.

es, the rationale for the retention seems questionable. *California* was sold for scrap in 1959.

Author's Note

The Big Five looked much different than the other standard type battleships, with far more solid and robust superstructures. They also lacked casemates, as the USN (along with every other navy) had learned that casemates were ineffective in bad weather, lacked sufficient scope for fire, and were completely useless against aircraft.

The reconstructions of *California*, *Tennessee*, and *West Virginia* produced a remarkable transformation, but one that didn't necessarily make sense given the time and the expense. Better fire control, radar, and anti-aircraft arrangement certainly made *California* a more powerful ship, but by the time she returned to service her ability to make an impact was deeply limited. Of course, had the USN found a job for the Big Five to do in the postwar world, the expense might have been justified, but it couldn't even put the newer battleships to good use.

A truly radical reconstruction plan, along the lines pursued by the Regia Marina with its old dreadnoughts, might have tried to bring the Big Five up to modern standards by increasing their speed. This probably would have required the elimination of part of the main armament, but nine 14" guns traveling at 28 knots would have found far more use than twelve 14" guns traveling at 21. However, such a reconstruction undoubtedly would have been expensive, and technically challenging.

Related Entries:

Contemporary of... HIJMS *Nagato*
Fought against... HIJMS *Yamashiro*
Fought at... Pearl Harbor

USS Maryland

Laid Down: 1916

Launched: 1917

Completed: March, 1920

Displacement: 32,600 tons

Main Armament: eight 16" guns (four twin turrets)

Secondary Armament: twelve 5" guns (individual mounts)

Speed: 21 knots

Major Actions: Pearl Harbor, Leyte Gulf, Okinawa

Treaty: Pre-Washington Naval Treaty

Fate: Scrapped, 1959

USS *Maryland* represented the zenith of "standard type" US battleship development. The "standard type" ships had compatible speeds, turning circles, and armaments, allowing them to form a squadron that could operate as a cohesive unit. *Maryland* was one of the "Big Five," the last five standard-type battle-ships completed by the United States. She and her two sisters (USS *Colorado* and USS *West Virginia*) differed from the first two ships (USS *Tennessee* and USS *California*) in that they carried eight 16" guns in four twin turrets rather than twelve 14" in triple turrets.

Maryland's interwar service was uneventful. The Washington Naval Treaty resulted in the destruction by gunfire of her last sister, USS *Washington*, leaving *Maryland* and her four sisters the most modern ships in the fleet. Nevertheless, the Navy decided not to modernize the Big Five after determining that they would be unable to keep up with the new battleships under construction. A moderate refit improved *Maryland*'s anti-aircraft protection. *Maryland* entered the Second World War on December 7, 1941 with her original profile intact, cage masts included.

On December 7, *Maryland* was moored inboard of USS *Oklahoma*, insulating her from torpedo attack. She suffered two bomb hits but received only superficial damage. Once freed from Battleship Row, *Maryland* proceeded with *Tennessee* and *Pennsylvania*,

USS Maryland transiting the Panama Canal, 1923

USS Maryland in column, 1930s

both of which had suffered similarly minor damage, to Puget Sound Naval Yard for repair and refit. Much work was done in a short period of time to modernize *Maryland* for the Pacific War. She lost her aft cagemast, and her foremast was reduced in height and complemented by a larger superstructure. Her beam was slightly increased to improve torpedo protection, and she received additional AA mounts. For the next year and a half she and a squadron of older battleships operated as convoy escorts and a "fleet in being" in the Pacific, without ever engaging the enemy. In late 1943 *Maryland* undertook her first shore bombardment mission, a role which would occupy her for most of the rest of the war.

In October 1944, *Maryland* and five other battleships (*West Virginia, California, Tennessee, Mississippi,* and *Pennsylvania*) were tasked with shore bombardment and escort of Leyte island in the Philippines. Warned by recon aircraft that a Japanese force was approaching, the American battleships took up a position in the Surigao Strait, crossing the "T" of the oncoming Japanese fleet. Led by the battleship *Yamashiro,* the Japanese ships sailed right into the American trap, and came under withering fire from the American ships. Three of the US battleships possessed modern radar arrays, and quickly found the range to *Yamashiro. Maryland* had an older array, but nonetheless managed to straddle *Yamashiro* with several salvos. *Yamashiro* suffered brutal shelling, and sank following a torpedo attack.

Maryland continued with her shore bombardment duties for the rest of the war. She was hit by three kamikazes, two causing serious damage. In early April, 1945, *Maryland* was assigned to shore bombardment off Okinawa when word came that a Japanese task force, led by the battleship *Yamato,* had left port. *Maryland,* along with *Colorado, West Virginia, Tennessee, Idaho,* and *New Mexico* was detailed to destroy *Yamato* if she survived air attacks along the way. The air attacks did succeed, and *Maryland* returned to her former duties. After the war *Maryland* and her four sisters were placed in reserve, and not finally disposed of until 1959. It is unfortunate that a more serious effort was not made for her preservation, since she was the only survivor of the Pearl Harbor attack to remain in substantially original condition (*California, Tennessee,* and *West Virginia* were transformed by wartime reconstruction).

USS Maryland, April 1944

Author's Note

Yamato fell victim to US carrier aircraft, but it's worth thinking about what an engagement with the huge battleship might have looked like. *Yamato* had considerable advantages in size, speed, and range over any of the American ships. The engagement would have been fought in darkness, which earlier in the war had worked to the Japanese advantage. In this case, I suspect that improvements in US radar and the long range of the battle would have worked in US favor, and that USS *West Virginia*, a ship with 16" guns and an advanced array, would have been the first ship to draw blood. Using her relatively high speed, *Yamato* could have tried to fight the battle at long range to her advantage, but I think that her suicide mission would have led to more aggressive tactics, and that she would have engaged with the US battleline. The US ships would no doubt have suffered severely from *Yamato's* 18" guns, but hit anything with enough 14"

USS Maryland in final condition, April 1945

shells and it will sink. The US advantage in destroyers would also have had an effect, as *Yamato* had virtually no defense against surface torpedo attack. However, as *Yamato* might easily have sunk one or more US battleships, with thousands of resultant dead, the Americans made the right decision by destroying her from the air.

The USN probably could have done more than it did with *Maryland* and the other Pearl Harbor survivors in the first years of the war, but forcing an engagement was a struggle for slow battleships. The single, cut down cage mast look adopted for *Maryland* (and *Colorado*) worked out very well from an aesthetic point of view. Surely, however, the state of Maryland (a state with deep, longstanding naval connections) could have made a more aggressive effort to preserve this artifact of the superdreadnought era.

Related Entries:

Inspired... HMS *Rodney*
Contemporary of... HIJMS *Nagato*
Fought at... Pearl Harbor

HIJMS Nagato

Laid Down: 1917

Launched: 1919

Completed: 1920

Displacement: 32,000 tons

Main Armament: eight 16" guns (four twin turrets)

Secondary Armament: twenty 5.5" guns (eighteen casemates, two individual mounts)

Speed: 26 knots

Major Actions: Midway, Leyte Gulf, Japan's Surrender

Reconstruction: 1926, 1934–6

Treaty: Pre-Washington Naval Treaty

Fate: Sunk as target during Bikini atom bomb tests

Even before the Washington Naval Treaty limited new construction, the Imperial Japanese Navy determined that it could never match the USN in numbers. The Japanese decided to solve this problem by ensuring ship-to-ship superiority. The IJN was the first navy to use the 14" gun (on *Kongo*), although the Americans soon matched this with *New York* and the British exceeded it with the 15" guns of *Queen Elizabeth*. The IJN, which continued to have close ties with the Royal Navy, found the British fast battleships particularly impressive, and decided to combine speed, armor, and hitting power in its next class.

The result was *Nagato*. Commissioned in 1920, Nagato was the first battleship in the world to carry 16" guns. At 32,000 tons she was one of the largest battleships in the world, and her 26 knot top speed exceeded even that of the *Queen Elizabeths*. *Nagato* was not as well armored as contemporary American battleships, but her speed allowed both operational and tactical flexibility. Along with HMS *Hood* and the American "Big Five," *Nagato* and her sister *Mutsu* represented the pinnacle of pretreaty battleship construction. After her 1926 refit, with her main funnel swept back, *Nagato* also looked dangerous and powerful.

Nagato was modernized twice in the interwar period, the second refit giving her much heavier deck armor. She served as the flagship of the Combined Fleet for most of the interwar period, including the Pearl Harbor attack. Strangely for a ship of her speed and power,

HIJMS Nagato in original condition

Nagato, early 1946. USN photo.

Nagato had a relatively quiet war record. She was part of the Main Body at Midway, but because Japanese naval practice of the time did not include deploying aircraft carriers with battleship protection, she saw no action. This was a grievous flaw in Japanese naval doctrine; *Nagato*, *Yamato*, and their sisters were fast enough to escort the Japanese carriers, and might have provided some anti-aircraft protection against American attacks. *Nagato* also did not participate in the Solomons campaign, although, again, her speed was sufficient to "run the Slot" and attack Henderson Field. This resulted from the Japanese decision to conserve ships and resources (especially fuel), but given the growing American material advantage almost certainly represented a strategic error.

In June 1943 *Nagato* lost her sister, *Mutsu*, to a magazine explosion. The Combined Fleet evacuated Truk for ports in Southeast Asia at the end of 1943, and prepared to fight the US invasion of the Philippines. *Nagato* participated in the Battle of Philippine Sea as a carrier escort, vainly attempting to prevent the destruction of her charge *Hiyo* by American aircraft. In October 1944, *Nagato* was attached to Admiral Kurita's strike force, designed to attack the American escort carriers and trans-

ports of Leyte. Although the Japanese plan successfully drew off the escorting American battleships, a group of destroyers and destroyer escorts disrupted the attack. Four battleships of the Imperial Japanese Navy managed to sink a couple of destroyers and a single escort carrier before fleeing under air attack. *Nagato* took several bomb hits during and after the action.

Nagato eventually limped back to Japan with the remnants of Kurita's force, which lost the battlecruiser *Kongo* along the way. *Nagato* was drydocked, but the IJN lacked both the materials needed for repair and the fuel necessary to making *Nagato* operational again. Reclassified as a coastal defense ship, *Nagato* did not participate in the final actions of the war. A few additional air attacks damaged, but failed to destroy, the aging battleship. Indeed, the Japanese were able to conduct enough repairs and assemble enough fuel to make a final sortie in case of an American landing attempt. The destruction of Hiroshima and Nagasaki rendered this moot, however. Present at the September 2, 1945 surrender ceremony, *Nagato* was the last surviving Japanese battleship.

There was no need to incorporate a twenty-five-year-old, badly damaged Japanese battleship into the USN. Nevertheless, the United States found a use for *Nagato*. The Bikini atom bomb tests were about to begin, and the Navy wanted to know what happened when atomic bombs were dropped on ships. Along with *Prinz Eugen*, the last heavy cruiser of the German navy, and dozens of old American ships, *Nagato* would serve as a guinea pig for the atomic age. An American crew took control of *Nagato* and began the necessary repairs, under the advice of its former Japanese officers. On March 18, 1946 *Nagato* set out for Eniwetok under her own power. The journey almost proved too much; *Nagato* began taking on water, and a blown boiler stopped her dead. Shipboard repairs sufficed to get her underway, however, and *Nagato* took her place for the bomb tests. The first bomb, dropped on July 1, exploded about 1,500 yards from *Nagato* and did only insignificant damage to her superstructure. Notably, *Nagato* held up better than the American battleships nearby, and was studied for several days by American engineers. On July 24, a second bomb was detonated underwater. *Nagato* rode out the blast without incident, but was rendered far too radioactive for further boarding. She began to settle, and sank on July 29.

Author's Note

Nagato was beautiful, one of my very favorite warships. The combination of the pagoda mast with the four-turret arrangement lent a sense of elegance and power. Technically impressive, she compared well with her foreign contemporaries, and could play a useful role through the end of World War II. Her great speed meant that she could support carrier operations when her American counterparts could not. The last surviving dreadnought battleship of the Imperial period, *Nagato* ideally would have been preserved, but the political context in both Japan and the United States at the end of World War II made this difficult. Still, an imaginative preservation strategy might have left the former flagship of the Combined Fleet as an American war trophy, berthed at Pearl Harbor not too far from the wreck of USS *Arizona*. In time, this might have served not only to memorialize the war, but also to symbolize the long peace between Japan and America.

Related Entries:

Inspired by... HMS *Barham*
Contemporary of... USS *Maryland*
Preceded... HIJMS *Kaga*

Nagato after Japanese surrender. Courtesy of State Library of Victoria.

Interlude

The Treaties

Stopping the Next Arms Race

World War I didn't end, at least not in the traditional sense of the term. Fighting continued in the East for several years as the successor states to the Russian and Ottoman empires struggled to sort themselves out. Still, the fragile peace on the Western Front held, even as the German High Seas Fleet scuttled itself at Scapa Flow. The framing of the peace, however, was intimately tied to assessments of why the war started.

Many blamed the war on the naval race between Germany and the United Kingdom. History has not been kind to this view; the Anglo-German antagonism was only one aspect of the complex knot of causes of the First World War, and probably not the most important. The British had effectively won the race by 1914, and in any case Germany, Austria-Hungary, Russia, and France had ample reason to fight. Especially in British minds, however, the naval race loomed large as the cause of animosity between Germany and the UK. Policymakers in the United Kingdom and elsewhere determined that the peace should deal not only with the specific problem (the potential growth of German naval power), but also with the general cause (naval arms races).

Even as the war ended, Japan, the United States, and the United Kingdom embarked on ambitious programs of naval construction, designed to provide supremacy over any would-be foe. In Japan and the United States, building programs emerged organically from pre-war and wartime planning. The United States continued to build its "standard type" battleships, and had finally begun to lay down battlecruisers. The Japanese pursued the "eight and eight" program designed to provide the IJN with eight modern battleships and eight modern battlecruisers. The Royal Navy had taken a brief battleship holiday in order to

digest the lessons of Jutland, and also to divert resources to the U-boat war. It shortly drew up plans, however, to build the next generation of huge capital ships.

There was no doubt, however, that the expense of a new arms race would prove beyond the means of several of the competitors. In the wake of the war, the United Kingdom simply lacked the resources to match US construction. Japan was willing to make a game of it, but the ambitious construction program of the IJN would have overwhelmed the Japanese economy. Only the United States could afford to build the desired ships, but

Herbert Yardley

Congress and the public were not yet in a mood to make extravagant defense expenditures possible.

The Washington Naval Conference began in November, 1921, and lasted into early 1922. It included the five major naval powers (the United Kingdom, the United States, Italy, France, and Japan), as well as several other countries (China, Portugal, Belgium, and the Netherlands) interested in preserving the peace in East Asia. Over the course of the conference, American codebreaker Herbert Yardly supplied US negotiators with information on Japanese positions and red lines, allowing the Americans to take a harder stance than they otherwise might have.

As negotiated, the treaty set quotas for the five major powers. It limited battleship size to 35,000 tons, and battleship guns to 16". The treaty determined that any ship larger than 10,000 tons, or carrying guns heavier than 8", would be deemed a battleship. This inadvertently created the type "Washington Treaty cruiser," which carried 8" guns and displaced roughly 10,000 tons. The terms of the treaty were unequal. The RN and the USN could keep eighteen battleships each, while Japan was allowed only eleven. Japan accepted these terms because the United States agreed not to fortify any of its Asian bases (primarily in the Philippines), and because Tokyo realized that it could not compete in a free-for-all. The treaty allotted half the Japanese strength to each of Italy and France.

The Politics

The effects of the treaty were more than just technical. The treaty narrowed the scope of competition between the major powers, committing each of them to the maintenance of the international status quo. Provisions limiting arms construction were intended to support agreements that committed the great powers to maintaining the territorial integrity of the great colonial empires of East Asia. The Nine Power Treaty, which included all of the conference participants, committed them to respect for China's territorial integrity.

The inclusion of France and Italy had obvious implications for security in the Mediterranean. But the treaty excluded Germany and Russia, two of the great naval powers of the pre-war period. The Treaty of Versailles tightly bound the Kriegsmarine, forbidding it from constructing or operating modern battleships. Of course, whenever Germany decided to do so, it could use its industrial might to break the treaty and to challenge British naval supremacy, but in 1921 this eventuality seemed far off.

Soviet Russia was a trickier problem. The Soviets, once they gained command of the full human and natural resources of Russia, could certainly threaten to build a large fleet. However, the Soviet Union remained in great disorder after World War I, with the fleet and the shipyards in disarray. None of the other great powers desired to engage with Moscow, a level of disdain that the Soviets shared. The Soviets were not invited to the conference, although the Soviet government eventually agreed to abide by many of the restrictions. This had no real impact on Soviet naval construction, as Soviet shipbuilding never recovered sufficiently to build anywhere near treaty limitations, and Soviet efforts to build classes of massive, treaty-breaking battleships and battlecruisers just prior to World War II were interrupted by the German invasion.

The Military Impact

The treaty system effectively froze battleship development for a decade. *Dreadnought* is remembered as the great inflection point for the modern battleship, a warship that rendered every existing battleship in the world obsolete, but HMS *Queen Elizabeth*, commissioned in 1915, probably held a greater advantage over *Dreadnought* than the latter did over her immediate predecessors. The battleships and battlecruisers proposed by great powers following World War I would similarly have eclipsed the super-dreadnoughts.

Each of the three major powers had already planned to build ships larger than treaty limits specified, and both Japan and the United States had actually laid down the next generation of capital ships. The Americans were allowed to complete three new battleships with 16" guns, and the Japanese two. In recompense, the Treaty allowed the Royal Navy to build two new battleships armed with 16" guns, which took important elements from the canceled designs.

Limited in their ability to build new units, the great naval powers decided instead to modernize and rebuild the old ones. Following the treaty-mandated scrappings, the oldest battleships in the world had generally served less than a decade. Nevertheless, improvements in technology and a changing threat environment (including primarily the advent of the submarine and the aircraft) meant that older ships required renovation, sometimes radical renovation. Typical light modernizations added such features as advanced rangefinders, light anti-aircraft weapons, aircraft catapults, higher elevation turrets, and a conversion from coal to oil propulsion. More full reconstructions improved deck armor, reorganized and replaced the secondary armament, and in some cases increased speed or even upgraded the main armament.

The Axis powers, primarily Japan and Italy, pursued these reconstructions with the greatest enthusiasm. Japan rebuilt all of its battleships and battlecruisers twice, leading to increased speed and armor and a radically changed appearance. The Italians sent all of their ships through radical reconstructions that increased the size of their main guns and added several knots of speed.

The United States rebuilt nine of its fifteen battleships, removing most of the cage masts but not increasing speed (which would become the most important commodity for a World War II battleship). The USN delayed reconstruction of the "Big Five," its most modern, powerful battleships, until it was too late; three were reconstructed during the war after receiving damage at Pearl Harbor. The United Kingdom also started late, rebuilding only four of its fifteen battleships and lightly modernizing two others. France, always more concerned by the threat of the Wehrmacht than of any navy, only lightly updated its ships.

The treaty also sped the transition from battleship to aircraft carrier. In order to match the conversions that the Royal Navy had already completed (primarily the "light cruisers" *Furious*, *Glorious*, and *Courageous*), both Japan and the United States were allowed to

HIJMS Tosa, after suspension of construction, 1922. Kure Maritime Museum.

convert two existing hulls into aircraft carriers. On the American side this resulted in *Lexington* and *Saratoga*, on the Japanese *Akagi* and (eventually) *Kaga*. The treaty limited carrier construction along similar ratios as battleships, but did not mandate any scrappings, and allowed each power to experiment with new types of ships.

Follow On, and Collapse

The London Naval Treaty of 1930 took arms limitation one step further. It mandated a reduction in the number of battleships that each of the great powers could keep, extended the naval construction holiday, and set limits (along a 10:10:7 ratio) on the number of heavy cruisers that each navy could build. This resulted in the construction of "light" cruisers that sported a massive array of 6" guns while still displacing 10,000 tons.

By the early 1930s, however, the collective security system that had held in the 1920s was breaking down. Japan in particular sought to revise its position in East Asia, and its relationship with the two Anglo powers. Italy had little interest in restricting its naval power in the Mediterranean. The twin shadows of German and Soviet power also loomed over the treaty system; either, but particularly Germany, could threaten to break out of the limits entirely.

Negotiations in London began in late 1935, but made little headway. The Japanese negotiating team, which included Vice Admiral Isoruku Yamamoto, would likely have faced assassination at home if it had conceded to maintaining the limits developed in previous treaties. The commitment of the parties to the maintenance of the territorial integrity of China had also become a dead letter with the 1931 Japanese invasion of Manchuria.

Japan and Italy declined to sign the treaty, which kept battleship size at 35,000 tons and limited gun caliber to 14". The London Naval Treaty of 1936 included an escalator clause if any of the original signatories declined to sign, which allowed the construction of 16" gunned battleships. The United States immediately up-gunned its planned battleships (the *North Carolina* class), but British plans for the *King George V* class were too far advanced.

The Japanese, by this time, already had their own plans.

III

The World War II Era

HIJMS Kaga

Laid Down: 1920

Launched: 1921

Completed: March, 1928

Displacement: 33,700 tons

Main Armament: ten 7.9" guns (two twin turrets, six casemates)

Secondary Armament: twelve 4.7" guns (twin mounts)

Speed: 27.5 knots

Major Actions: Pearl Harbor, Midway

Treaty: Washington Naval Treaty

Reconstruction: 1933–1935

Fate: Scuttled after damage from American carrier aircraft, June 4, 1942

In the wake of World War I, the Imperial Japanese Navy decided to pursue the "8-8" program, designed to provide Japan with eight modern battlecruisers and eight modern battleships. The follow-up Japanese designs included the *Amagi* class battlecruisers and the *Tosa* class battleships. *Kaga* was the second ship of the former class, initially designed to carry ten 16" guns in five twin turrets, displace 40,000 tons, and make 26.5 knots. Her most likely opponents would have been the American *South Dakota* class, which was more heavily armed and armored but much slower.

Because of the 1922 Washington Naval Treaty, only two ships from these projects (*Nagato* and *Mutsu*) were completed as designed. Construction on *Kaga* and several other ships was suspended. The terms of the treaty allowed the United States and Japan to convert two ships into aircraft carriers in order to match carriers converted by the Royal Navy. The Americans converted the battlecruisers *Lexington* and *Saratoga*, and the Japanese intended to convert the battlecruisers *Akagi* and *Amagi*. *Kaga* and her almost complete sister *Tosa* were slated for destruction.

At 11:58 AM on September 1, 1923, a massive earthquake struck Japan. The magnitude of the earthquake measured at least 7.9. Fires broke out all over Tokyo, and it is thought that over 100,000 Japanese died in the earthquake and the ensuing chaos. In the wake of the earthquake, rumors spread that Korean gangs were looting the wreckage of downtown Tokyo. In spite of the protection of the Japanese Army, nearly 2,000 Koreans were murdered by Japanese mobs. *Amagi*, in the process of conversion to an aircraft carrier, was damaged beyond repair. *Kaga* won a reprieve.

Unlike the nearly identical *Lexington* and *Saratoga*, Kaga differed considerably from her "cousin" *Akagi*. As initially constructed, she carried three launching decks and no superstructure island. Because Japanese battleship construction emphasized speed, she could keep

HIJMS Kaga, prior to reconstruction.

HIJMS Kaga. Courtesy of Australian War Memorial

up a respectable pace, but was still slower than *Akagi*.

Along with *Akagi*, she formed the core of Japan's interwar aircraft carrier force. Experience with *Akagi* and *Kaga* helped form Japanese carrier doctrine during the interwar period, leading to a tightly integrated force that could combine the power of several air wings. In 1933, the IJN rebuilt *Kaga* to increase her speed, eliminate the redundant decks, and improve her capacity to launch heavy strike aircraft. *Kaga* participated in the Sino-Japanese War, providing cover for the Japanese fleet and conducting aerial bombardment of Chinese targets.

In November 1941, *Kaga* proceeded with *Akagi*, *Hiryu*, *Soryu*, *Shokaku*, and *Zuikaku* on a secret mission to attack Pearl Harbor. On December 7, her aircraft helped sink six American battleships, along with several other vessels. Following the Pearl Harbor raid, *Kaga* participated in operations against Rabaul, Darwin, and various targets in the Dutch East Indies. She missed the IJN's Indian Ocean raid because of damage incurred by a reef grounding.

In May 1942 the Japanese high command decided to launch an operation to seize Midway, a small island northwest of Hawaii. *Akagi*, *Soryu*, *Hiryu*, and much of the strength of the Japanese Combined Fleet were also committed to the operation. American codebreaking revealed the Japanese force, and three USN carriers intercepted the invasion attempt. Although

Japanese fighters defeated an attack by American torpedo bombers, a group of dive bombers from *Hornet*, *Yorktown*, and *Enterprise* found the Japanese carriers and attacked. *Kaga* was hit by four bombs, which started uncontrollable fires on her flight and hangar decks. *Kaga*'s crew was evacuated, and torpedoes from a pair of escorting destroyers provided the coup de grace. *Soryu*, *Akagi*, and *Hiryu* were also destroyed by American carrier aircraft during the battle.

Author's Note

Kaga was the slowest of the six Japanese fleet carriers, but she nonetheless participated effectively in the operations of 1941 and 1942. Lax Japanese damage control practices doomed her at Midway. Of the eight large warships ships converted to aircraft carriers because of the Washington Naval Treaty (including *Eagle*, *Furious*, *Courageous*, *Glorious*, *Kaga*, *Akagi*, *Lexington*, and *Saratoga*), only two (*Furious* and *Saratoga*) would survive the Second World War.

Related Entries:

Contemporary of... USS *Lexington*
Preceded by... HIJMS *Nagato*
Fought at... Pearl Harbor

USS Lexington

Laid Down: 1921

Launched: 1925

Completed: December, 1927

Displacement: 36,000 tons

Main Armament: four 8" guns (four twin turrets)

Secondary Armament: twelve 5" guns (individual mounts)

Speed: 33 knots

Major Actions: Coral Sea

Treaty: Washington Naval Treaty

Fate: Scuttled after attack by Japanese carrier aircraft, May 8, 1942

The United States made a very late entrance into the battlecruiser game. The Royal Navy built the world's first battlecruiser in 1908, with the Germans and Japanese quickly following suit. Since the USN viewed the Royal Navy and the Imperial Japanese Navy as its most likely foes in the early part of the twentieth century, it's surprising that the Americans would concede the battlecruiser race to enemy navies. The most charitable interpretation is that the USN recognized the basic problem with the battlecruiser form: its inability to participate in the line of battle because of light armor. The Japanese recognized this problem as well, but decided that, given the size of the Pacific theater of operations, battlecruisers would nonetheless be useful. To the credit of the USN, it consistently built the best protected battleships in the world, which may have made the battlecruiser unpalatable on an organizational culture basis.

The USN began to think seriously about battlecruisers in 1912 and 1913. The first designs were genuinely appalling; one early design was over a thousand feet long, and could make over 36 knots, but was armed with only eight 12" guns. The first serious design was commissioned in 1916, and envisioned a ship with seven funnels, ten 14" guns, boilers on two levels, and a speed of 35 knots. When the United States became involved in World War I, the Royal Navy handed over the plans to HMS *Hood*, which revolutionized the US design. In the final design, the *Lexington* class

USS Lexington off Oahu, 1933

USS Lexington at sea, 1930s.

battlecruisers would carry eight 16" guns in four twin turrets, displace 43,500 tons, and make 33.25 knots. The design was competitive with but probably inferior to that of the Japanese *Amagis*, which would have carried heavier armor. Both the Japanese and the American ships would likely have been outclassed by the British G3 class, 48,000 ton ships with a 32 knot speed, nine 16" guns, and a well-balanced armor scheme.

The naming program for the battlecruisers lacked any particular strategy, unusual for the US Navy. While the USN had historically been very programmatic about its ship names (submarines after fish, battleships after states, cruisers after cities, destroyers after people), the proposed names of the battlecruisers were *Lexington*, *Constellation*, *Saratoga*, *Constitution*, *Ranger*, and *United States*. This represented an odd collection of battles and historical vessels.

The Washington Naval Treaty intervened, and almost all the new battlecruisers were scrapped or canceled. The Treaty spared *Lexington* and *Saratoga*, which immediately began conversion into aircraft carriers. The conversion worked out beautifully, with *Saratoga* and *Lexington* being far more effective as aircraft carriers than they would have been as battlecruisers. Of course, it took a while for the USN to figure out what to do with its huge new ships, and *Lexington* spent most of the prewar period participating in exercises and simulations designed to determine the proper employment of the fast carrier. The most famous of these involved surprise air attacks on the Panama Canal and Pearl Harbor.

Lexington was one of three carriers in the Pacific at the beginning of World War II. Fortunately, all three were away from Pearl Harbor during the attack. *Lexington* was ferrying aircraft to Midway, but participated in the search for the Japanese task force after the attack. In early 1942, *Lexington* participated in raids against Rabaul and other targets in the South Pacific before returning to Pearl in March. On April 15, *Lexington* left Pearl Harbor to rendezvous with the carrier *Yorktown* in an effort to stop the Japanese advance on New Guinea. The Japanese were

USS Lexington on fire, Battle of Coral Sea, May 8, 1942. USN photo

launching a maritime effort to seize Port Moresby, which would allow them to severely degrade communications between the United States and Australia.

The Battle of Coral Sea began on May 7 with the sighting of the small Japanese carrier *Shoho*. *Lexington's* dive bombers destroyed *Shoho* in less than ten minutes, but failed to locate the two much larger Japanese carriers, *Shokaku* and *Zuikaku*. Both sides launched strikes on May 8, and both airgroups found their targets. Planes from *Lexington* and *Yorktown* severely damaged *Shokaku*, but failed to sink her. *Lexington* was hit by two torpedoes and three bombs, but because of her large size and sound construction, was able to maintain speed and begin to recover her aircraft. Unfortunately, damage control techniques remained at a relatively primitive stage. Gasoline fumes spread on the lower decks of the ship, resulting in a huge explosion. With uncontrolled fires raging, *Lexington* was aban-

USS Lexington during Battle of Coral Sea, May 8, 1942.

doned by her crew. Shortly thereafter she was scuttled by an accompanying destroyer. Historians have rated the battle as both a tactical and strategic victory for the United States, despite the loss of a fleet carrier, as the Japanese invasion failed and *Shokaku* and *Zuikaku* could not participate in the Battle of Midway. *Lexington*'s sister, *Saratoga*, survived the war and was sunk in the Bikini atom bomb tests.

Author's Note

The United States would have been far better served to have saved four of the *Lexingtons*, two carriers and two in place of a pair of the *Colorado* class (had such an outcome been possible). Both the Royal Navy and the IJN used modernized battlecruisers to good effect in World War II, while the slow American battleships largely remained relegated to escort and shore bombardment duty. Battlecruisers, on the other hand, could have served as carrier escorts at most of the battles in the early part of the war, potentially supplying critical anti-aircraft fire at Midway, Coral Sea, and Santa Cruz.

Related Entries:

Contemporary of... HIJMS *Kaga*
Preceded by... USS *Maryland*
Inspired by... HMS *Hood*

HMS Rodney

Laid Down: 1922

Launched: 1925

Completed: August, 1927

Displacement: 33,700 tons

Main Armament: nine 16" guns (three triple turrets)

Secondary Armament: twelve 6" guns (six twin turrets)

Speed: 23 knots

Treaty: Washington Naval Treaty

Major Engagements: Sinking of the *Bismarck*, Operation Torch

Fate: Scrapped, 1948

The Washington Naval Treaty struck the Royal Navy harder than any of its counteparts. In 1921 the RN posssesed 32 dreadnoughts and 9 battlecruisers, compared to the 22 dreadnoughts of the USN and the 8 dreadnoughts and 4 battlecruisers of the IJN. Moreover, the battleships (N3 class) and battlecruisers (G3

class) on the Royal Navy drawing board were distinctly superior to their Japanese and American equivalents. The fact that the United Kingdom was nearly bankrupt in the wake of World War I, and that her resources were far outmatched by those of the United States, didn't help alleviate the sting of having to scrap more than half of her dreadnought fleet, abandon her magnificent new battleships, and accept naval parity with the Americans and only modest naval superiority over the Japanese. British negotiators wrung a major concession, however. Because Japan and the United States had both completed battleships with 16" guns, Great Britain would be allowed to construct two of its own.

These ships became *Nelson* and *Rodney*. *Rodney* was the fourth ship named after Admiral George Brydges Rodney, a Royal Navy officer who made his name in the American War of Independence. Originally, the name Rodney belonged to one of the four "Admiral" class battlecruisers, of which only HMS *Hood* was completed.

In designing the two ships, the British

HMS Rodney viewe from Plymouth Pier

HMS Rodney during World War II

tried to combine the best elements of the can-celed battlecruisers and battleships. The treaty limited the displacement of the ships to 35,000 tons, slightly larger than the *Nagato* and *Colorado* class battleships of the other two major navies. Designers decided to preserve the armament of the battlecruisers while reducing the speed. To save weight, the *Nelsons* carried their entire main armament forward, ahead of the tower superstructure. One of the turrets was superfiring, but one was not, leaving it with a firing arc restricted to broadsides. The gun disposition also led to blast problems, and it was general policy that the guns should never be fired all at the same time.

For the first time, the Royal Navy adopt-ed the "all or nothing" armor scheme that had been incorporated in US battleships since 1916. This scheme left much of the ship unprotected, on the assumption that the vital areas (magazines, boilers) should be heavily defended and that the light armor covering the non-vital areas could not resist battleship guns in any case. Consequently, the *Nelsons* were very heavily armored, including a 14" main belt, although in practice the belt proved diffi-cult to repair.

Although quite powerful, the ships were of a hybrid design and consequently had some serious problems. The ships had a massive tower superstructure that, while looking impressive, sometime acted as a sail in high winds. Because of the desire to save weight the ships only used two propellers, which reduced their maneuverability and made them vulnera-ble to underwater attack.

In hindsight, several changes could have made them much more effective ships. The third turret should have been placed aft, which likely would have improved structural stability as well as firing arcs. Although it was hard to predict at the time, sacrificing protection in favor of speed would have resulted in much more useful ships, as *Rodney* could not keep up with even the *Queen Elizabeth* class battle-ships.

Rodney was commissioned in 1927, and despite these problems it is probably fair to argue that she and her sister were the most powerful battleships in the world until 1940. The United Kingdom was still strapped for cash, and the Depression didn't help matters. In 1931, the government decided to cut pay for some sailors by 25%. Unsurprisingly, the sailors didn't care for this line of thinking. On September 15, 1931, sailors on board *Rodney* and three other Royal Navy battleships mutinied, and refused to take orders from their officers. The Invergordon Mutiny, as it came to be called, threatened to spread until the Cabinet took action, reducing the pay cut to 10%. Several hundred sailors were either jailed or discharged for participating in the mutiny. Partially in consequence of the resultant fiscal crisis, the United Kingdom abandoned the Gold Standard several months later.

In the early part of World War II, *Rodney* served as a convoy escort, meeting *Scharnhorst* and *Gneisenau* in March 1941, although the wary Germans avoided engagement. In May, *Rodney* joined the hunt for the battleship *Bismarck*. Because of damage to her rudder, *Bismarck* could not escape the slow British battleship, and *Rodney* (along with *King George V*) engaged *Bismarck* on May 27. The most serious damage that *Rodney* suffered during the battle was self-inflicted, as the crew could not be dissuaded from launching full salvos that warped the main deck. *Bismarck* proved difficult to sink, with *Rodney* finally closing to point blank range and firing torpedoes before breaking off. *Bismarck* would later be sunk/scuttled by a combination of British torpedoes and her own scuttling charges. This appears to be the only case of a battleship successfully torpedoing another battleship.

After her encounter with *Bismarck*, *Rodney* returned to convoy escort in the Mediterranean, the North Atlantic, and the Arctic. Due to heavy use and insufficient repairs, she became incapable of further action in 1944, and was put in reserve in December. *Rodney* was sold for scrap in 1948.

Author's Note

From a visual perspective, *Nelson* and *Rodney* were certainly interesting ships. The front-loaded armament and huge superstructure set them apart from any other class of battleship. These were useful ships, if hampered by slow speed and by the pacing of Royal Navy reconstructions. The role *Rodney* played in the destruction of *Bismarck* remains her central contribution to the war.

Related Entries:

Inspired by... USS *Maryland*
Fought against... *Scharnhorst*
Contemporary of... HIJMS *Nagato*

A and B 16" turrets of HMS Rodney.

Admiral Scheer

Laid Down: 1931

Launched: 1933

Completed: November, 1934

Displacement: 13,700 tons

Main Armament: six 11" guns (two triple turrets)

Secondary Armament: eight 5.9" guns (single mounts)

Speed: 28.3 knots

Major Actions: Convoy HX-84, Convoy PQ-17

Treaty: Treaty of Versailles

Fate: Sunk by Royal Air Force bombers, April 9, 1945

At the end of World War I, the Royal Navy (and international opinion) identified the Anglo-German naval race as one of the key causes of World War I. Consequently, the postwar settlement drastically limited Germany's right to build a navy. The Treaty of Versailles limited the German navy to vessels of 10,000 tons or less, with the intention to prevent Germany from constructing any ships larger than coastal defense vessels. In practice, the letter of Versailles allowed Germany to build ships as large as Washington Treaty heavy cruisers, but without the limitations on the armament that the Washington Treaty subjected. Using the most advanced construction techniques possible, the Germans decided to circumvent the treaty by building capital ships within the legal limits. Thus resulted the "Panzerschiff," a battleship on the displacement of a heavy cruiser.

Germany had used surface commerce raiders to good effect in World War I, and decided that purpose-built ships might be even more effective, especially with increases in armor, speed, armament, and range. Given the treaty restrictions, Germany could not hope to equal the Royal Navy in any case, so commerce raiding was a natural option. *Admiral Scheer* took its name from Admiral Reinhard Scheer, commander of the High Seas Fleet at the Battle of Jutland.

The Germans saved weight through the use of welding and a relatively light armor scheme. The German hope was that *Admiral Scheer* and his (*Admiral Scheer* is often cited as one of a very few ships referred to in the masculine) siblings could outrun any foe that they could not outgun. Despite his light armor, *Scheer* probably had the advantage against traditional Washington Treaty cruisers, which could not hope to resist his 11" guns. However, *Scheer* and his siblings were clearly outclassed by the British battlecruisers *Renown*, *Repulse*, and *Hood*, all of which could both outrun and outgun the Panzerschiff. The construction of *Dunkerque* and *Strasbourg* by France reinforced the vulnerability of the type, and the last two ships were canceled in favor of the battleships *Scharnhorst* and *Gneisenau*.

Obsolescence is a relative term, and has never stood in the way of employment during war. *Admiral Scheer* was used by the Nazis to aid the Nationalist side in the Spanish Civil War, firing on Republican positions and escorting Nationalist convoys. He underwent an

Admiral Reinhard Scheer. Library of Congress.

Admiral Scheer prior to World War II

overhaul and refit at the beginning of the war, and did not participate in the invasion of Norway. In October 1940 *Scheer* set out on a raiding cruise that lasted nearly eight months and took him into the Indian Ocean. On the cruise *Scheer* managed to sink sixteen ships with a total displacement of over 100,000 tons. Although the raid was a success, it didn't compare all that favorably in cost-effectiveness to U-boats or even to converted merchant cruiser raiders. In August 1942, *Admiral Scheer* sortied against Arctic convoy PQ-17, which was scattered in response with extremely heavy loss to submarines and Luftwaffe aircraft. In August he sortied again, shelling a Soviet weather station and sinking a Soviet icebreaker. Hitler became disillusioned with the surface fleet after 1942, and *Scheer* left Norway for Germany in December.

In late 1944 the German situation in the Baltic began to rapidly deteriorate because of the Soviet advance, combined with the ever more effective bombing of the Royal Air Force. *Scheer* escorted ships escaping from German-controlled pockets along the coast, and supplied artillery support for retreating German forces. He returned to Kiel in April 1945, and was sunk by a massive RAF raid. The wreck was partially broken up after the war, and the area in which the hull lay filled in with rubble and covered to serve as a parking lot.

Author's Note

Most ships are referred to in the feminine. The exceptions mostly come from German and Russian navies, and take their names from men (*Prinz Eugen, Tirpitz, Scheer*). The commander of *Bismarck*, apparently, ordered his crew to use the masculine because of *Bismarck's* great power, although most German ships were referred to by the general public with the feminine "die."

The Panzerschiff are easy to criticize; they were hybrid creatures, built solely to work around the restriction of Versailles. Within those limitations, however, they were extremely effective ships. They certainly forced the Royal Navy to exert far more resources in pursuit than Germany spent in design and construction.

On a personal note, I spent much of 2003 in Kiel. I often walked upon the Horn, not realizing that the grave of *Scheer* lay directly beneath me. The nearby naval memorial at Laboe had a silhouette of *Scheer*, along with his siblings and every other German warship sunk in the First and Second World Wars.

Related Entries:

Preceded... *Scharnhorst*
Inspired... *Strasbourg*
Served alongside... *Tirpitz*

Littorio
Italia

Laid Down: 1934
Launched: 1937
Completed: May, 1940
Displacement: 41,000 tons
Main Armament: nine 15" guns (three triple turrets)
Secondary Armament: twelve 6" guns (triple turrets)
Speed: 30 knots
Major Actions: Taranto
Treaty: Washington Naval Treaty
Fate: Scrapped, 1948

The Regia Marina was one of the busiest navies of the interwar period. Four old battleships were rebuilt so completely that they barely resembled their original configuration. This helped Italy achieve what was really, by the late 1930s, significant ship-to-ship superiority over the French Navy. The reconstruction of these ships helped generate ideas as to what their new battleships should look like. The new ships were to have enough speed to catch *Dunkerque* and *Strasbourg*, and enough firepower to destroy them. The result was the first post-treaty class of genuine fast battleships, the *Littorio* class.

Littorio displaced 42,000 tons, could make 32 knots, and carried nine 15" guns in three triple turrets. Although well protected from shellfire, Littorio was built with an experimental underwater protection system designed by Italian naval architect Umberto Pugliese. This system proved disastrous in practice, and limited the effectiveness of Littorio and her sisters, as they were forced to be unusually wary of torpedo attacks. Like the German *Tirpitz* but unlike Allied battleships of the day, *Littorio* did not carry a dual purpose secondary armament, a measure that would have saved weight and improved her anti-aircraft capabilities. The Italian 15" gun was also something of a disappointment, as it fired a very heavy shell at a high velocity, but was difficult to reload, inaccurate, and incurred serious barrel wear. Finally, *Littorio* had a very short range, although this was of little concern in the Mediterranean. All in all, *Littorio* and her sisters were probably the least capable of the final generation of fast battleships, with the likely exception of *Bismarck* and *Tirpitz*. Nevertheless, they were useful ships, and in battle the difference between *Littorio* and, say, *Prince of Wales*, *Richelieu*, or *Washington* probably would have been minimal.

Littorio had an active war career. She par-

RN Littorio, 1940

RN Littorio in column ahead of her sister, Vittorio Veneto

ticipated in numerous convoy escort actions, resulting in the first and second Battles of Sirte, in which she briefly exchanged fire with Royal Navy vessels. *Littorio* also engaged in occasional missions to hunt and intercept British convoys. Her most notable battle service, however, was less than distinguished. On November 11, 1940 HMS *Illustrious*, escorted by a few Royal Navy cruisers and destroyers, launched an air attack on the Italian fleet anchorage at Taranto. One of three ships hit, *Littorio* suffered three torpedo impacts. The damage sank *Littorio* at anchor, although the damage was not so severe that she couldn't be salvaged. Repairs took about four months, limiting the effectiveness of the Italian Navy at a critical point in the war. The Taranto attack was carefully studied by Japanese naval planners, and provided a model for the Pearl Harbor attack of December, 1941.

Later in the war, the Regia Marina was beset by fuel problems, precluding the aggressive use of *Littorio* and her two sisters (*Roma* and *Vittorio Veneto*). However, the Italian fleet-in-being, built around these modern units, remained a major strategic problem for the Allies until the end of combat in Tunisia.

In September 1943, the Italian govenment decided to seek an armistice with the Western Allies. The surrender of the Italian fleet was a prominent condition of this agreement. *Littorio* had been renamed *Italia* upon the fall of the Fascist government, and was in preparation with her two sisters to attack the Allied landing force at Salerno when the armistice was signed. Instead of heading to Salerno, *Italia* and her sisters laid a course for Malta. Along the way, the fleet was attacked by German glider bombs, of the same sort that later damaged HMS *Warspite*. *Italia* narrowly avoided one of the bombs, but *Roma* was hit twice, exploded, and sank with nearly all hands. *Italia* and *Vittorio Veneto* arrived at Malta without further molestation, and were then transferred to Egypt.

Some consideration was given to the idea of incorporating *Italia* and her sister into the USN or the RN. *Italia* technically became US war booty, while *Vittorio Veneto* was given to the United Kingdom. The ships certainly had the speed to operate with fast carrier groups in the Pacific, but there were several problems. Neither the USN nor the RN had the appropriate ammunition or spare part stores to operate the ships over a long period of time. Moreover, the short range of *Italia* would have proven a severe handicap in the Pacific. Had the war situation been more critical, the two ships might have been used nonetheless, but by 1944 the USN, the RN, and the Marine Nationale had overwhelming superiority in fast battleships over the IJN. *Italia* saw no further service, although she was physically returned to Italy after the war. Struck from the US list in 1948, she was scrapped in the 1950s.

Author's Note

The idea of an international squadron in the Pacific, with the two surviving fast Italian battleships, is very appealing. The French *Richelieu* operated with the Royal Navy in the Pacific at the end of the war, and under desperate circumstances *Littorio* and *Vittorio Veneto* also might have joined. It speaks to the degree of Allied dominance in 1944–5 that the Allies felt they could leave modern, capable capital ships behind while they tightened the noose around Japan.

The idea of *Littorio* in Soviet service is also interesting. The Soviets planned a fleet of large battleships based (very loosely) on the *Littorios*, although none were ever completed. The Soviets kept *Giulio Cesare* in limited service until she sank in 1955. A more modern ship might have remained in service much longer.

These were lovely ships aesthetically, with crisp lines and a well-proportioned superstructure. They came into service before most of the rest of the "fast battleship" generation, and had flaws commensurate with their pace-setting.

Related Entries:

Contemporary of...*Tirpitz*
Meant to fight... *Strasbourg*
Served alongside... *Giulio Cesare*

Strasbourg

Laid Down: 1934
Launched: 1936
Completed: April, 1939
Displacement: 27,300 tons
Main Armament: eight 13" guns (two quadruple turrets)
Secondary Armament: sixteen 5.1" guns (three quadruple, two twin turrets)
Speed: 30 knots
Treaty: London Naval Treaty
Major Engagements: Mers El Kebir, Toulon
Fate: Scuttled 27 November 1942, scrapped 1955

France's early efforts at battleship construction suffered from slow building, full slips, and a concentration on the more pressing issues of World War I. Early French ships could not compete against foreign contemporaries, and the Marine Nationale failed to remedy these problems with reconstruction projects during the interwar period. The Washington Naval Treaty allotted France 70,000 tons for battleship construction, which the French wisely delayed using for a decade.

Germany, of course, suffered under far more serious restrictions than France. Germany was allowed to construct no battleships of over 10,000 tons, which should have limited them to coastal defense vessels. The Germans, however, were not content with this plan, and developed "pocket battleships," a trio of cruiser-size ships with battleship armament and very long cruising ranges. Each of the pocket battleships carried six 11" guns in two triple turrets, could make about 29 knots, and had diesel engines that gave them ranges ideal for commerce raiding. These cruisers could either outrun or outgun any French ship afloat, putting French colonial communications in jeopardy. Upon the construction of the pocket battleships, France began to design ships that could destroy the German vessels. The result was the *Dunkerque* class fast battleships, relatively small ships that fit within the demands of the Washington Naval Treaty.

The *Dunkerques* were efficiently designed vessels. Sometimes described as battlecruisers, their strong protection effectively made them light battleships. *Strasbourg*, the second ship of the class, devoted an enormous percentage of her displacement to armor. Although exact figures differ a bit and depend on interpretation, armor constituted between 41% and 44%

Strasbourg after USAAF bombing, 1944. US Army Air Force photo.

of *Strasbourg*'s displacement, making her one of the best armored battleships ever built, for her size. (Armor took up roughly 33% of the displacement of a typical modern battleship, although the later *Richelieus* also achieved a percentage in the low forties.) The French were able to achieve such numbers through excellent, efficient design work and also through the practice of quadruple turrets, which significantly reduced the weight of the main armament. The armor was well distributed, and *Strasbourg* also had excellent underwater protection and a fine anti-aircraft armament. Altogether the French battleship construction effort was much more impressive than that of the Germans or the Italians, and on a ton for ton basis was competitive with that of the Royal Navy.

Strasbourg's activities at the beginning of World War II involved convoy escort and the pursuit of German commerce raiders. *Strasbourg* was more than capable of catching and destroying a pocket battleship, and she likely would have fared well against the lightly armed German *Scharnhorst* class, although an interception would have resulted in a tough fight. In any case, *Strasbourg* never caught a German ship, and the French surrender found her at the harbor of Mers El Kebir.

The French fleet, by and large, hoped to sit out the war following the French surrender. Notwithstanding the Fascist sympathies of Admiral François Darlan, many of the sailors and officers of the Marine Nationale resisted the idea of giving ships to the Germans or the Italians. Winston Churchill, however, felt that the French fleet was too great of a threat to let lay, and decided to take vigorous action. He ordered a task force including HMS *Hood* and two older battleships to Mers El Kebir in order to capture or destroy the French squadron. The French squadron included two old battleships (*Provence* and *Bretagne*), but the main British concern was with *Dunkerque*, *Strasbourg*, and six large, modern French destroyers. In Axis hands they would have the speed

and firepower to stiffen the Italian battlefleet. The same qualities made the two battlecruisers valuable to the Royal Navy; in British or Free French hands, they might have been used to hunt German raiders (imagine them at the Battle of Denmark Strait, with *Hood* and *Prince of Wales*), or stiffen British forces in the Pacific.

The negotiations between the French and British naval officials at Mers El Kebir went poorly, and the British ships eventually opened fire. *Strasbourg* was handicapped by the fact that her entire main armament (two quadruple 13" turrets) were forward, and could not fire to the aft, where the British happened to be. Nevertheless, *Strasbourg* managed to get underway, and with five of the six destroyers made a break for the open sea. The rest of the French squadron did not fare so well, with *Bretagne* exploding and *Dunkerque* and *Provence* beaching themselves.

HMS *Hood* was the only ship that could have caught *Strasbourg*, and a battle between the two would have been interesting. *Hood* was much larger and carried a heavier armament, but *Strasbourg* was newer and better protected. She was also faster, and *Hood* damaged herself during the pursuit. *Strasbourg* and the five large destroyers made their way to Toulon, where they sat, mostly inactive, until November 1942. They were eventually joined by *Dunkerque* and *Provence*, which had received serious but not critical damage in the British attack.

On November 10, 1942, the Germans abrogated the armistice with France, and occupied Vichy controlled areas. The Marine Nationale decided to retain its honor, however, and on November 27, 1942, scuttled itself. *Strasbourg*'s military equipment was destroyed and she settled on the bottom of the harbor. Her hulk was refloated in 1943 by the Italians, and was transferred several times between Italy, Germany, and the skeleton of the Vichy state. In August 1944, *Strasbourg* was hit by eight American bombs, and grounded to pre-

Strasbourg after scuttling at Toulon. Courtesy of World War II Database.

vent capsizing. The French refloated her in 1946, and considered, but rejected, converting the hulk into an aircraft carrier. She was used for explosives tests before finally being scrapped in 1955.

Author's Note

The idea of *Strasbourg* and *Dunkerque* in foreign service is surely appealing. The addition of two fast battleships to the Italian battle squadron would have given the Regia Marina presumptive dominance in the central Mediterranean, although fuel shortages likely would have continued to cause severe problems. On the other hand, had the French squadron at Mers El Kebir joined the British, we can easily imagine *Strasbourg* and *Dunkerque* as part of the pursuit group of *Bismarck*, or as part of the squadron deployed to the Far East in preparation for the Japanese attack. In either the Pacific or the Atlantic, these handsome, effective ships could have fought well. Sadly, neither the British nor the French had the courage and imagination necessary to make this happen.

Related Entries:

Meant to fight... *Admiral Scheer*
Fought against... HMS *Hood*
Served alongside... *Bretagne*

Scharnhorst

Laid Down: 1935

Launched: 1936

Completed: January, 1939

Displacement: 31,000 tons

Main Armament: nine 11" guns (three triple turrets)

Secondary Armament: twelve 5.9" guns (six twin turrets)

Speed: 32 knots

Major Actions: Operation Weserubung, Channel Dash, Battle of North Cape

Treaty: Anglo-German Naval Agreement

Fate: Sunk by gunfire from HMS *Duke of York*, 26 December 1943

The Treaty of Versailles drastically limited the size of the postwar Kriegsmarine, precluding Germany from owning any dreadnought battleships. The Germans could keep (and replace) pre-dreadnought vessels of 10,000 tons or less, roughly the size of a heavy cruiser in most navies. Presented with a problem, the German engineers designed the pocket battleships, warships of relatively small size (12,000 tons or so), with relatively heavy armaments (six 11" guns) that were faster than any ship more powerful than they and more powerful than any ship faster. Alas, the concept behind the pocket battleships went the way of all technology. The Royal Navy retained three of its battlecruisers, each of which would have no difficulty catching and destroying the German ships. More troubling, the French built *Dunkerque* and *Strasbourg*, a pair of battlecruisers that similarly would have meant doom for the German vessels.

In 1933, the new Nazi government was looking for ways to break out of the Treaty of Versailles. London believed that maintaining some control over German shipbuilding was better than nothing, and negotiations resulted in the Anglo-German Naval Agreement, which gave Germany the right to build warships up to 33% of the Royal Navy. The Kriegsmarine

Scharnhorst firing on HMS Glorious

realized that building additional pocket battle-ships would serve no compelling purpose. Accordingly, the navy developed plans for two new ships, *much* larger than the pocket battle-ships.

These ships became the battlecruisers *Scharnhorst* and *Gneisenau*, named after a pair of crack armored cruisers destroyed at the Battle of Falkland Islands, themselves named after Prussian commanders in the Napoleonic Wars. Like most German battleships, *Scharnhorst* was under-armed for her size. The German 11" gun was a very effective weapon, with a high rate of fire, but it lacked sufficient punch to seriously endanger enemy battleships. The designers built in the capability for re-equipping *Scharnhorst* with 15" tur-rets, but the opportunity for conversion never emerged.

Scharnhorst had an extremely active career. After a couple early raiding cruises, *Scharnhorst* and *Gneisenau* helped cover the German landings in Norway. They engaged HMS *Renown*, without much effect. A month later, the British aircraft carrier *Glorious* somehow blundered into *Scharnhorst* and *Gneisenau*. The German ships quickly destroyed the British carrier, with *Scharnhorst* scoring a hit at 26,000 yards, although *Scharnhorst* took a torpedo hit during the engagement.

In early 1941, *Scharnhorst* and *Gneisenau* left Kiel for a very successful two month raid-ing cruise before pulling into the French naval base at Brest. The Kriegsmarine planned a massive naval operation for May 1941. *Scharnhorst* and *Gneisenau* would depart from Brest and lead the Royal Navy to the south. In the meantime, the newly commissioned *Bismarck*, accompanied by the cruiser *Prinz Eugen*, would enter the Atlantic through Denmark Straights and wreak havoc on Atlantic convoys. *Bismarck*, being a battleship, could deal with the older British battleships used to escort convoys. Unfortunately for the Germans, RAF attacks on Brest disabled the

General Gerhard David von Scharnhorst.

facilities and prevented *Scharnhorst* and *Gneisenau* from sortieing. *Bismarck*'s cruise was famously unsuccessful.

Scharnhorst remained at Brest for the rest of 1941, but increased RAF bombing attacks made the German naval presence untenable. The German ships could not sortie, and could not remain in Brest. The Germans developed a risky plan in which *Scharnhorst*, *Gneisenau*, *Prinz Eugen*, and six destroyers would dash up the English Channel, hopefully avoiding British surface ships, aircraft, and submarines, in an effort to make it to Wilhelmshaven. The plan worked beautifully, and the German fleet escaped with only minor damage. The dash was a great embarrassment to the Admiralty and the Royal Air Force.

Scharnhorst remained at Kiel for most of 1942. In early 1943, she proceeded to Norway with *Prinz Eugen* (*Gneisenau* had been badly damaged by an RAF attack on Kiel, and would not return to service). While in Norway,

Scharnhorst operated as part of a "fleet in being" with *Prinz Eugen*, *Tirpitz* (the sister of *Bismarck*), and other ships. These vessels threatened British convoys to Russia, inducing the convoys to occasionally disperse (making them easy prey for U-boats), and forcing the Royal Navy to keep assets in the area.

On Christmas, 1943, *Scharnhorst* departed Norway in an attempt to catch a British convoy. Unfortunately for the Germans, the Royal Navy received intelligence of the German movements, and dispatched *Duke of York* with several cruisers and destroyers to intercept. *Duke of York* was a fast battleship, more heavily armed and armored than *Scharnhorst*, and enjoyed the support of four cruisers, which maintained contact throughout the battle. The German battleship withstood several hits before losing speed, at which point the British cruisers and destroyers closed to make a torpedo attack on *Scharnhorst*. The ship capsized and sank at 7:45 PM on December 26. Only 36 men from the crew of 1,968 were rescued.

Author's Note

Scharnhorst is one of the world's most famous battleships. Her strategic value, though, was limited. The Kriegsmarine never threatened Royal Navy control of the North Atlantic, and German surface raiders never approached the lethality of their undersea cousins. The Germans could have used *Scharnhorst* and the rest of the surface fleet more aggressively, but then several efforts at aggressive action ended badly. It's also unclear how *Scharnhorst* would have fit into the "Plan Z" fleet that Hitler and Raeder contemplated on the eve of war.

Nonetheless, an aesthetically lovely ship that led one of the most exciting careers of World War II. That her sister very nearly survived the war (albeit inactive for its last two years) was a miracle.

Related Entries:

Preceded by…*Admiral Scheer*
Fought against… *HMS Rodney*
Preceded… *Tirpitz*

Tirpitz

Laid Down: 1936
Launched: 1939
Completed: February, 1941
Displacement: 42,000 tons
Main Armament: eight 15" guns (four twin turrets)
Secondary Armament: twelve 5.9" guns (twin turrets)
Speed: 30 knots
Major Actions: None
Treaty: Post-Washington Naval Treaty
Fate: Sunk by Royal Air Force aircraft, November 12, 1944

Tirpitz was the culmination of forty (interrupted) years of German battleship design. In construction she was very similar to her sister *Bismarck*, although slightly larger and with a few minor modifications. When commissioned in February 1941 she became the largest battleship in the world, a title she would retain until the commissioning of the Japanese *Yamato* in December of that year.

Fittingly, *Tirpitz* took her name from Admiral Alfred von Tirpitz. Admiral Tirpitz was critical in driving the coalition that made Imperial Germany a major naval power. State-financed naval construction helped unite German industrialists with German labor unions, reducing class conflict and creating a large domestic constituency for an aggressive foreign policy. Tirpitz presided over the construction of the High Seas Fleet, helping to push his country into a naval race with Great Britain. In an important sense, Bismarck and Tirpitz represented the beginning and end of the German Empire. Bismarck famously created the Empire in 1871, by engineering a successful war against France. Tirpitz helped lead it into war with Great Britain, and eventual destruction, between 1900 and 1918. Indeed, the scuttling of the High Seas Fleet at Scapa provides a grim coda to the history of Imperial Germany.

Like the other fast battleships, *Tirpitz* combined a heavy armament with high speed and strong armor. However, neither *Tirpitz* nor her sister compared favorably with foreign battleship designs. German naval architects were only partially at fault for this, as the Treaty of Versailles not only prohibited German battleship construction, but confiscat-

Tirpitz. Office of Naval Intelligence recognition drawing.

ed Germany's existing battleships. Whereas every other navy had older ships that could be refit, rebuilt, and experimented upon, the Kriegsmarine was forced to start from scratch.

Tirpitz had a lot of problems. She was heavily armored, but the armor was not well-arranged. Like all German battleships, *Tirpitz* had a very wide beam, which made the ship very difficult to sink. However, she was much easier to disable. Electrical systems necessary to full function were left unarmored. The excellent fire control points were easily knocked out even by small caliber shells. *Tirpitz* had a very poor anti-aircraft armament, at a time when aircraft were becoming especially lethal to battleships. Finally, *Tirpitz* was dreadfully under-armed for a ship of her size. The German 15" gun had excellent range, muzzle velocity, and accuracy, but lacked the weight of other weapons. While *Tirpitz* and her sister were the third largest class of battleships constructed, the weight of their broadside was somewhat less than that of USS *New York*, a ship constructed in 1914. In this *Tirpitz* was no different than any other German battleship; with the exceptions of *Baden* and *Bayern*, every German battleship from 1908 until 1944 was under-armed relative to foreign contemporaries.

Thus, while *Tirpitz* and her sister *Bismarck* had a formidable reputation, they were not competitive with the modern ships constructed in other navies. *Prince of Wales*, had she not suffered teething difficulties in the Battle of Denmark Straits, could probably have defeated *Bismarck*. *Tirpitz* had the good fortune to avoid enemy capital ships. A meeting with any of the modern US battleships, all of which carried more powerful main batteries and radar controlled firing systems, would likely have been disastrous for the Germans. The French *Richelieu* was also an all-around superior unit. This did not mean, however, that *Tirpitz* posed no threat. As the Battle of Denmark Straits demonstrated, a single lucky hit could result in the destruction of any capital ship.

The marginal superiority of the Allied battleships could not be relied upon as a guarantee of victory. As it turned out, despite her problems *Tirpitz* managed to tie down serious Allied naval assets for most of World War II.

Tirpitz was still conducting trials when *Bismarck* undertook her disastrous cruise of May 1941. Following the destruction of *Bismarck*, *Tirpitz* was deployed, along with the other major surviving German surface units, to Norway. From Norway, *Tirpitz* could threaten to attack Allied convoys to the Soviet Union or to make a break for the Atlantic. *Tirpitz* engaged in three major actions, including two convoy raids and an attack on Allied installations on Spitsbergen. Although *Tirpitz* did not actually engage any foes, one of the raids disrupted the convoy PQ 17, leading to the destruction of most of its ships. *Tirpitz* spent most of her time docked in various Norwegian fjords, and acquired the nickname "Lonely Queen of the North" from locals.

Admiral Alfred von Tirpitz. German Federal Archives.

In mid-1943, the Allies decided to seek a permanent solution to the *Tirpitz* problem. If *Tirpitz* would not emerge to be destroyed, then the Allies would take the war to Norway. The first attack on *Tirpitz* involved miniature submarines, and successfully disabled *Tirpitz* for a few months. Six major air attacks later, the British turned to the Royal Air Force, which started using five-ton "tallboy" bombs delivered by Lancaster bombers to attack *Tirpitz*. The first such attack crippled *Tirpitz* and ended her career as a useful major unit. Subsequent attacks did further damage, and on November 12 *Tirpitz* was hit by three tall-boys during Operation Catechism. Despite the presence of sandbars intended to keep her upright, she capsized and sank with a thousand men. After the war, *Tirpitz* was scrapped over the course of nine years.

Although *Gneisenau* and some other major German units survived, *Tirpitz* represented the last real Atlantic threat faced by the Allies. She also represented the end of an epoch of German naval design.

German Empire could have found a better use of resources than the construction of the High Seas Fleet. However, in World War II the surface fleet of the Kriegsmarine served a real purpose, even as most of its ships found their way to the bottom. Battleships like *Tirpitz* and *Scharnhorst* helped draw off tremendous Royal Navy (and eventually US Navy) resources from the Mediterranean and the Pacific, giving Germany's Axis partners a chance to make an impact. This wasn't the intended role of the Kriegsmarine, but it was important.

After *Tirpitz* was permanently disabled in 1944, the British could have simply left her alone, applying the Lancasters to other areas of war. Had she survived the final days of the conflict, which saw the scuttling of much of the Kriegsmarine, she might eventually have found her way to Bikini Atoll to witness the early atomic bomb tests. Alternatively, she might have ended up in Russian hands, where she undoubtedly would have served for a very long time in the Red Banner Northern Fleet.

Author's Note

The German fixation with a powerful surface fleet arguably proved its undoing in the two World Wars. Surely, in World War I the

Related Entries:

Contemporary of... USS *Washington*
Preceded by... *Scharnhorst*
Meant to fight... HMS *Prince of Wales*

Jean Bart

Laid Down: 1936
Launched: 1940
Completed: 1952
Displacement: 38,000 tons
Main Armament: eight 15" guns (two quadruple turrets)
Secondary Armament: nine 6" guns (three triple turrets)
Speed: 32 knots
Treaty: London Naval Treaty
Major Engagements: Battle of Casablanca, Suez Crisis
Fate: Scrapped, 1969

The Marine Nationale followed up *Dunkerque* and *Strasbourg* with the *Richelieu* class. Although fine ships, the *Dunkerques* could not compete with the latest heavy battleships emerging from Germany and Italy. *Richelieu* and her sister, *Jean Bart*, represented the Marine Nationale's first truly competitive battleship design since the ill-fated *Dantons*. Essentially, the *Richelieus* were enlarged *Dunkerques*, with heavier armament and better armor. Like the *Dunkerques* and the British *King George V* class, their main armament was disposed of in quadruple turrets. This allowed them to combine very heavy armor with very high speed, almost certainly rendering them superior to their Italian, German, and British contemporaries. Apart from the *South Dakotas*, they would probably have been the most powerful battleships built under the London Naval Treaty restrictions.

The name *Jean Bart* is one of the most common in French naval history. The original Jean Bart was a privateer of Flemish descent from Dunkirk, who served in several conflicts in the seventeenth century. He has given his name to over two dozen French warships, including the Marine Nationale's first dreadnought, a battleship of the *Courbet* class.

As was the case in 1914, the onset of war played havoc with French naval construction. Neither *Richelieu* nor *Jean Bart* were ready when France fell to German forces in June, 1940. The almost complete *Richelieu* escaped to Dakar, enduring a series of confrontations with the Royal Navy before eventually departing for New York. *Jean Bart*, however, was not nearly as complete in 1940. Escaping a German bombing raid under her own power, *Jean Bart* made it to Casablanca shortly before the French surrender. Since the French authorities in Casablanca had no facilities with which to complete the ship, *Jean Bart* remained moored for the next two years. Both *Richelieu* and *Jean Bart* were fortunate to avoid the twin disasters of Mers El Kebir and Toulon, where the bulk of the Marine Nationale either fell to British shellfire or scuttled itself.

In November 1942, the United States and the United Kingdom invaded French North Africa as part of Operation Torch. The USN was tasked with landings near Casablanca, which needed to contend with the remaining French naval presence. To match the incom-

Jean Bart in 1955. French Navy photo.

plete *Jean Bart*, the Americans detailed the new battleship USS *Massachusetts*. To the surprise of the Americans, *Jean Bart* was ready to play; she exchange fire with *Massachusetts* twice, taking severe damage from the USN ship but remaining afloat. Following the successful American invasion, *Jean Bart* was turned over to Free French authorities.

The Allies floated several schemes for completing and modernizing *Jean Bart*, but none of these seemed likely to come to fruition in time to have an impact on the war. Consequently, *Jean Bart* remained in Casablanca until the end of the war, still in her damaged, incomplete condition. After the war she was returned to France, with her future uncertain. One proposal involved reconstructing the ship as an aircraft carrier, but the Marine Nationale found it cheaper to purchase off-the-shelf carriers than to build their own. Eventually, the French government decided to complete *Jean Bart* as a battleship, despite the utter lack of any potential enemy battleships. *Jean Bart* re-entered service gradually between 1949 and 1952, the last battleship to be commissioned by any navy in the world.

Jean Bart's purpose now was clearly not to defeat enemy fast battleships, but rather to supply shore bombardment and demonstrate French power and prestige. *Jean Bart* participated in the 1956 Suez conflict, although only one of her main turrets was serviceable, and she only fired a handful of shells. After Suez she became a gunnery training ship. Later proposals for modification included turning *Jean Bart* into a guided missile ship, but none seemed cost-effective. The battleships was decommissioned in 1968, and scrapped in 1970. Save for *Yavuz Selim*, she was the last dreadnought battleship owned by any European navy.

Author's Note

Jean Bart owed her long life, in large part, to French conceptions of national prestige. Having one of the last existing battleships played to particularly Gallic ideas of national greatness. The decision to complete her made little sense, especially given the obvious presence of her sister, *Richelieu*. While it's possible to imagine scenarios in which France could have used a battleship (contributions such as *Jean Bart* made in the Suez Crisis), it's much more difficult to envision how the Marine Nationale could have required a pair of battleships in serviceable condition.

Related Entries:

Contemporary of...*Littorio*
Inspired by... *Strasbourg*
Fought against... USS *Massachusetts*

HMS Prince of Wales

Laid Down: 1937

Launched: 1939

Completed: March, 1941

Displacement: 43,000 tons

Main Armament: ten 14" guns (two quadruple, 1 twin turrets)

Secondary Armament: sixteen 5.25" guns (twin turrets)

Speed: 28 knots

Major Actions: Denmark Straits, Malaya

Treaty: London Naval Treaty

Fate: Sunk by Japanese aircraft, December 10, 1941

Battleships are generally best known by their guns, and for good reason. A ship carrying eight 16" guns may have the same weight of broadside as one carrying twelve 14" guns, but the larger guns have a longer range and more penetrating power than the smaller weapons. Increasing gun sizes during and after World War I, therefore, were a matter of considerable attention. The best British battleships carried 15" guns, as did the most advanced German vessels. American and Japanese ships carried 14" guns. Near the end of the war, both the Americans and Japanese laid down ships with 16" guns. After the war, the Royal Navy planned to trump the IJN and the USN by arming a new class of battleships with 18" guns.

The Washington Naval Treaty of 1922 ended that dream, and limited guns to 16". For the Second London Naval Treaty, the financially constrained British wanted to limit the size and expense of the new battleships as much as possible. Accordingly, the British proposed that all new battleships would be limited to 14" guns. In a bout of wishful thinking, the Royal Navy designed its newest class of battleships around the 14" weapon. The 1936 London Naval Treaty established a 14" limit, but contained a clause that lifted the limit to 16" if any one of the original signatories did not sign. Japan opted out of the treaty (and began building battleships with 18" guns), and the United States took advantage of this clause by designing its new ships to carry the 16" gun.

This left the Royal Navy at a disadvantage. The naval architects tried to solve the problem by equipping the new class of warships with twelve 14" guns in three quadruple turrets. Unfortunately, this led to a top-heavy design, and the "B" turret on the design had to be reduced to a twin. Thus, while the new American battleships carried nine 16" guns

HMS Prince of Wales in 1941.

Winston Churchill at Atlantic Conference, onboard HMS Prince of Wales, August 1941.

and the new Japanese ships nine 18" guns, the British ships carried only ten 14" guns. Moreover, the complexity of the quadruple turrets created problems in several early engagements, with fire slowing because of faulty mechanisms and overcrowding.

The *King George V* class had other design flaws, including a very poor turning circle, and relatively short range. Their armor scheme was uneven, with areas of heavy protection (main belt) alternating with relatively light protection to the superstructure and main turrets. Their underwater protection was similarly uneven, although probably better than that of the Italian *Littorios*. All in all, these were effective but not excellent ships, which is surprising given the experience of the Royal Navy and the quality of RN naval architecture at the end of World War I.

Prince of Wales, third ship of the class,

entered service in early 1941. While still under construction, she suffered a bomb hit that led to severe flooding. Her commissioning was hurried due to the threat posed by the German battleships *Bismarck* and *Tirpitz*. When *Bismarck* and *Prinz Eugen* broke for the Atlantic, *Prince of Wales* was put to sea before fully working out in trials, with civilian engineers remaining on the ship. *Prince of Wales* accompanied *Hood*, constituting a fast squadron with the best chance of catching and destroying the Germans. The two battleships, accompanied by several destroyers, steamed north in an attempt to intercept the German task force in the Denmark Straits.

Hood and *Prince of Wales* successfully made contact, and the battle was joined on the night of May 24, 1941. *Hood* was struck by a salvo from the *Bismarck* and promptly exploded and sank. *Prince of Wales*, although still fac-

HMS Prince of Wales and HMS Repulse under attack from Japanese aircraft, December 10, 1941.

ing some teething troubles, gave a good account of herself against the German battleship. Although she suffered seven hits (plus several dud shots), she managed to hit *Bismarck* three times, causing a fuel leak and limiting *Bismarck*'s speed. Her main armament no longer operative, *Prince of Wales* broke off the action and began to shadow *Bismarck*. Because of low fuel, however, *Prince of Wales* was forced to withdraw from the chase, and played no role in the final destruction of German battleship.

After six weeks of repairs, *Prince of Wales* transported Winston Churchill to Newfoundland, where he met with Franklin Roosevelt and helped hammer out the naval strategy of the Western Allies. In October, *Prince of Wales* was dispatched to Singapore in order to counter the increasing Japanese threat to British possessions. She and the battlecruiser *Repulse* formed the nucleus of the British Far Eastern Fleet.

The Japanese were well aware of their presence, and of the threat that *Prince of Wales* and *Repulse* posed to Japan's offensive plans. They detailed the battlecruisers *Kongo* and *Haruna* (the former itself built in a British yard) to meet the two Royal Navy ships and protect the invasion fleets.

There was no need. Admiral Tom Phillips did not believe that Pearl Harbor conclusively demonstrated the lethality of air power against battleships. The Pearl Harbor attack was a surprise; the American ships were at anchor and could not maneuver. Unspoken, perhaps, was the belief that while American ships might be vulnerable to such attacks, British ships certainly were not. On December 8, Admiral Phillips sortied his two ships in an effort to intercept and destroy the Japanese task forces attacking Malaya.

On December 10, *Prince of Wales* and *Repulse* were caught in the open sea by 87 Japanese aircraft. *Repulse* suffered five torpedo hits, *Prince of Wales* four. Both ships sank, although most of the crews of each were saved. The attacking Japanese planes behaved, by all accounts, in an exceptionally honorable manner. They made no effort to attack British destroyers during rescue operations, and it is held that the Japanese squadron leader flew low and waggled his wings above the surviving British ships as *Prince of Wales* sank. Admiral Phillips gallantly decided to go down with the ship. Winston Churchill felt that the destruction of *Prince of Wales* and *Repulse* was a greater blow to Allied seapower than the Pearl Harbor attack. Certainly, it demonstrated that battleships could not hope to survive without support from aircraft, either from carriers or land bases.

Author's Note

We can overstate criticism of the *King George V* class; they were good ships, competitive with their foreign contemporaries, and clearly superior to the leftovers from World War I. At the same time, they were a bit disappointing, especially from a navy with the most battleship experience in the world.

Prince of Wales could have made an important contribution in the Pacific, had Phillips not put her in an impossible situation. The Japanese *Kongos* were excellent ships, but no match for a modern battleship. The Japanese might have approached the conquest of Southeast Asia with considerably more caution if they still had a pair of fast battleships to contend against. *Prince of Wales* was the only modern battleship lost by the Allies during the war.

Related Entries:

Served alongside... HMS *Hood*
Contemporary of... USS *Massachusetts*
Meant to fight... HIJMS *Kongo*

HIJMS Yamato

Laid Down: 1937

Launched: 1940

Completed: December, 1941

Displacement: 65,000 tons

Main Armament: nine 18.1" guns (three triple turrets)

Secondary Armament: twelve 6.1" guns (four triple turrets)

Speed: 27 knots

Treaty: Post–London Naval Treaty

Major Engagements: Midway, Philippine Sea, Leyte Gulf, Okinawa

Fate: Sunk April 7, 1945 by US carrier aircraft

Japan withdrew from the London Naval Treaty in 1936. The chief Japanese negotiator, Admiral Isoruku Yamamoto, feared that concessions on the part of his negotiating team would lead directly to their assassination upon return to Japan. Japanese nationalists believed that the Washington Naval Treaty system was holding Japan back and preventing it from becoming a first-rate power. Freed from the constraints of international treaties, Japan could build a world-beating fleet that would push the Western powers out of Asia and help usher in a new era of Japanese dominance. The partisans of this position didn't call their organization "Project for a New Japanese Century," but they might as well have.

Yamato was the first of a new generation of

HIJMS Yamato under construction.

battleships. The IJN believed that the United States would never build battleships too large to move through the Panama Canal, and calculated that the maximum displacement of such ships would amount to about 60,000 tons. Ships of that size could not, it was thought, carry guns larger than 16". The IJN's engineering problem was thus to design and build battleships that could destroy the largest ships the Americans were likely to build. These ships were to have a speed of at least 30 knots, carry 18" or larger guns, and have a long range with good fuel economy. With three triple 18.1" gun turrets, *Yamato* met one of the three conditions. A well-armored 31 knot version was rejected as too large, and the IJN unwisely decided to sacrifice speed for armor. As it was, her armor weighed more than an entire World War I dreadnought, and could absorb enormous damage.

Yamato was initially designed with diesel engines for economical cruising, but problems with the diesels led to the use of a standard, fuel-intensive power plant. *Yamato* was an immensely powerful ship, but the Japanese sacrificed operational mobility for surface tactical effectiveness. Four more ships of the class were ordered, but only *Musashi* was completed as intended. *Shinano*, the third sister, was completed as an aircraft carrier support vessel.

Upon completion *Yamato* became the flagship of the Combined Fleet, a designation she held until replaced by *Musashi* in 1943. Admiral Yamamoto sat on *Yamato*'s bridge as the USN destroyed four of his carriers at the Battle of Midway. Because of her speed and enormous fuel requirements, the IJN did not use *Yamato* in the Guadalcanal campaign. While Japanese reticence in the context of oil shortages is understandable, her presence might well have changed the character of several of the engagements of Savo Island. This was not a time at which the IJN should have emphasized fuel economy. *Yamato* withdrew from the Central Pacific with the rest of the fleet as American carrier groups launched ever more devastating attacks on Japanese bases.

Yamato was present at both the battles of Philippine Sea and Leyte Gulf. At the latter she, *Musashi*, *Nagato*, *Kongo*, and *Haruna* served as the core of Admiral Kurita's strike force. Although American battleships were successfully decoyed away, the Japanese attack on US transports and escort carriers was foiled by the extraordinary courage of a few American destroyer captains. *Musashi* sank under the weight of nearly 30 bombs and 20 torpedoes, demonstrating that unsinkable super-battleships could, indeed, be sunk. After the battle *Yamato* withdrew to Japan, where she rode out several air attacks.

By April 1945 the Imperial Japanese Navy was largely spent. In response to the invasion of Okinawa, the Army guaranteed that it would devastate the American fleet with kamikaze attacks on unprecedented scale. Upon being informed of this, the Emperor asked "And what of the Navy?" This set in motion a plan under which most of the remainder of the IJN, including *Yamato*, a light cruiser, and eight destroyers would sail for Okinawa, fight their way through the defending warships and transports, and beach themselves on the island. The crews would then abandon ship and reinforce the Okinawa garrison. Although the IJN was noted for its bravery and loyalty, this plan did not meet universal acclaim. Several admirals and captains thought this a waste not only of their remaining ships but also of the lives of their crewmen. They pointed out that *Yamato*, super-battleship that she was, could not hope to destroy the entire USN. Moreover, the approach to Okinawa would require ten hours of sailing in daylight without air cover. The US carriers would certainly find and destroy the task force before it reached its target. Such concerns were brushed aside.

The task force set sail on April 5, and was detected almost immediately by US submarines and reconnaissance aircraft. Admiral Raymond Spruance initially ordered his battleship squadron to prepare to meet *Yamato*. This squadron included *New Mexico*, *Idaho*, *Tennessee*, *Colorado*, *Maryland*, and *West Virginia*. The American carrier commander, however, had other ideas, and wanted to destroy the Japanese with air strikes. The decision was eventually made to launch the air strikes and rely on the battleships as a backup. This was certainly the correct call. Although the six elderly battleships would almost certainly have been too much for *Yamato* to contend with, it is quite possible that she would have take one or two, along with several thousand American sailors, with her.

The airstrikes began five hours into *Yamato*'s daylight trek. They immediately inflicted heavy damage, and soon sank several of *Yamato*'s escorts. *Yamato* continued at speed, but suffered heavy damage from bombs and torpedoes. She began to list, and her steering failed. The final wave of American torpedo aircraft delivered the coup de grace, and *Yamato* rolled over and sank with nearly 3,000 of her crew. To their eternal dishonor, the American pilots then strafed the Japanese survivors, destroying lifeboats and life-rafts, and interfering in the rescue operations of the remaining escorts. These attacks on shipwrecked sailors also violated all applicable laws of war.

The effort that went into *Yamato*'s construction would better have been spent on aircraft carriers and other ships. Her final journey was a sickening waste; while some of the Japanese admirals realized that the 3,000 men who died on *Yamato* might better have been employed building a new Japan, others did not. When Japan surrendered, the IJN attempted to destroy all photographic and technical data on *Yamato* and her sister, leaving Western analysts guessing as to her exact characteristics well into the Cold War.

Yamato has had an enduring pop culture presence. For American audiences of a certain age, the most evocative depiction of *Yamato* came in the form of the animated television show *Star Blazers*, in which the Earth repurposed the hulk of *Yamato* to fight a series of galactic wars. *Star Blazers* was an edited and redubbed version of the Japanese *Space Battleship Yamato*, which made explicit reference to the lost battleship. In a pointed reference to Japan's wartime experience, the first alien attack comes in the form of a radioactive bombardment that leaves the surface of the earth poisonous and desolate. Most of this escaped the notice of the American audience at the time, however.

Memory of *Yamato* remains alive and well in Japan. Junya Sato directed a relatively successful film on the historical *Yamato* in 2005. In 2010, a live action version of *Space Battleship Yamato* performed very well in Japan, although it didn't enjoy much crossover success in the United States.

In "Fusing Nationalisms in Postwar Japan: The Battleship Yamato and Popular Culture" Shunechi Takekawa studied this issue in some depth. *Yamato* began appearing in Japanese film in the 1950s, and has remained a relatively popular subject for film, television, and manga since the 1970s. Takekawa argues that the stylized memory of *Yamato* provides a space for working out contradictory messages about Japanese nationalism, and about the historical experience of World War II. This goes well beyond a straightforward right-wing interpretation of Japanese nationalism, as the *Yamato* narrative evokes complex and contradictory understandings of the war, some of which even verge into left-wing pacifism.

It perhaps shouldn't be surprising that the colossal *Yamato* has become symbolic of multiple interpretations of Japan's colonial period. Her construction represented a doomed effort to match and exceed the capabilities of the Western powers, and yet her entire career was characterized by dysfunction within the Japanese war machine. The final destruction of *Yamato* evokes a vision of heroic, but also pointless and futile, sacrifice.

The bigger story, perhaps, is the enduring relevance of World War II to the construction of national identity within Asia. Not only the sheer drama, but also the machinery of the Second World War remain key mileposts in how nations define themselves. In this context, it's surely unsurprising that more controversial elements of the legacy of World War II (including the Yakusuni Shrine, which commemorates Japanese war dead, among them acknowledged war criminals) continue to embitter Japan's relations with the rest of Asia.

Author's Note

Over the years, a variety of reports of turned up on the expected successor classes to *Yamato*. The next iteration would have been slightly larger, slightly more heavily armored, and would have carried six 20" guns in three twin turrets, probably with roughly the same speed and range as *Yamato*. Designs for these ships were finalized, but wartime demands meant that they were never laid down. Expectations of a further follow-on class, with a speed above 30 knots and four twin 20" guns, have emerged over the years, although the construction of such ships would have been purely notional.

She was beautiful; she was graceful; she was referred to by her crew as "more beautiful than any woman." The *Yamatos* were the zenith of the Japanese battleship aesthetic, with a beautiful swept back pagoda mast that managed to convey speed, grace, and power. This, undoubtedly, is one of the reasons why *Yamato* has continued to hold a place in the public imagination, even seventy years on.

Related Entries:

Contemporary of... USS *Wisconsin*
Fought alongside... HIJMS *Kongo*
Preceded by... HIJMS *Kaga*

The Battleships That Never Were

The navies of the world constructed dozens of battleships, but planned on many more.

War often disrupted battleship construction plans. To follow up the *Tegethoffs*, the Kaiserliche and Konigliche Kriegsmarine planned the four ship *Monarch* class, 25,000 ton super-dreadnoughts that would have carried ten 14" guns in two twin and two triple turrets. The Germans canceled seven battlecruisers at the end of the war, including a trio of 38,000 ton monsters that would have carried eight 15" guns apiece. The Royal Navy planned three additional "Admiral" class battlecruisers, only to cancel them after Jutland.

World War II had a similar effect. The British *Lion* class, designed to carry nine 16" guns in three triple turrets, would have been a major improvement on the *King George V*s. The United States expected to build the *Montana* class, Yamato-sized ships that would have carried twelve 16" guns in four triple turrets, but canceled them in favor of aircraft carrier construction. The Japanese eventually gave up on the A-150s, a class of warship that carried six 20" guns on a hull slightly larger than *Yamato*. The Germans laid down but eventually canceled a variety of improvements on the *Bismarck* class, while the Soviets held out hope to complete the gigantic *Sovetsky Soyuz*, which would have displaced 60,000 tons and carried nine 16" guns, until 1949.

But the biggest losses of imaginary battleships came just after World War I. The American *South Dakotas*, Japanese *Tosas*, and a group of gigantic British battleships and battlecruisers so terrified the legislators of the world that the Washington Naval Treaty resulted. The *South Dakotas* would have carried twelve 16" guns in four triple turrets. The 50,000 ton "N" class battleships of the Royal Navy would have carried nine 18" guns in three triple turrets.

Fortunately for everyone (except battleship aficionados), none of these ships made it into service.

USS Washington

Laid Down: 1937

Launched: 1938

Completed: May, 1941

Displacement: 35,000 tons

Main Armament: nine 16" guns (three triple turrets)

Secondary Armament: twenty 5" guns (ten twin turrets)

Speed: 28 knots

Treaty: London Naval Treaty

Major Engagements: Second Naval Battle of Guadalcanal, Battle of Philippine Sea, Battle of Leyte Gulf

Fate: Scrapped, 1960

The London Naval Treaty of 1936 was intended to preserve the battleship size limitation at 35,000 tons and to restrict the size of battleship gun size to 14". The United States designed its first generation of London Treaty battleships to carry twelve 14" guns in three quadruple turrets, a formidable armament equal to that of the pre-treaty "Big Five."

However, the London Naval Treaty had an escape clause. If any one of the original three signatories failed to ratify, the gun limitation rose to 16". Japan did not sign the treaty (her representatives would have been assassinated if she had), so the 14" limitation did not apply. The Royal Navy had already begun construction of the 14" weapons for its *King George V* class, and could not alter their design. The design of *North Carolina* and *Washington*, however, allowed the use of either 14" or 16"

USS Washington at sea, September 1945

USS Washington at sea, May 1944

weapons. Accordingly, the Americans quickly substituted the heavier weapons.

USS *Washington* entered service in May 1941. At least nine American warships have borne the name Washington. The first six took their name directly from President George Washington. The last four took their name from the state named for George Washington. Since the founding of the state, two additional ships (a ballistic missile submarine and an aircraft carrier), have taken the name "George Washington," so as to eliminate any confusion.

Washington and her sister, *North Carolina*, were the first American battleships built since 1921. The first plans for the *North Carolina* class envisioned their speed at 23 knots. This was in keeping with the pre-treaty battleships, which the USN expected *North Carolina* and *Washington* to operate with. However, an investigation of foreign battleship designs, as well as exercises that demonstrated the need for battleships to operate with aircraft carriers, pushed designers to a much higher speed. The *North Carolinas* sacrificed some armor protection, but their anti-aircraft armaments were very strong, making them extremely effective as aircraft carrier escorts.

As the first of a new generation of ships, *Washington* suffered from considerable teething troubles, and required an extensive period of trials and training. This kept

Washington in the Atlantic, where she was, incidentally, closer to the war in Europe. It is fortunate that *Washington* and *North Carolina* were not deployed with the Pacific Fleet. Although they would have had a better chance at surviving than the older battleships at Pearl Harbor, their loss or even damage would have been a severe handicap for the US Navy.

Washington deployed to the United Kingdom for service with the Home Fleet in March 1942. *Washington* helped guard convoys to Murmansk, hedging against a sortie from *Tirpitz* or *Scharnhorst*. A confrontation would have favored *Washington*, as her armament and armor were superior to that of *Tirpitz*, and she had much better fire control. That fall, after a refit, she would head to the Pacific for the balance of the war.

In late September Washington was deployed to the Solomon Islands. The battle of Guadalcanal revolved around the control and operation of Henderson Airfield. Japanese forces had been pushed back on the island of Guadalcanal, but still held large parts of the island. Japanese naval units resupplied the Army forces at night, and heavy Japanese units bombarded Henderson Field on a regular basis. The US Navy's job was to prevent this from happening.

On November 13, 1942, *Washington* was deployed, along with the battleship *South*

USS Washington on training cruise, 1946.

Dakota and four destroyers, to intercept a Japanese task force steaming toward Henderson Field. The Japanese fleet included *Kirishima*, one of four *Kongo* class battlecruisers. The USN force was superior on paper, but the Japanese had considerable skill at night-fighting and had better torpedoes. In a confused night action, all four US destroyers were crippled or sunk, and *South Dakota* managed to wander into the searchlights of the Japanese heavy ships. The Japanese lacked radar, however, and didn't notice the approach of *Washington*. *Washington* did exactly what a modern battleship should have done to a thirty-year-old battlecruiser, reducing *Kirishima* to sinking condition in about ten minutes. The rest of the Japanese force retired shortly afterward. *Washington* suffered no damage.

Washington spent most of the rest of the war in convoy escort. Her closest brush with disaster came in February 1944, when she rammed the battleship *Indiana*. *Indiana* received the brunt of the damage, but *Washington* was still forced to retire to Puget Sound Naval Yard for a refit. Later, *Washington* served as an escort at the Battle of Philippine Sea and the Battle of Leyte Gulf. *Washington* also delivered shore bombardment at Iwo Jima and Okinawa.

Washington was taken out of commission in June 1947. The US Navy went through three major cycles of battleship disposal in the twentieth century. The first came in 1922–23, when most of the pre-dreadnoughts and older dreadnoughts were scrapped in accordance with the Washington Naval Treaty. Between 1946 and 1948, all of the pre-war battleships, with the exception of the Big Five and *Mississippi*, were either scrapped or sunk as targets. The last cycle came in the late 1950s, when the Big Five (*Colorado, Maryland, West Virginia, California*, and *Tennessee*) and six of the ten fast battleships were disposed of, either through scrapping or through donation. *Alabama, Massachusetts*, and *North Carolina* were all adopted by their respective states. *Washington* was not, and went to the scrapyard.

Author's Note

The existence of the large reserve fleet in the Puget Sound probably sealed *Washington's* fate. What was the point of keeping *Washington* around when several other battleships remained in reserve? There's little question, however, that USS *Washington* would now make a splendid memorial along the waterfront in Tacoma or Seattle.

Washington's wartime service was exemplary. Had the USN pursued its original plan of keeping the ships at 23 knots, they would have had little influence over the Pacific War. Their relatively light armor notwithstanding, *Washington* and her sister were excellent ships, comparing favorably with those foreign contemporaries that remained restricted by the naval treaty system.

Related Entries:

Preceded…USS *Massachusetts*
Contemporary of… HMS *Prince of Wales*
Served alongside… USS *Wisconsin*

Battleship Movies

Battleships have never provided the same degree of cinematic grist as submarines. The scale of shooting battleship combat pushes budgets well beyond the breaking point, and the massive crews reduce interpersonal intimacy, making individual heroism more difficult to depict. Still, over the years many directors have tried to put battleships on celluloid.

In the aftermath of World War I, the British film industry produced several excellent documentaries on the naval war. By general acclaim, the *Battles of Coronel and the Falkland Islands* is the best of these, depicting the Royal Navy's hunt for the squadron of Graf von Spee. Although often listed as a documentary, the film consists mostly of footage shot in the post-war period, and thus really represents more of a lightly fictionalized representation of the battles.

Sergei Eisenstein's *Battleship Potemkin* will likely remain the finest film to ever feature a battleship, even if Eisenstein's interests ran more to the revolution than to the ship itself. The *Potemkin* herself had been scrapped by the time filming began, so *Dvenadstat Apostolov* served in her place. The most memorable sequence from the film, a fictional massacre on the Odessa Steps, happens well away from the battleship.

Sink the Bismarck (1960) is often regarded as the best battleship film to concentrate on the ship itself. HMS *Vanguard*, nearing retirement, stood in for *Bismarck*, *Hood*, and *King George* V, while a few ships involved in the actual hunt for *Bismarck* played themselves (although generally not in original configuration). The film fictionalizes the personalities associated with the search, but generally remains true enough to real life to sufficiently represent the technical and strategic problems on both sides.

The best film about Pearl Harbor is undoubtedly *Tora Tora Tora* (1970). Tantalizingly, producers initially hoped that legendary director Akira Kurosama would direct the Japanese scenes, with David Lean directing the American. Lean never materialized, and Kurosawa withdrew from the project after a series of disputes with the studio. Very little of Kurosawa's footage remained in the film; long shots of Admiral Yamamoto walking along the decks of HIJMS *Nagato* eventually found their way onto the cutting room floor. Nevertheless, the finished film is capably done and altogether entertaining.

By contrast, Michael Bay's *Pearl Harbor* (2001) was terrible in every way that it is possible for a movie to be terrible. The story revolved around anything but the actual Japanese attack, the visuals of the attack were unimpressive, and none of characters were interesting. The only halfway compelling moment involved the capsize of *Oklahoma*, but the film is such a mess that it's hard to enjoy even the small moments.

Under Siege (1992) appeared when studios struggled to imagine *Die Hard* in every possible locale, from a plane, to a train, to a ship. The plot revolves around a group of extortionists seizing control of the USS *Missouri* (on her way to deactivation), and threatening to fire a cruise missile at Honolulu. Steven Segal saves the day, ending the plot with a memorable knife fight against Tommy Lee Jones.

Filmmakers revisited USS Missouri in Peter Berg's pathetic *Battleship* (2012), with a story that involved restoring *Missouri* in order to fight alien invaders. Plot aside, the film bore little resemblance to the much stronger *Space Battleship Yamato*. The only real upsides were a few clever sight gags based on the board game.

I discuss *Space Battleship Yamato* at length on the entry on that ship. The live action *Yamato* (2005) depicts the last mission of the battleship, using a combination of expensive and faithful reproductions of the ship with some models and computer generated imagery. The film doesn't break any new ground dramatically or stylistically, but fans of battleship footage should appreciate it.

USS Massachusetts

Laid Down: 1939
Launched: 1941
Completed: May, 1942
Reconstruction: None
Displacement: 35,000 tons
Main Armament: nine 16" guns, three triple turrets
Secondary Armament: twenty 5" guns (dual purpose twin turrets)
Speed: 28 knots
Major Actions: Casablanca, Leyte Gulf, Okinawa
Treaty: Washington Naval Treaty
Fate: Preserved as museum, 1962

The United States Navy followed up the two battleships of the *North Carolina* class with the four *South Dakotas*. Initial plans for the *South Dakotas* had called for a reduction in speed from the 27 knots of *North Carolina* to 23, which would allow them to operate with the older ships of the battle line. However, it soon became apparent that most new foreign battleships had speeds in excess of 27 knots. The designers decided to increase the speed of the *South Dakotas*, while at the same time keeping the improved protection that had been worked into the design.

The resulting ships were quite powerful, but not completely satisfactory. The *South Dakotas* were more heavily armored than the *North Carolinas* on a slightly smaller hull, but at the expense of weaker underwater protection and a cramped engineering section. Nevertheless, the *South Dakotas* were extremely effective ships, the only ships to fulfill the Washington Naval Treaty requirements while carrying 16" guns, having protection against 16" shells, and enjoying a speed of 27+ knots. They also had a large and effective anti-aircraft armament.

Third of the class, USS *Massachusetts*

USS Massachusetts at Ulithi Anchorage, November 1944

USS *Massachusetts, early in World War II. USN photo*

commissioned in 1942, and five months later joined Operation Torch, the US invasion of French North Africa. Although both British and American planners hoped that French resistance to the invasion would be minimal, a major French naval presence at Casablanca threatened to disrupt the operation. The French squadron at Casablanca included several large destroyers and *Jean Bart*, an incomplete but operational battleship that had escaped just prior to the Nazi conquest of France. *Massachusetts* and several escorts were detailed to subdue this force. On November 8, while supporting landings near Casablanca, *Massachusetts* came under fire from *Jean Bart*. *Massachusetts* replied, silencing *Jean Bart* with five hits. *Massachusetts* and her escorts then opened fire on and sank a pair of destroyers. French shore batteries inflicted superficial damage on *Massachusetts*, the scars of which are still evident on her decks today. Thus, *Massachusetts* had the first honor of surface combat against battleships of any American dreadnought, beating out USS *South Dakota* and USS *Washington* by six days.

With the French subdued and the threats from the German and Italian fleets in decline, USS *Massachusetts* was dispatched to the Pacific, arriving in March 1943. The rest of her career would be consumed with carrier escort, convoy escort, and shore bombardment. At the Battle of Leyte Gulf, *Massachusetts* was part of the force that narrowly missed engaging Kurita's battleships off Samar Island. She and the carriers she escorted operated against Formosa, Kwajelein, Iwo Jima, Okinawa, and mainland Japan in 1944 and 1945. Her final mission was against an industrial complex at Hamamatsu on August 9, 1945, and many believe that the last 16" shell fired in anger in World War II came from *Massachusetts*.

USS *Massachusetts* returned to the States, and decommissioned in 1947. She would remain in reserve for fifteen years. Because of the cramped conditions of the *South Dakotas*, the Navy preferred to use *Washington* and *North Carolina* as training vessels. Their slow speed relative to the *Iowas* precluded their reactivation for the Korean War. In the late 1950s, the USN began disposing of its remaining slow battleships, first the "Big Five," then

USS Massachusetts at Battleship Cove. USN photo Don S. Montgomery.

the *South Dakotas* and the *North Carolinas*. Fortunately, a group of veterans from the Bay State put together a campaign to raise the money to save USS *Massachusetts* and convert her into a memorial. She was berthed at Battleship Cove in Fall River, Massachusetts in 1965, and remains there today.

Author's Note

USS *Massachusetts* is the first battleship I ever visited. *Massachusetts* is positioned beautifully at Battleship Cove, along with several other warships, and remains in excellent condition. (Her sister, USS *Alabama*, has been preserved at Mobile Bay.) Other ships on display at Battleship Cove include USS *Joseph P.* *Kennedy*, USS *Lionfish*, the former East German corvette *Hiddensee*, and a pair of PT boats.

The *South Dakotas* were classic interim ships, but the naval architects achieved remarkable things while remaining within the constraints of the Washington Naval Treaty. For my money, the single funnel *SoDaks* are more beautiful vessels than the *North Carolinas*.

Related Entries:

Fought against... *Jean Bart*
Preceded... USS *Wisconsin*
Contemporary of... *Tirpitz*

USS Wisconsin

Laid Down: 1941

Launched: 1943

Completed: April, 1944

Displacement: 45,000 tons

Main Armament: nine 16" guns (three triple turrets)

Secondary Armament: twenty 5" guns (ten twin turrets)

Speed: 33 knots

Treaty: Post–London Naval Treaty

Major Engagements: Final raids on Japan, Gulf War

Fate: Memorial, Norfolk, Virginia

The *North Carolina* and *South Dakota* class battleships were designed with the limits of the Washington Naval Treaty in mind. Although much more could be accomplished in 1938 with 35,000 tons than in 1921, sacrifices still had to be made. As had been practice in the first round of battleship construction, US Naval architects accepted a low speed in return for heavy armor and armament. Consequently, both the *South Dakotas* and the

North Carolinas had speeds a knot or two slower than most foreign contemporaries. The *Montanas*, and the final battleship design authorized by the USN, would also have had a 28 knot maximum speed. In any case, Japan's failure to ratify the 1936 London Naval Treaty bumped the maximum standard tonnage from 35,000 to 45,000, giving the designers some extra space to work with. The result was the *Iowa* class, the most powerful and best-designed battleships ever built.

USS *Wisconsin*, last laid down but third completed of the *Iowa* class, carried a slightly heavier main armament than the *South Dakotas*, and could make five extra knots. The *Iowas* were the first USN battleships to make speed a primary value, and achieved the speed through a longer hull and more powerful machinery. Indeed, the *Iowas* are the fastest battleships ever built, outpacing even the Italian *Littorios* by a knot or two. While no *Iowa* ever recorded a speed higher than 31 knots, rumors over the years suggested that the battleships might be able to make 35 knots over short distances. Part of the rationale for building the *Iowas* was to have ships capable of chasing down and destroying the Japanese *Kongo* class battlecruisers, themselves built in

USS Wisconsin operating off Korea, 1952

1913, but the USN also wanted to ensure that it had battleships capable of keeping up with the *Essex* class carriers.

Wisconsin's guns were also a step up from previous classes. The 16"/50 cal could fire a heavier shell, at a longer range, and with more penetrating power than the guns carried by the *South Dakota* class. Indeed, while the 18.1" guns of HIJMS *Yamato* launched a heavier shell, the 16"/50s have more penetrating power and can be fired at a slightly faster rate. On the downside, *Wisconsin's* great length and narrow beam (necessary for transit through the Panama Canal) made her a mediocre seaboat in heavy oceans, and probably would have left her vulnerable to underwater attack.

USS *Wisconsin* entered service in April 1944 and joined Bull Halsey's Third Fleet in December. *Wisconsin's* primary mission was aircraft carrier escort, although she participated in the bombardment of Okinawa in 1945. After the destruction of what was left of the IJN and the Japanese air force, *Wisconsin* bombarded Japan directly. After Operation Magic Carpet and some occupation related activities, *Wisconsin* retired to the United States and was employed as a training ship.

In 1948 *Wisconsin* was mothballed, only to be brought back to service two years later for the Korean conflict. For two years she carried out shore bombardment missions along the Korean peninsula. After the war, *Wisconsin* again served as a training ship. In 1956 she collided with the destroyer *Eaton*, necessitating bow-replacement surgery that transplanted the bow of the incomplete battleship *Kentucky* to *Wisconsin*. In 1958 she went back into reserve.

Various proposals were floated for reactivating the *Iowas* over the next twenty-five years. *New Jersey* returned to service in 1968 to bombard North Vietnam, but was soon sent back to mothballs. Some proposals in the late 1970s envisioned the replacement of the aft turret with a flight deck capable of operating helicopters and VSTOL aircraft, but these

were rejected because of high cost. At the beginning of the Reagan administration, however, funds began to flow more freely, and plans were hatched to reactivate the four remaining battleships. That the Soviets were putting into service the *Kirov* class battlecruisers, the largest surface combatants in the world, helped the battleship advocates make their case. *Wisconsin* returned to service in October 1988 with four fewer 5" guns, but with mounts for Harpoon and Tomahawk cruise missiles, as well as Phalanx point-defense guns and Stinger short-range surface-to-air missiles. *Wisconsin's* aircraft were replaced with a helipad, and she was given the capability to launch and recover unmanned drones. In 1990 *Wisconsin* deployed as part of Operation Desert Shield, and in January contributed to the air offensive against Iraq with several salvos of Tomahawk missiles. When the ground invasion began, *Wisconsin* and her sister *Missouri* began bombarding Iraqi positions with 16" and 5" guns. *Missouri* narrowly avoided an Iraqi anti-ship missile when HMS *Gloucester* shot the missile down. The last bombardment of the war was made by USS *Wisconsin*, shortly prior to the cessation of hostilities.

With the Cold War over, *Wisconsin* decommissioned in September, 1991. She and her sister *Iowa* remained on the Naval List until early 2006. The viability of returning the ships to service was debated for much of the 1990s and early 2000s. The Marine Corps argued that the battleships were necessary for the provision of amphibious gunfire support, and was skeptical that the Advanced Gun System (AGS) to be installed upon the Zumwalt class destroyer would perform the role adequately.

Even at the turn of the twenty-first century, *Wisconsin* remained a formidable platform. As naval architecture since the end of World War II turned decisively away from the armored ship and the concept of survivability, a good case could be made that anti-ship mis-

USS Wisconsin in final configuration, 1988-1991

siles would struggle to penetrate the armor of *Wisconsin* and her sisters. The torpedo remained a threat, however, and the narrow beam of the *Iowa* class always lent credence to concerns about underwater attack. The costs of restoring *Wisconsin* to service and maintaining her would have been prohibitive. Her Tomahawk launchers were obsolete (Tomahawks are now launched through a Vertical Launch System), and the rest of her systems (even those installed in the 1980s) had grown old. The Navy hated the idea of returning the battleships to service because of the high cost and immense crew requirements.

From 1996 Wisconsin sat in Norfolk in a nether world, her upper parts open to visitors while her interior was closed in anticipation of reactivation. She was stricken from the Navy List in 2006, and finally in 2009 donated to the city as a memorial. In 2012, Republican Presidential candidate Mitt Romney (who had made naval construction a key plank of his campaign, and who had identified both Virginia and Wisconsin as electoral battlegrounds), announced that his running mate would be Representative Paul Ryan (R-Wisconsin) from the decks of USS Wisconsin.

Battleships, in the end, are simply a delivery system for ordnance. When other platforms became capable of delivering ordnance more efficiently, the battleship began to disappear. The Navy plans to fill its shore gunfire responsibilities with the new Zumwalt class (DDG-1000) stealth destroyers, which displace about 14,000 tons and carry a modern, long range, high accuracy 6" gun. The Navy expects to commission three Zumwalts, although in the future other ships may use the advanced gun system.

Author's Note

I have had the opportunity to visit Wisconsin several times in Norfolk. The first time, I stumbled upon the battleship by accident; I left a Japanese garden, and suddenly here sat an Iowa class battleship! She remains in excellent condition, reputedly the best of the four Iowas (although she did suffer an electrical fire in the 1960s). No doubt because of a local community which has deep, long-term ties to the Navy, the memorial seems well-staffed and serves a constant stream of visitors.

All of the late American battleship designs combined a grim practicality with a streamlined aesthetic. Because of their length and narrow lines, the Iowas were the pinnacle of the effort. They are truly beautiful ships, and it is fortunate that all four are now on display. Wisconsin resides in Norfolk, New Jersey in Camden, Iowa in Los Angeles, and Missouri at Pearl Harbor. We might have hoped that a more diverse set of battleships would have survived (Maryland or California would have been treasures), but we can't complain overmuch about what we have today.

Related Entries:

Contemporary of... HMS Vanguard
Inspired by... HIJMS Kongo
Served alongside... USS Massachusetts

HMS Vanguard

Laid Down: 1941
Launched: 1944
Completed: May, 1946
Displacement: 44,500 tons
Main Armament: eight 15" guns (four twin turrets)
Secondary Armament: sixteen 5.25" guns (eight twin turrets)
Speed: 30 knots
Major Actions: None
Treaty: Post–London Naval Treaty
Fate: Scrapped, 1960

One of Jacky Fisher's goofier schemes involved the Pomeranian Landings, a scheme to operate in the Baltic and support landings on the German coast. To this end, Fisher championed construction of a group of three "light cruisers" armed with heavy guns, designed to provide heavy gunfire support in the shallow Baltic. HMS *Courageous* and HMS *Glorious* would each carry four 15" guns in two twin turrets, while HMS *Furious* was expected to carry two 18" guns in single turrets. Neither the ships nor the operation proved practical, and after the war the Royal Navy converted all three ships to aircraft carriers.

This left four twin 15" turrets lying about, guns which couldn't be used on new ships because of the Washington Naval Treaty. Gun turrets are among the most expensive and difficult-to-construct parts of a battleship, so they were retained in the hope of future use.

The Royal Navy intended to follow up the *King George* V class with the *Lions*, which would have been the apogee of British battleship design. A class of six, they would have displaced 43,000 tons and carried nine 16" guns in three triple turrets. The *Lions* would have carried heavier armor than the US *Iowas*, but they could only have made 28 knots. But the war intervened, and the Admiralty determined

HMS Vanguard in 1947.

that smaller ships should take precedence.

However, the availability of the four 15"
turrets meant that a seventh *King George V*
class ship, *Vanguard*, could be completed
more quickly than the *Lions*. Intended for use
in the Pacific, the ship would be fast enough to
catch and powerful enough to destroy the
Japanese *Kongo* class battlecruisers. The
design went through several evolutions (at one
point the Royal Navy declared that the ship
would be a replacement for HMS *Royal Oak*,
sunk by *U-47* in 1939) before the keel was
finally laid in 1941. Work proceeded slowly,
and *Vanguard* was not finally completed until
late 1946. She was the last battleship ever
launched, although not the last one completed.
Only *Iowa* and *Yamato* were larger, but numerous battleships carried a more heavy armament. *Vanguard* was well-armored and an
excellent seaboat, but because of her light
main battery she likely would have fared poorly against the other super-fast battleships. In
pictures, her great size dwarfs the 15" turrets
that she carries.

Completed after the war, *Vanguard* didn't
see much action. In 1947 she carried King
George VI, Queen Elizabeth, and a young
Princess Elizabeth on a royal visit to South
Africa. *Vanguard* was placed in reserve in
1956. After efforts to preserve her as a museum failed she was scrapped in 1960.

Author's Note

The United Kingdom has never had a strong
policy with respect to the preservation of ships,
and the Royal Navy has done a poor job of
grappling with its own decline. The scrapping
of HMS *Warspite* was a tragedy for historians
and antiquarians. In this context, the existence
of preservationist sentiments with respect to
Vanguard is surely interesting. Even among
the battleships that survived immediate postwar austerity, *King George V* and *Duke of York*
(which had played key roles in the destruction
of *Bismarck* and *Scharnhorst*, respectively),
surely had a better case for preservation.

Vanguard was a curiosity, but she would
likely have been effective in her role if she'd
been completed in reasonable time. Though
she was not comparable to her contemporaries
of modern design and armament, she was a
beautiful ship, and well worthy of service to
the Royal Family.

Related Entries:

Contemporary of... USS *Wisconsin*
Preceded by... HMS *Prince of Wales*
Meant to fight... HIJMS *Kongo*

Interlude

Pearl Harbor

The Setting

The stage for US–Japanese naval competition was set early in the twentieth century, when the two countries began competing for empire in the Pacific, and for access to China. The Japanese defeat of Russia at Tsushima effectively eliminated one major Pacific naval player, and the Royal Navy decided to concentrate its interwar efforts on the Atlantic and the Mediterranean.

This left the IJN and the USN, two navies that had taken their own innovative paths to battleship design. The Japanese believed that tactical and operational mobility would carry the day, as faster battleships could fight under conditions of their own choosing, and could bring their weapons more effectively to bear against slower-moving targets. The Japanese also appreciated their materiel deficit, which they attempted to remedy through maximizing the effectiveness of each unit. This left Japan with a force of fast battleships and battlecruisers that could offer battle anywhere in the Pacific, even if the naval architects sometimes attempted too much.

The Americans, on the other hand, believed that battleships would fight most effectively as a single unit, and designed their battlefleet around a common conceptual architecture. The "standard type" battleships carried similar weapons, traveled at the same speed, and enjoyed the same basic armor scheme. In battle, the Americans would have relied on armor and concentrated firepower to give them the chance to break apart the Japanese line before it could outmaneuver them.

The Washington Naval Treaty system

Japanese model of Pearl Harbor. Courtesy of the Naval Historical Center.

altered the expectations of both combatants, but had the effect of freezing the two fleets in amber. Instead of building new ships, the Americans and Japanese improved the old, with Japan approaching the project more consistently and conscientiously. Most of the battleships operated by both sides on the eve of World War II had come into service during, or immediately after, the First World War.

The Washington Treaty and its successor, the London Treaty, also left Japan at a numerical disadvantage. The United States kept fifteen battleships, against only nine for Japan. In return, the United States guaranteed that it would not fortify its bases in the Philippines. Because distance tended to reduce the effectiveness of a battlefleet, even a larger US force would struggle to prevail against the IJN in battle. And the demands of defending two oceans meant that the USN would always reserve some of its strength for the Atlantic.

The Ships

In mid-1940, the nine battleships and three carriers of Pacific Fleet deployed from San Diego to Pearl Harbor in response to continuing Japanese expansion. The intention was to deter Japan from aggression against British, Dutch, and Australian assets in Southeast Asia. The nine battleships of the Pacific Fleet were all of the "standard type" and had all entered

service over a period of six years in the 1910s and 1920s. Two of the three carriers (USS *Lexington* and USS *Saratoga*) had begun life as battlecruisers.

The United States planned, under War Plan Orange (Red was for war against the British Empire) to send the US fleet across the Pacific to destroy the IJN before the latter could conquer the Philippines. The Philippines, of course, had been taken from Spain in the Spanish-American War, leading to a brutal insurgency that persisted for decades. Several other Pacific islands had also been seized from Spain, but the Hawaiian Islands themselves had come into US possession via a coup instigated by American landowners against the Hawaiian monarchy.

By 1941 War Plan Orange was largely considered obsolete, given what was expected to be local Japanese superiority in the Western Pacific. Against the battleships of the Pacific Fleet, the IJN could marshal ten of its own battleships, and had the advantages of nearby bases and effective support craft. Japan had reconstructed its battleships more diligently, and had begun re-arming sooner.

Nevertheless, Admiral Isoruku Yamamoto of the Imperial Japanese Navy decided that Japan's war plans would be best served by a surprise attack on Pearl Harbor. The destruction of the Pacific Fleet, he reasoned, would give Japan the opportunity to seize Southeast

US battleships on fire at Pearl Harbor, December 7, 1941. Courtesy of the Naval Historical Center.

US battleships on fire at Pearl Harbor, December 7, 1941. Courtesy of the Atlantic.

Asia and build a defensive cordon in the Pacific before the USN could respond effectively. The imposition of an oil embargo by the Roosevelt administration in August, 1941, narrowed the window in which the IJN could act.

Pearl Harbor was not the first carrier air strike against enemy battleships. In July 1918, HMS *Furious* had undertaken the first carrier strike against an enemy naval base, attacking the Kaiserliche Marine's zeppelin base at Tondern. More recently, twenty-one Swordfish bombers operating from HMS *Illustrious* had attacked the Italian naval installation at Taranto, sinking three battleships (two of which eventually returned to service). The Japanese had vastly greater resources at their disposal than the British.

The Strike

The plan involved Japan's six modern fleet carriers (Kido Butai) and was to concentrate on the American capital ships. The two battle-

ships (*Hiei* and *Kirishima*) escorting Kido Butai had entered service in the 1910s as battlecruisers. Two of the carriers (*Akagi* and *Kaga*) had originally been intended as superdreadnoughts, the latter a battleship and the former a battlecruiser.

Unfortunately for the Japanese, all three of the US carriers and one of the battleships (USS *Colorado*, one of the "Big Five") had left Pearl Harbor on various missions. This left eight older battleships, one battleship that had been converted to a target and training ship (USS *Utah*), and a wide variety of smaller warships.

The first Japanese aircraft reached Pearl at 7:53 AM (local) on December 7, 1941. Most of the US battleships lay in two columns along "Battleship Row," although USS *California* sat apart, USS *Pennsylvania* lay in dry dock, and USS *Utah* was on the other side of Ford Island. Within two hours, all eight US battleships took damage, although three remained battleworthy. Four lay at the bottom of Pearl, as did USS

Propaganda poster, 1942. Library of Congress.

Utah, and one (*Nevada*) was intentionally run aground to avoid sinking in the channel. It was obvious from the start that *Arizona* and *Oklahoma* would never return to service. Apart from the scuttling of the High Seas Fleet at Scapa Flow, no single day saw the destruction of so many dreadnoughts.

The attack was a tactical and operational success but a strategic failure, as it ensured that the United States would pursue the Pacific War with enthusiasm and anger. The success of the attack depended, in part, on a series of intelligence failures by the United States. In spite of access to Japanese codes, US intelligence ignored or misinterpreted several warning signs about the attack. In hindsight Japanese intentions seemed clear, which led to allegations that President Roosevelt had known about the attack and allowed it to go forward in order to embroil the United States in war.

The intelligence failures associated with the Pearl Harbor attack helped lead to the reorganization of 1947 and the structure of the modern national security state. Rebecca Wohlstetter's *Pearl Harbor: Warning and Decision* remains a classic of military intelligence history, highlighting the analytical shortcomings that preceded the attack, and setting the terms of discussion for evaluating future intelligence disasters, such as the Cuban Missile Crisis and the September 11 attacks.

The conspiracy theories associated with the Pearl Harbor attack should serve to remind us that there's nothing particularly new about the paranoid style of American politics. Several investigations during the war probed the reasons for the intelligence failure that led to Pearl Harbor, coming to no particularly earth-shattering conclusions. That few presidents seek to start a war by having their main naval assets destroyed, that the damage to the Pacific Fleet could have been minimized with even an hour's preparation before the attack, and that the intelligence failures are entirely consistent with how we know intelligence and military organizations function should lead to deep skepticism about the claims of the conspiracy theorists. Unfortunately, evidence and logic can never kill a conspiracy theory.

USS Guam

Laid Down: 1942
Launched: 1943
Completed: 1944
Displacement: 30,000 tons
Main Armament: nine 12" guns (three triple turrets)
Secondary Armament: twelve 5" guns, (six twin turrets)
Speed: 33 knots
Major Actions: Okinawa
Treaty: Post–Washington Naval Treaty
Fate: Scrapped, 1961

At the turn of the twentieth century, the divide between battleship and cruiser had yet to take full form. Armored cruisers were large, relatively fast ships that carried a large number of small caliber guns. Battleships were large, relatively slow ships that carried a mixed armament, including a small number of large guns. The almost exact contemporaries HMS *Warrior* and HMS *King Edward VII*, for example, differed in displacement by only 2,000 tons. At Tsushima, battleship and cruisers fought in the same line of battle.

The construction of HMS *Dreadnought* amplified the divide, putting cruisers in a clearly subordinate class in terms of size and armament. Battlecruisers straddled the divide, with the speed of a cruiser but the size and armament of a battleship. The Washington Naval Treaty gave this development a legal form, creating a specific definition for cruisers (maximum displacement 10,000 tons, maximum guns 8") and classifying all larger ships as battleships.

As the treaty system deteriorated in the late 1930s, this classification began to break down. Germany (not subject to Washington Naval Treaty requirements in any case) built a trio of cruisers armed with 11" guns. The United States began to develop several classes of large cruisers, ranging from the 14,000 ton *Baltimore* class to the 17,000 ton *Oregon City* and *Des Moines* classes. Despite their size, these ships maintained a main armament of 8" guns, and appeared to safely remain "cruisers."

But the *Alaska* class "large cruisers" were something else. Early in World War II, the United States received intelligence suggesting that Japan was building a class of 18,000 ton heavy cruisers designed to raid deep into the Eastern Pacific. The USN also worried about the commerce raiding potential of the remaining German pocket battleships. In order to counter these threats, the United States Navy

USS Guam on trials.

developed plans for a class of ships in between heavy cruisers and battleships (of which the most recent were 35,000 tons, carrying 16" guns). The results were USS *Alaska*, USS *Guam*, and four ships never completed. Oddly enough, the Japanese were neither building nor planning to build any such ships, although

USS Guam (foreground) and USS Alaska off China, 1945.

they considered the possibility after learning of *Alaska* and *Guam*.

The Navy insisted (and still insists) that *Alaska* and *Guam* were not battleships, or even battlecruisers, but instead something called a "large cruiser." The naming protocol for large cruisers was unclear. Cruisers were named after cities, and battleships after states. The battlecruisers planned in the early 1920s were named after famous battles, such as *Lexington* and *Saratoga*, but kept their names after conversion to carriers. It was decided that these not-quite-battleships-but-more-than-cruisers should be named after US territories. The four members of the class never completed were listed as *Hawaii*, *Samoa*, *Philippines*, and *Puerto Rico*. The USN may have been reluc-

tant to call *Guam* a battlecruiser because of the high casualty rate among battlecruisers in World War II. The *Alaska's* only major flaw was the lack of good underwater protection.

Guam saw only a few months of service at the end of the war. She participated in fleet air defense of carrier battle groups off Okinawa and off Japan, and also conducted shore bombardment in both areas. Near the end of the war she and her sister *Alaska* conducted one of the only efforts at surface commerce raiding by the USN in World War II. The raid netted nothing, however, as submarines had already sunk most of the Japanese merchant marine.

The US Navy placed *Guam* and *Alaska* in reserve shortly after World War II, along with most of the rest of the battleship fleet. A large number of ships were disposed of in the immediate postwar period, leaving only the Big Five (*California*, *Tennessee*, *Maryland*, *West Virginia*, and *Colorado*), the two ships of the *North Carolina* class, the four of the *South Dakota* class, the four of the *Iowa* class, and the two *Alaskas*. The Navy purged itself of all but the *Iowas* in 1960.

Author's Note

The contention that *Alaska* and *Guam* were not battlecruisers is indefensible. *Guam* was more than twice the size of the heaviest heavy cruiser ever built, and carried an armament superior to the contemporary *Scharnhorst* class. Moreover, they were designed for specifically the mission that the first battlecruisers were created for, which was the pursuit and destruction of enemy heavy cruisers. In action, *Guam* fulfilled precisely the same missions as the other battleships in the fleet, which primarily meant fleet air defense. Had *Guam* encountered *Yamato* or another modern battleship, her characterization as a "large cruiser" wouldn't have made a damn bit of difference.

I wonder if scrapping *Alaska* and *Guam* was a mistake. Their armor and armament were superior to any ships afloat other than the *Iowas* (and the French *Jean Bart*). They could perform shore bombardment duties nearly as well as the Iowas, and could be operated at a lower cost and with a smaller crew. They might well have proved a more palatable option than retaining *Wisconsin* and *Iowa* on the Navy List until the first Zumwalt class destroyer came into service. The South American navies, which purchased a number of gun cruisers after the war, might also have found them attractive at the right price.

Related Entries:

Contemporary of... *Scharnhorst*
Preceded by... USS *Wisconsin*
Inspired by... *Admiral Scheer*

USS Guam, Pearl Harbor, February 21, 1945. USN photo.

RFS Pyotr Velikiy

Laid Down: 1986

Launched: 1996

Completed: April, 1998

Displacement: 24,300 tons

Main Armament: 20 P-700 Granit Anti-ship Missiles

Secondary Armament: 16x8 3K95 Surface-to-air Missiles

Speed: 32 knots

Major Engagements: CTF-151 counter-piracy operations

Fate: In service

The Soviet Navy emerged from World War II a hodgepodge, possessed of a few ancient battleships and numerous smaller craft. Geography has not been kind to Russian maritime endeavors, as the Black and Baltic Seas are easily choked off, the Russian Far East is distant from the industrial base, and the far north is both often choked with ice and very far from conventional shipping lanes. Nonetheless, naval power was considered important by Stalin, and the Soviet Navy became a formidable force in the 1950s and 1960s. The Soviet Navy differed in important ways from the USN, however, as the Soviets never fully adopted a Mahanian outlook on naval power. Rather than pursue the construction of a few large capital ships designed to attack and destroy their Western counterparts, Russian efforts focused on submarines, patrol boats, destroyers, and cruisers. As the Soviet SSBN force developed, naval doctrine began to concentrate on the problem of defending Russian submarine patrol areas from US submarines, surface combatants, and aircraft carriers. Thus, even the Soviet aircraft carriers designed late in the Cold War focused on defensive fighter squadrons rather than on strike aircraft.

RFS Pytor Velikiy under escort from HMS Dragon, May 7, 2014. Royal Navy photo.

The *Kirov* class represented something of a break from this philosophy. Designed in the early 1970s, the *Kirovs* were the largest class of surface combatants built anywhere in the world since the end of the Second World War.

The *Kirovs* were named after important Soviet leaders. *Yuri Andropov*, fourth ship in the class, was laid down in 1986. The collapse of the Soviet Union and the end of the Cold War led to neglect of the Soviet (then Russian) Navy, and the ship was not completed until 1996, when it entered service as *Pyotr Velikiy* (Peter the Great). *Pyotr Velikiy* carries a main armamament of 20 P-700 Granit surface-to-surface missiles. She is powered by a nuclear reactor, allowing her to maintain top speed for considerable distances, but also has oil-fired boilers in case problems develop with the reactors. *Pyotr Velikiy* also has significant intrinsic anti-submarine and anti-air capabilities, although in a combat situation other vessels would likely accompany her.

Pyotr Velikiy is capable of carrying out multiple operations. Her surface armament (the P-700 is a large, heavy missile) makes her a danger to US carrier battle groups. *Pyotr Velikiy* can also defend Russian naval task forces, as well as SSBN patrol areas. The very size of the *Kirovs* disturbed the US Navy, and strengthened the hand of elements desiring to reactivate the four *Iowa* class battleships, three of which had been in reserve since the 1950s. As surface combatants the Kirovs were no match for the larger, more heavily armed, and more heavily armored *Iowas* (indeed, the *Kirovs* had little if any armor) and it's unclear that even a P-700 missile could do much damage to USS *Iowa*, a ship designed to resist 16" shells. However, the anti-air and anti-submarine capabilities of the *Kirovs* were much greater than that of the *Iowas*, making them more flexible ships.

Pyotr Velikiy has had a spotty career since her commissioning. As Russia really has little need for a deep water Navy, funds have been scarce. All three of *Pyotr Velikiy's* sisters have been decommissioned, although one may eventually return to service. Named flagship of the Northern Fleet upon completion, she has participated in several notable exercises. In 2000 she was the designated target ship for RFS *Kursk*, the submarine that exploded and sank with all hands. An exercise off Iceland in 2004 was designed to simulate an attack on a US carrier battlegroup, and involved *Pyotr Velikiy*, the carrier *Kuznetsov*, and several other major assets. Because of mechanical problems, *Pyotr Velikiy* remained stationary off the Iceland coast for the duration of the simulation. It was later decided that the exercise went so badly that, in order to minimize embarassment in the future, the Russian Navy should exercise as little as possible.

Perhaps most disturbing, in 2004 the chief of the Russian Navy said that *Pyotr Velikiy* could "explode at any moment," a troubling statement at any time, but particularly when made in reference to a nuclear powered battlecruiser. Admiral Koroyedov later withdrew the statement, and it has since been argued that the statement was more about internal Russian Navy politics than about the actual state of *Pyotr Velikiy*. In any case, *Pyotr Velikiy* remains in service as the flagship of the Northern Fleet. Although not technically a battleship, she serves a similar symbolic purpose to the dreadnoughts of the early twentieth century. She has undertaken a number of "show the flag" cruises, and even participated in counter-piracy operations in support of Combined Task Force 151 off of Somalia for a time. At 26,000 tons, she is likely to be the last large surface combatant constructed by any navy for a very long time.

Author's Note

The *Kirovs* are odd creatures. They are certainly powerful warships, and could provide a major threat to a US carrier group. At the same time, their size would make them a magnet for bad attention, especially from NATO submarines. In Tom Clancy's *Red Storm Rising*, one of the *Kirovs* is put down by a Norwegian diesel electric submarine.

Of *Pyotr Velikiy's* three sisters, one (*Admiral Nakhimov*) appears to be genuinely in the process of refit, while the Russian Navy periodically announces plans to return the other two ships to service (all left service in the 1990s). However, most analysts believe the ships are in such poor condition that refits would prove financially impossible. But given that Russia no longer has the capacity to build such large ships, and given the taste for symbolism in the Kremlin, it's hardly impossible that the others could return to service at some point in the future.

Related Entries:

Preceded by... *Giulio Cesare*
Contemporary of... USS *Wisconsin*
Inspired by... USS *Mississippi*

Conclusion

Nine battleships remain afloat today, four more if we include the Russian *Kirovs*. The United States has preserved eight ships, including all four battleships of the *Iowa* class (*Iowa*, *New Jersey*, *Missouri*, *Wisconsin*), two *South Dakotas* (*Alabama* and *Massachusetts*), USS *North Carolina*, and USS *Texas*. All but *Missouri*, *Wisconsin*, and *Iowa* reside in their namesake states; *Wisconsin* remains in Norfolk, *Iowa* in Los Angeles, and *Missouri* at Pearl Harbor, not far from the wreck of USS *Arizona*. HIJMS *Mikasa*, flagship of Admiral Togo Heichahiro, sits on display at Yokosuka. As for the Russian ships, one (*Pyotr Velikiy*) remains in service, one (*Admiral Nakhimov*) is undergoing an extensive refit, and two others sit in the limbo peculiar to retired nuclear warships, too expensive to refit, but too expensive to dispose of.

Role Played

Although battleships would play some of their most memorable parts in World War II, they were fundamentally a legacy of the First World War. Eighty-six dreadnoughts, super-dreadnoughts, and battlecruisers had entered service by 1914, with another thirty or so joining

global fleets by 1918. Of these ships, only eight were lost to enemy action: four to gunfire at Jutland, one to a mine, one to a torpedo boat, one to human torpedoes, and one (*Leonardo Da Vinci*) to causes that remain murky.

The Second World War was far more deadly to battleships than the first. Sixty-three battleships were in service worldwide in 1939, with new construction adding about two dozen more across the course of the war. Twenty-three battleships were lost to enemy action: eight to surface vessels, three to submarines, and twelve to air attack.

Things we know: The great powers constructed far fewer battleships in the years leading up to World War II than they had constructed in the years prior to World War I, even as the treaty system decayed. The ships themselves had grown more expensive, but navies also had other priorities; they had found important roles for cruisers, destroyers, submarines, and aircraft carriers, in addition to the traditional line of battle.

The navies of World War II would fight their battles with ships that were, on balance, much older than those of the First World War. At Jutland, the High Seas Fleet was constrained by the presence of six pre-dreadnought battleships, which had entered service between 1904 and 1906, between ten and twelve years prior to the battle. At Leyte Gulf, both sides used battleships that were nearly thirty years old.

The battleships that remained useful, generally speaking, were those that had sufficient speeds to stay tactically useful (nighttime shore bombardment, carrier escort), and operationally mobile. As Surigao Strait and countless other actions demonstrated, however, the old battleships could still serve effectively in many situations.

How they were built

The world reached "peak battleship" in 1918, when 118 dreadnoughts served in thirteen different navies. By 1923, in the wake of the Washington Naval Treaty, this number would drop to seventy-five. It would reach a low of sixty-one in 1938, before rising to seventy-two in 1942. Wartime losses and postwar retirements dropped the number dramatically. Twenty-six battleships were laid down in 1912, and seven of the nine years between 1907 and 1915 would see double digit battleship starts. The only other years to see ten or more ships laid down came in 1920 and 1939, although few of the former group of ships would ever see service.

The chief builders of battleships were the United Kingdom and the United States, followed by Germany. Japan stands in distant fourth. Spain was the smallest country to build its own battleships, with three España class vessels entering service around World War I. The Netherlands considered building battlecruisers to patrol the East Indies, but World War II intervened before the plans could be brought to fruition. Other aspirants that never quite acquired a battleship include Greece and China. The United Kingdom easily led in battleships built for foreign buyers, including Chile, Brazil, and Japan. Indeed, the productivity of British yards in the first two decades of the twentieth century was truly remarkable.

How they were lost

Scrapping outpaces all other causes of battleship loss, by a wide margin. Next comes scuttling, including the losses at Scapa Flow, at Toulon, and in the American atom bomb tests at Bikini. Surface ships, air attacks, and accidents come next. Curiously, only three battleships were lost to submarine attack, despite (or perhaps because of) major concerns before both wars.

The single greatest permanent loss of battleships came at Scapa Flow, where eight German battleships and battlecruisers scuttled themselves under a mistaken assumption. Four battlecruisers were lost at Jutland. Three battleships were permanently destroyed at Pearl Harbor, three at Leyte Gulf, three at Toulon, and three in a great air raid against Kure in late July, 1945.

We can interpret this distribution of losses in several ways. It is surely true that battleships saw open combat much less often than there architects envisioned, especially against one another. It is also clear that while the architects prepared battleships well for certain kinds of threats, they underestimated the threat that aircraft could present, and that navies (at least in World War I), misallocated resources to battleships that should have gone to a more multifaceted approach to naval power.

Why no more?

The battleship era ended not because the ships themselves lacked utility, but rather because they could no longer fulfill their roles in a cost-effective manner. Even into 1945, the battleships of the USN, RN, and IJN remained important, useful units.

Our retrospective history of the transition between carrier and battleship tends to overstate how quickly the latter overtook the former, and our efforts to find blame for procurement mistakes in "Big Gun" admirals and other hidebound dinosaurs leads us to understate the usefulness of battleships in World War II.

Most of the Royal Navy battleships that served in World War II engaged in combat against enemy surface warships. The same is true of German, Italian, and French battleships. The long distances and wide open spaces of the Pacific favored the aircraft carrier over the battleship, but even in that ocean many of the great battleships fought surface engagements.

Battleships could still resist battle damage better than aircraft carriers, or any other ship. They had more space for anti-aircraft weapons than any other kind of vessel. Battleships lacked intrinsic anti-submarine weapons, but modifications (including the addition of helicopter decks) could have added such capabilities. Finally, battleships could provide shore bombardment more effectively than any class, with the possible exception of the automatic-firing cruisers that came into service shortly after World War II.

The problem was that battleships could no longer perform these missions in a cost-effective manner. Especially with the shift to the jet age, smaller, less expensive ships could provide the same anti-aircraft defense as the hulking battleships of the *Iowa* and *South Dakota* classes. Architects could design these ship around anti-air and anti-submarine missions, providing useful platforms at a fraction of the cost of building a new battleship. Moreover, these smaller ships had smaller crews, and less demanding training requirements.

Battleships were good for a lot of things, but they were only strictly necessary for fighting other battleships, and then only before good alternatives presented themselves. As it became apparent that submarines, and particularly aircraft, could also sink battleships, the best reasons for building a big ship with big guns and heavy armor plate faded.

The big hulls persisted, and for a while many argued for rebuilding and repurposing the battleships, as had happened during the interwar period. But the costs of reconstruction were extremely high, and the resulting ships could rarely fulfill their new roles as effectively as purpose-built vessels. The reconstruction mania of the interwar period was driven almost entirely by legal restrictions on ship construction.

In the end, only the United States would reactivate any of its battleships, and only for a relatively short period of time. Had the Soviets possessed more modern and effective ships than they did (say, if they had received one of the *Littorio* class battleships in the postwar settlement), they might have done the same, but it was not to be.

Memories

The veterans of the World War I battlefleets are all gone. Henry Allingham, the last survivor of Jutland, died in 2009 at the age of 113. The veterans of World War II are now passing rapidly, although if the First World War is any indication we should enjoy the company of a few of them well into the next decade. Veterans of the four *Iowas* will remain with us for a good long time, of course.

Fortunately, we enjoy accounts of battleship history that are far more detailed than those created and made available in previous centuries. The twentieth century was, if nothing else, a century of paperwork, and the rise and fall of the battleship has been amply chronicled in a dozen national archives.

And we're also fortunate that the age of the dreadnought battleship coincided with the wide spread of accessible photography. We have a rich stock of photos of nearly every battleship ever constructed. The internet age has made it all the easier to collect these images, as they find their way from archives and even private collections into publicly available spaces. Thanks to the internet, good video records of some battleships have become available. We have video of the losses of HMS *Barham* and SMS *Szent Istvan*, available on Youtube to whomever might have an interest, along with countless newsreels about battleships from the early- and mid-twentieth centuries.

As alluded to in a few of the entries (particularly the *Yamato* chapter), battleships have appeared repeatedly in popular film, with mixed results. 1960's *Sink the Bismarck!*, directed by Lewis Gilbert, is generally regarded as the best battleship film. The director combined the use of models with a few footage shot on a few older warships, including HMS *Vanguard* (which did not enter service until five years after *Bismarck*'s sinking). Other efforts include a variety of attempts to film the Pearl Harbor attack, of which 1970's *Tora Tora Tora* is the best. Recent efforts have included Michael Bay's awful *Pearl Harbor*, and 2014's reprehensible *Battleship*, in which USS *Missouri* fights aliens.

My great hope is that a competent director, with a significant budget capable of taking advantage of the latest in computer animation technology, will some day take on Jutland. At one point Ben Kingsley was attached to a Jutland film in which he would have played Admiral John Jellicoe, but the project seems to have fallen apart. However, as good CGI becomes ever more cost manageable, we can hope that we will someday get good depictions of Jutland, Denmark Straits, Guadalcanal, and perhaps even Surigao Straits.

Further Reading

Ballantyne, Iain. *H.M.S. Rodney* (*Warships of the Royal Navy*). Barnsley: Pen and Sword Books, 2008.

Ballantyne, Iain. *Killing the Bismarck: Destroying the Pride of Hitler's Fleet.* Barnsley: Pen and Sword Books, 2014.

Ballantyne, Iain. *Warspite* (*Warships of the Royal Navy*). Barnsley: Pen and Sword Books, 2001.

Costello, John. *The Pacific War, 1941–1945.* New York: Quill, 1982.

Goldman, Emily O. *Sunken Treaties: Naval Arms Control Between the Wars.* University Park: Penn State University Press, 1994.

Gordon, Andrew. *Rules of the Game: Jutland and British Naval Command.* London: John Murray, 1996.

Halpern, Paul G. *A Naval History of World War I.* Annapolis: Naval Institute Press, 1994.

Keegan, John. *The Price of Admiralty: The Evolution of Naval Warfare.* New York: Penguin, 1988.

Lyon, Hugh. *The Encyclopedia of the World's Warships: A Technical Directory of Major Fighting Ships from 1900 to the Present Day.* Secaucus: Chartwell, 1985.

Mahan, A. T. *The Influence of Sea Power Upon History 1660–1783.* Boston: Little, Brown, and Company, 1890.

Massie, Robert K. *Castles of Steel: Britain, Germany, and the Winning of the Great War at Sea.* New York: Ballantine Books, 2003.

Massie, Robert K. *Dreadnought: Britain, Germany, and the Coming of the Great War.* New York: Random House, 1991.

Morison, Samuel Eliot. *The Two-Ocean War: A Short History of the United States Navy in the Second World War.* Annapolis: Naval Institute Press, 1963.

O'Connell, Robert L. *Sacred Vessels: The Cult of the Battleship and the Rise of the U.S. Navy.* Oxford: Oxford University Press, 1991.

O'Hara, Vincent. *The U.S. Navy Against the Axis: Surface Combat, 1941–1945.* Annapolis: Naval Institute Press, 2007.

Pleshakov, Constantine. *The Tsar's Last Armada: The Epic Voyage to the Battle of Tsushima.* New York: Basic Books, 2002.

Rohwer, Jurgen and Mikhail S. Monakov. *Stalin's Ocean-Going Fleet: Soviet Naval Strategy and Shipbuilding Programmes 1935–1953.* London: Frank Cass, 2001.

Spurr, Russell. *A Glorious Way to Die: The Kamikaze Mission of the Battleship Yamato.* New York: New Market Press, 1981.

Westwood, J. N. *Fighting Ships of World War II.* Chicago: Follett, 1975.

Photo Credits